The State and the Politics of Knowledge

The State and the Politics of Knowledge

Michael W. Apple

Petter Aasen   Anita Oliver
Misook Kim Cho   Youl-Kwan Sung
Luis Armando Gandin   Hannah Tavares
Ting-Hong Wong

RoutledgeFalmer
Taylor & Francis Group

NEW YORK AND LONDON

Published in 2003 by
RoutledgeFalmer
29 West 35th Street
New York, NY 10001
www.routledge-ny.com

Published in Great Britain by
RoutledgeFalmer
11 New Fetter Lane
London EC4P 4EE
www.routledgefalmer.com

10 9 8 7 6 5 4 3 2 1

Library of Congress Cataloguing-in-Publication Data

Apple, Michael W.
    The state and the politics of knowledge / Michael W. Apple; [assisted by] Petter
Aasen . . . [et al.].
        p.   cm.
    Includes bibliographical references and index.
    ISBN 0-415-93512-1 — ISBN 0-415-93513-X (pb.)
        1. Education and state—Cross-cultural studies.   I. Aasen, Petter.   II. Title.
LC71 .A67 2003
379—dc21   2002034968

Contents

Acknowledgments

Books such as these are collaborative efforts in a variety of ways. Obviously, this book has multiple authors, a fact that has necessitated a considerable amount of meetings and discussions over the period of time it was being planned and being written and rewritten. Yet *The State and the Politics of Knowledge* is collaborative in another way. In the process of putting this volume together, a number of people provided valuable advice and assistance or helped me think in a more coherent manner about the issues with which this book deals. Among these individuals were James Beane, Roger Dale, David Gillborn, Diana Hess, Cameron McCarthy, Fazal Rizvi, Susan Robertson, Antonio Novoa, João Paraskeva, Tomas Tadeu da Silva, Michael Singh, Steven Selden, Amy Stambach, Steven Stoer, Carlos Alberto Torres, Amy Stuart Wells, and Geoff Whitty.

A special word of thanks must go to Marcus Weaver-Hightower. Marcus served as my assistant on this book. The care with which he dealt with the manuscript and with the bibliographical tasks associated with it and his conceptual ability as a sounding board for some of the ideas included in it are very much appreciated. Bekisizwe Ndimande also provided assistance during the final stages of the manuscript.

Joe Miranda, my editor at Routledge, was one of the first people with whom I discussed this project. His encouragement and insights were important in the formation and production of this volume.

I need as well to say something about the Friday Seminar at the University of Wisconsin, Madison. For over thirty years, the Friday afternoon meetings with my graduate students and with visiting faculty members from universities and research institutes all over the world have played a crucial role in honing my arguments and in forming a counterhegemonic community that enables all of us to engage in crucial intellectual and political work. This particular book owes even more to past and present members of the Friday Seminar. Its members come from all over the world. Currently, for example, participants come from South Africa, Japan, Korea, Taiwan, Jamaica, Brazil, India, Portugal, New Zealand, and from various parts of the United States. Their insistence that we all think internationally provided much of the impetus behind this book. A simple acknowledgment is insufficient to signify how much we have all learned from each other. But let me do it anyway.

As always, Rima D. Apple gave me intellectual, political, and emotional support throughout the entire process. This was even more necessary than usual in this case because of constant worries about the health of our younger son.

CHAPTER 1

The State and the Politics of Knowledge

Michael W. Apple

Introduction

Formal schooling by and large is organized and controlled by the government. This means that by its very nature the entire schooling process—how it is paid for, what goals it seeks to attain and how these goals will be measured, who has power over it, what textbooks are approved, who does well in schools and who does not, who has the right to ask and answer these questions, and so on—is by definition political. Thus, as inherently part of a set of political institutions, the educational system will constantly be in the middle of crucial struggles over the meaning of democracy, over definitions of legitimate authority and culture, and over who should benefit the most from government policies and practices. That this is not of simply academic interest is very clear in the increasingly contentious issues surrounding what curricula and methods of instruction should be used in our schools. Think for instance of the whole language-versus-phonics debate and the immense political controversies this has demonstrated in local communities and in state legislatures. Or think of Diane Ravitch's (largely erroneous) arguments that "real knowledge" is no longer taught and that political and educational "progressives" have captured the teaching and curriculum in most schools throughout the past century (Ravitch, 2000). Even though her assertions are both empirically and historically incorrect (Apple, 2001b), these and similar arguments have been circulated largely uncritically by the mainstream media, by increasingly conservative foundations, and by political groups.

The political nature of education is also made more than a little visible in the current attempts in many nations to change the mode of governance

1

of education (Robertson & Lauder, in press). This involves conscious policies to institute neoliberal "reforms" in education (such as attempts at marketization through voucher and privatization plans), neoconservative "reforms" (such as national or statewide curriculum and national or statewide
testing, a "return" to a "common culture," and the English-only movement
in the United States), and policies based on "new managerialism," with its
focus on the strict accountability and constant assessment that so deeply
characterize the "evaluative state" (Clarke & Newman, 1997). When the efforts of authoritarian populist religious conservatives to install *their* particular vision of religiosity into state institutions are also added to this mix,
this places education at the very core of an entire range of political and cultural conflicts.

In *Educating the "Right" Way* (Apple, 2001a), I raised serious questions
about these kinds of current educational reform efforts now under way in
a number of nations. I used research from England, New Zealand, the
United States, and elsewhere to document some of the hidden differential
effects of two connected strategies—neoliberal and authoritarian populist-
inspired market proposals and neoliberal, neoconservative, and middle-
class managerial-inspired regulatory proposals. I described how different
interests with different educational and social visions compete for domin-
ion in the social field of power surrounding educational policy and practice. In the process, I documented some of the complexities and imbalances
in this field of power. These complexities and imbalances result in "thin"
rather than "thick" morality and in the reproduction of both dominant
pedagogical and curricular forms and ideologies and the social privileges
that accompany them. I also criticized some of the dominant forms of supposedly counterhegemonic literature that urge us to move in more "emancipatory" directions. Thus, for example, I argued that the rhetorical flour-
ishes of the discourses of critical pedagogy need to come to grips with these
changing material and ideological conditions. Critical pedagogy cannot
and will not occur in a vacuum. Unless we honestly face these profound
rightist transformations and think tactically about them, we will have little
effect either on the creation of a counterhegemonic common sense or on
the building of counterhegemonic alliances among those people who,
rightly, have raised serious questions about the ways our schools currently
function. The growth of that odd combination of marketization and regulatory state, the move toward pedagogic similarity and "traditional" academic curricula and teaching, the ability of dominant groups to exert leadership in the struggle over this and the accompanying shifts in common
sense—all this cannot be wished away. Instead, these need to be confronted
honestly and self-critically.

Yet education is thoroughly political in an even more practical and gritty way. In order to change both its internal dynamics and social effects as well as the policies and practices that generate them—and in order to defend the more democratic gains that committed educators and activists have won in many nations over the years (see, e.g., Apple & Beane, 1995)—we need to act collectively. Multiple movements around multiple progressive projects surrounding education and its role in all of the complex politics to which I have pointed above are either already formed or are currently in formation. Collective dilemmas warrant collective political responses.

These concerns raise important issues. How do we understand the role of education in responding to and helping to form collective and progressive political action? What is the place of politics in this? Is it possible to alter these politics? To cope with these and similar questions, we need critical theoretical, empirical, and historical tools; and we need *examples* of how these tools might be used productively. That is what this book is about.

For over three decades, critical scholarship in education has focused on the relationship between education and differential power. At first, much of the focus was reductive. A simple connection was presumed. Education was seen as simply a reflection of economic forces and relations. This "reproduction" approach—a variant of what has been called "identity theory" (things get their meaning by mirroring something else) in social theory—was criticized, reconstructed, and made much more dynamic and subtle over the years (Apple & Weis, 1983; McCarthy & Apple, 1988). In the process, approaches emerged that were considerably less reductive and essentializing and that recognized a much more complex set of contradictory relationships. These approaches have grown considerably over the years. Influenced by Gramscian frameworks, by cultural studies, by feminist and postcolonial theories, by the theoretical, empirical, and historical work of figures such as Pierre Bourdieu, Basil Bernstein, and Michel Foucault, and by other traditions, a good deal of the most creative work in critical sociological scholarship in general is now found within critical educational studies (see Apple, 1999; Arnot, 2002; Carlson & Apple, 1998; Dimitriadis & McCarthy, 2001).

Some of the very best analyses on education and power have been concerned with the way the *state* functions. The state can be loosely defined as "a distinct ensemble of institutions and organizations whose socially accepted function is to define and enforce collectively binding decisions in the name of popular interests or the general will" (Wong, 2002, p. 1). This general definition has still required a considerable amount of conceptual, historical, and empirical work in order to go further. How do we think about the state? What role does "it" play? How is it challenged? What are the contradictory power relations within it and between the state and civil society? Perhaps the best ways of understanding and answering these questions can be found in the conceptual apparatuses developed around the concept of hegemony. As an entire range of critical scholarship has clearly demonstrated, this kind of approach can be employed creatively to uncover some of the truly major dynamics that determine the politics of education and that lead to social and cultural transformation. The most recent work complements, extends, and goes beyond some of the most cited investigations of the relationship between education and the state (see, e.g., Wong, 2002).

In thinking about the state, there are a number of things that must be done if we are to avoid the dangers of previous analyses. First, we need to recognize that the state is not simply *there*. It is constantly evolving, always in formation, as it responds to demands from social movements. Thus we need to restore motion to what with very few exceptions had been an all-too-static tradition of critical analysis, something that will clearly be seen in the work on the growth of rightist social movements around education in this volume.

But this is not all. Nearly all of the work on the state has focused its attention either on single nations or on nations in the West or the North. This simply will not do. Truly international studies are necessary. But just as important, we need comparative studies that both continue but also refocus our attention away from, say, England or Sweden, where a good deal of research on the state and education has been done. By decentering the West and the North, by refocusing our attention on those areas that have been historically neglected, a much more subtle picture of the relationship between the state and education can be built. Given this attention to the "non-West," our analyses can become much more subtle and dynamic. We can study many more dynamics of power—not only class, but also race, gender, and colonial and postcolonial relations in all their complexities and contradictions—and do so with an eye to how these dynamics are formed in the contexts of histories and power relations that may be strikingly different from those we are used to focusing on. At the same time, we can also study the cultural politics of empire, of how empires engage in cultural control, of the social and cultural dynamics of what it meant to be a colony, and how social movements challenge such control from below and are themselves changed in the process. This kind of approach is important not only so that our analyses are more subtle; it is also crucial for critically oriented political and educational *action*.

In his discussion of schooling and class relations, David Hogan (1982) argued that education has often played a primary role in mobilizing oppressed communities to challenge dominant groups. It has been a set of institutions, an arena or site, in which groups with major grievances over culture and politics struggle for both recognition and redistribution (Fraser, 1997). In this complicated story, cultural struggles and struggles over schools in particular play a significant part in challenging the very legitimacy of political and cultural dominance. Thus education must not be seen as simply a reflection of forces outside itself. To paraphrase Ting-Hong Wong's words, educational systems, rather than being merely a dependent variable determined by processes of state-building, profoundly affect consciousness, identity, cultural cleavage, and social antagonism. Thus the connections between schooling and state formation are two-way, reciprocal, and interactive (Wong, 2002, pp. 9–10). This position restores the relative autonomy of educational systems and at the same time demonstrates how the building of hegemonic relations both incorporates and remakes cultural processes and these relations themselves. By dealing with the specificities of situations that have not been previously studied, we are able not only to criticize previous theories of the role of schooling that have been accepted and too easily generalized, but also to show how very different hegemonic strategies may lead to very different political and cultural results. We can also begin to see much more clearly how to challenge dominance. This in itself is a considerable achievement and will be visible in a number of the chapters in this book.

The approaches that guide the work in this volume are significant for another reason. As I noted above, all too much of current critical cultural and social research in education has been rhetorical. It seems to assume that detailed empirical and/or historical substantiation of one's arguments are beside the point. Because of this, it can too easily be dismissed as simply a set of slogans that can be ignored. And, predictably, this is what happens with depressing regularity. Of course, neoliberals and neoconservatives are already predisposed to reject such critical arguments (Apple, 2000, 2001a). But we help them along by writing as if evidence was an afterthought. The authors in this book will have none of this. In their detailing of the struggles over the state and over knowledge and meaning, and of what this means for a much more serious critical understanding of hegemonic struggles over culture and institutions in the state and civil society, a considerably more dynamic and nuanced set of pictures of the relationship between the state and education can be gained. And because their analyses are international—with chapters including detailed and insightful treatments of the politics of educational policy in for example the United States, Korea, Singapore, the nations of Scandinavia, Brazil, and internal nations and people within dominant nations—they are applicable to a much wider range of experiences and power relations than many other approaches.

Hegemony and the State

As I noted above, underpinning a number of the chapters in this book is one particular concept and the analytic framework that was developed to understand it—*hegemony*. The concept of hegemony was elaborated most productively in the work of Antonio Gramsci (1971). It refers to the ability of dominant groups in society to establish the "common sense" or "doxa" of a society, "the fund of self-evident descriptions of social reality that normally go without saying" (Fraser, 1997, p. 153). Hegemony is both discursive and political. It includes the power to establish "legitimate" definitions of social needs and authoritative definitions of social situations. It involves the power to define what counts as "legitimate" areas of agreement and disagreement. And it points to the ability of dominant groups to shape which political agendas are made public and are to be discussed as "possible." As a concept it has enabled us to ask how alliances are formed and what effects such alliances have. It has opened up an entire terrain of questions concerning the ways in which the struggles over social meanings are connected to the structures of inequality in society. Questions such as the following come to the fore: "How do pervasive axes of dominance and subordination affect the production and circulation of social meanings? How does stratification along lines of gender, 'race,' and class affect the discursive construction of social identities and the formation of social groups?" (Fraser, 1997, p. 153).

As I have shown at much greater length elsewhere, hegemony is a process, not a thing. Furthermore, it is not monolithic. It does not constitute a seamless web, nor does it refer to a process whereby dominant groups exercise top-down and near-total control over meanings. Exactly the opposite is the case. Hegemonic power is constantly having to be built and rebuilt; it is contested and negotiated (Apple, 1995, 2000, 2001a). Thus, because society has a plurality of competing ethical and political visions and discourses, conflicts and contestation are constitutive dynamics in any hegemonic relations (Fraser, 1997, p. 154). Because of this, counterhegemonic groups and alliances are also crucial to any understanding of the relationships of power. Hence, for the authors of this book, the state is neither a simple nor a fixed object. Rather, along with Gramsci, we take the position that "the life of the state is conceived of as a continuous process of formation and superceding of unstable equilibria" (Gramsci, 1971, p. 182). A sense of constant movement, of conflict and unstable compromises that ultimately lead to further movement, is a guiding understanding incorporated within this book. This is true not only of the state and its relations to civil society but also within the state itself. Even more important to the arena with which *The State and the Politics of Knowledge* deals, it is also true in terms of the constantly shifting role the state plays in producing and policing what counts as legitimate knowledge both within schools and in the larger society.

The State and the Production of Public Knowledge

Among the most crucial ways to understand the complex connections between education and power is to examine the politics of knowledge. One of the most powerful questions that can be asked in education is that offered by Herbert Spencer many years ago: "What knowledge is of most worth?" In the course of a number of books about the relationship between culture and power, I have sought to reword this question into "Whose knowledge is of most worth?" (Apple, 1986, 1990, 1995, 1996, 2000, 2001a; see also Whitty, 1985). Either way of wording the issue points to one of the central concerns of curriculum studies, the sociology of education, and critical educational studies in general. Out of the vast universe of possible knowledge, only some knowledge and ways of organizing it get declared to be legitimate or "official." Thus even the most practical of task in education—answering the question of what one should teach—has at its very basis a cultural politics. But the politics of curriculum doesn't end with the knowledge itself. It also involves who should select it, how it should be organized, taught, and evaluated, and once again who should be involved in asking and answering these questions.

Yet even these issues are insufficient. Official knowledge is taught within specific kinds of institutions, with their own histories, tensions, political economies, hierarchies, and bureaucratic needs and interests. Therefore, thinking about school knowledge involves at the same time thinking about its internal and external contexts. Whether we like it or not, curriculum talk is power talk. There is, of course, a long tradition within curriculum studies and the sociology of education of recognizing this. Like many of the chapters in this volume, some of the best work on these issues has been international in nature, since one of the very best ways of more fully understanding how power works internally and externally in education is to compare what is taken for granted in one's own nation or region with what is taken for granted in another (see, e.g., Green, 1990, 1997; Meyer, Kamens, & Benavot, 1992).

In order to engage in this kind of analysis, it is important to understand that official knowledge is the result of conflicts and compromises both within the state and between the state and civil society. This involves complex issues of political economy, of cultural politics, of the relationship between cultural legitimacy and state regulation, and of the ways in which and through which identifiable social movements and alliances form (Apple, 2000). Understanding these things has also involved tensions between different models of interpretation, including neo-Marxist, world-system, and poststructural/postmodern perspectives. It is in the sociology of curriculum particularly that the relationship between culture and power has continued to receive considerable attention, with what counts as "official knowledge" being one of the foci and what does *not* receive the imprimatur of legitimacy also being subject to attention. Thus the tradition represented in *Knowledge and Control* (Young, 1971) in the United Kingdom and first articulated in coherent form in the United States in *Ideology and Curriculum* (Apple, 1990) has been widened and deepened, not only both in its scope and sophistication but in the number of ways in which the connections between knowledge and power are interrogated (Apple, 1999). *The State and the Politics of Knowledge* extends this tradition even further to include some of the best new work both on the relations among education, power, and knowledge and on the struggles to defend or alter these relations. In addition, because many of the chapters included here focus directly on the current pressures to make schools conform to the ideological visions embodied in neoliberal and neoconservative policies, the book extends and widens the scope of many of the arguments I make in *Educating the "Right" Way* (2001a) and makes them truly global.

I noted above that the state clearly regulates the politics of official knowledge. Yet this recognition needs not to remain at an abstract level. It needs to be instantiated in real institutions and real examples, as this book does. In order to see the state's role in such regulation, it is helpful to think of this as having implications both inside and outside of education. In the United States, for example, a complicated process has evolved in which state textbook adoption committees found largely in the South and West have an immense influence on what gets published and sold for use in schools. Thus much of what teachers teach in Wisconsin, for example, is very strongly influenced by the political and educational tensions and problems of Texas and California. As I have demonstrated at much greater length elsewhere, this connects what counts as "legitimate" knowledge to the complex interrelations among market demands, the internal workings of publishers, social movements and political groups that try to influence the state, the needs of schools and teachers for relevant material, and the dynamics of deskilling and reskilling teachers. Hence the history of the politics surrounding this can be understood only by placing it in the larger history of class, gender, and especially race dynamics that have played such important roles in the struggles over redistribution and recognition in this nation (Apple, 1986, 2000; Apple & Christian-Smith, 1991). As we shall see in this book, this set of dynamics is not found "only" in the past. The tensions and conflicts involved in the role of the state in policing knowledge for use in schools place the state at the center of conflicts over what schools should do, over the larger role the state should play in society, and over the formation of social movements against the state itself. This is something to which I shall return later in this introductory chapter.

Yet we cannot limit our attention to the political realities inside education. It is important to focus on how the state regulates not just school knowledge but knowledge in the larger spheres of social life as well. The relationship between the state and the production of "public knowledge" to legitimate policy is clear in the following two examples. In England in the late 1970s to early 1980s, the Thatcher government saw the fight against inflation as a key both to its economic policies and to gaining the support of even larger parts of the citizenry for its policies. The government had to be *seen* to be successful in its efforts to reduce inflation. By 1983, an official spokesperson proudly proclaimed that the Thatcher government "would be the first in over twenty years to achieve in office a lower average increase in prices than that of its predecessor." In order to accomplish this aim, a new index of inflation was constructed, one which dropped the cost of mortgage interest payments out of the computational equation. Since Treasury officials had been expressly asked to produce the new index for exactly this purpose, the new measure unsurprisingly consistently showed a lower rate of inflation throughout this period (Evans, 1997, p. 28).

In the United States, there is an even more powerful example of the ways race and class work in the production and regulation of official knowledge. This again has to do with government-produced statistics. Throughout much of the 1980s and 1990s, official unemployment rates in the United States were consistently lower than those in many Western European countries. Government officials and economic pundits argued that this was due to the "lighter hand" of government regulation and a low, and falling, rate of unionization in the United States compared to Europe. The argument was that in these European nations unionization kept wages "artificially high." Unionization and government social programs actually depressed employment. Thus the welfare state needed to be radically changed; the government had to withdraw not only from its regulatory interventions but also from its provision of other welfare services. Only the minimalist state in both the economy and social welfare would keep unemployment low (Katz, 2001, p. 16). As we know, the vision of such a minimalist state lies as well behind the proposals in education to turn schools over to the competitive forces of the market.

However, as Michael Katz (2001) reminds us, in opposition to this story, official unemployment rates in the United States appear lower only because the statistics do *not* include the extremely large numbers of people who are incarcerated in prisons and jails, the majority of whom are poor and are persons of color. Factoring this in means at minimum that the unemployment rate here must rise by 2 percent.[1] Thus the production of official data by the state not only produces an economic reality that is decidedly "unreal" but it also makes invisible the hundreds of thousands of identifiable people whose lives and realities are expunged from the records of the classed and raced effects of the economy.

These examples point us to something I mentioned when I spoke about the politics of state textbook adoption policies—the fact that the state is classed, gendered, and raced. These dynamics are not "add-ons" but are part of the very constitution of the state. It is not as if there are government policies on the economy or on education, the (in)justice system, and welfare, and then there are additional policies on, say, race. Rather, state policies and structures are fundamentally structured along raced lines as they are on classed and gendered lines (see, e.g., Arnot, David, & Weiner, 1999; Arnot & Dillabough, 2000; Fraser, 1997; Mills, 1997). Think, for example, of the cuts in funding for health care, early childhood education, and child care and who benefits from that—and then compare it to the recent massive funding increases for defense and the military. The gendered divisions embodied in these funding priorities speak to the relations between what counts as state responsibility and what counts as "private."[2] By instituting such cuts in a way that constructs a reality around the discourse of "TINA" ("there is no alternative"), the state tells us what reality actually *is*, what is true and what isn't. This process of truth creation is very powerful.

Yet the state produces "truth" in more general ways as well. Take, for example, the current emphasis on the importance of markets and on the "new managerialism" (Clarke & Newman, 1997) in many government policies and practices that I pointed to earlier. Foucault was not inaccurate when he urged us not to think of, say, neoliberal or liberal versions of the market as "ideologies or truth claims." Instead, we need to think of them as discourses that help *produce* things like markets, the "rational" and economizing individual, and the world as made up of competitive relations. Yet such discourses do something else as well; they make such "things" as objects of government practices and they do so *through* government practices (Slater & Tonkiss, 2001). Bourdieu (1998), as well, points to the fact that neoliberalism is what might be called a "strong discourse." It has the means of "making itself true" because it orients "the economic choices of those who dominate economic relationships . . . [and is then] converted into a plan of political action" (Slater & Tonkiss, 2001, p. 194). Thus neoliberalism, which is usually seen as an attack on and a rolling back of the state, is not at all like this in practice. Rather, it represents a powerful approach to economic governance. It is remarkably statist in orientation, with the state "steering at a distance" and employing policy instruments and legislation to create, secure, and control market structures and relations instead of simply "freeing" them (Slater & Tonkiss, 2001, p. 140). One of the major points of reference in this book is the ways in which the discourse of markets and managerialism has indeed become "strong" and has helped to structure the terrain on which a large amount of educational policy and practice stands. We shall examine how this has happened and, just as important, what can be done to interrupt it.

Having said all of this about the role of the state in creating legitimate knowledge and in producing "truth" inside and outside of schools, however, there is a danger in focusing our attention only on "official knowledge." This can cause us to ignore the realities of popular knowledge and popular culture. To do so would be a very real error, since popular knowledge is crucial in the formation and legitimation both of identities and of what counts as "real" knowledge. Indeed, popular knowledge serves as the *constitutive outside* that causes other knowledge to be called legitimate. The ability of dominant groups and the state to say that something is real knowledge is contingent on something else being defined as merely popular. For this very reason, the popular itself is actually closely linked to the state in often unseen ways and hence cannot be ignored. This will be more than a little visible in the insightful discussion of, say, the connections among racializing discourses embedded in the state, tourist culture, texts for children in schools, and more general problems in education in this book. As we shall see, there are indeed close and clear interrelations between the history of colonial understandings and how indigenous peoples and lands are known both in popular culture and in educational materials—and these interrelations are themselves connected to histories of race and gender distinctions.

The State and Identity

The state/knowledge/power connection does not exhaust the issues with which we must deal. As I noted earlier, questions about who decides and about how bureaucratic and administrative needs and demands structure the participation of various kinds of people in this process are equally important. Perhaps the best way to begin a discussion of these issues is to recall that states also provide roles for people to play. In more technical terms, we can say that they establish "subject positions" that embody identities for people. For example, social-democratic states tend to see people as members of collective groups—unions for instance—while neoliberal modes of governance that are more positively oriented toward marketized relations tend to provide positions in which people act only as individual consumers. Think of institutions of the local state such as school systems. In most parts of the United States, elected school boards at a districtwide level are the ways in which citizens participate. The subject position on offer for most people is that of "voter." Any other participation is left to "voluntary" action, such as fund-raising through the Parent-Teacher Association (PTA). Or think of neoliberal policies such as voucher plans, in which the role of the citizen is simply that of the consumer who makes individual choices in a competitive school market. This is what we might call *thin* democracy in which people have very limited roles—voting or buying.

Compare this to schools in which community activists and parents, and in some cases the students themselves, are full participants in the development and articulation of policies and where even the principals of local schools are elected by the community. The subject positions on offer are much more collective and active and are not limited simply to the practices of voting.[3] As we shall see, there are places where such fully participatory roles—what is best seen as *thick* democracy—are being implemented in powerful ways, with Porto Alegre, Brazil being one of the most interesting places.

The case of Porto Alegre is important since sometimes the subject positions established by the state become sites of resistance. Individuals and groups reject the limited roles that the bureaucratic and/or increasingly neoliberal and neoconservative state establishes for them. Thus, in this book's discussion of Porto Alegre, this meant that a series of political and cultural mobilizations changed the governing party and put in place an entirely new set of relations between the state and the most dispossessed members of Brazilian society. We hope that the detailed discussion of Porto Alegre included here will provide a sense of realistic possibility for those of us who are becoming worn out by the constant struggles to build an education that is worthy of its name.

Yet we need to be cautious about romanticizing resistance. The fact that the limited subject positions on offer from either the traditionally bureaucratic state or the defunded shrunken state envisioned by neoliberals may become sites of resistance does *not* mean that such acts of resistance always lead to progressive policies. Indeed, one of the most important things we need to recognize is that when groups act against the roles and identities that the state has established for them, such struggles can just as easily lead to the formation of retrogressive identities. This may especially be the case now, since in all too many nations the discourses that circulate in the media and elsewhere and that have increasingly become "common sense" are neoliberal, neoconservative, managerialist, and/or authoritarian-populist-religious conservative ones (Apple, 2001a).

Thus, when people are (sometimes rightly) dissatisfied both with the ways the state is organized and with the roles it establishes for them, the manner in which they interpret their dissatisfaction is often based on the ideologies that circulate most powerfully in a society. Let us be honest here. In many nations currently, the dominant discourses are based on positions that are antipublic, antistate, and uncritically promarket; they are often based as well on a return to a romantic past and are religiously conservative. Not only does this mean that we should not automatically assume that resistance to state policies will be progressive, but it has major implications for a good deal of the literature on identity politics in critical educational research and theory. Much of this material assumes that identity work is always a "good thing." Yet, as we shall demonstrate in this book, while a politics based on identity and on struggles over the state's modes of "governing the soul" (see, e.g., Foucault, 1977a; 1977b; 1980; see also Popkewitz & Brennan, 1998) may at times be progressive, such struggles can and do occur in a context where a likely result often may be the formation of *retrogressive* identities. Apple and Oliver, in this volume, provide a powerful instance of exactly this result, where the state sought to uphold the "professional prerogatives" both of the state itself and of the teachers and administrators who are employed in it. This led to a situation in which a rejection of the state's subject positions also resulted in the taking up of antischool and right-wing identities by a large number of people within the community. Therefore, as this case will document, there is no guarantee that counterhegemonic identities may be to the liking of progressive educators and activists. In fact, this is one of the reasons that in earlier work I have spent so much time analyzing the creative processes involved in convincing large numbers of people who might otherwise not be susceptible to ideological "conversions" to come under the leadership of conservative causes (see Apple, 1996, 2001a). Neoliberals, neoconservatives, and authoritarian-populist-religious conservatives have themselves understood Gramsci's emphasis on building hegemonic blocs by using the elements of good sense that people have to incorporate such people under the leadership of dominant groups.[4] They know that to win in the state, you must win in civil society.

This emphasis on context, on understanding the balance of power in any situation, and on the complicated politics of what happens at a local level reminds us of a larger issue that will be important in this volume. Where something comes from—a subject position from the state, a commodified piece of popular culture such as a rap CD, or a product for use in schools such as a textbook—need not determine its political or educational use in any concrete situation. Context and the balance of power in the specific situation *do* count. This is one of the reasons why we need to be cautious of what might be called the productivist or genetic fallacy. This assumes, often wrongly, that the politics of a commodity's production and where something comes from totally determine its ultimate use. Thus, for example, we might assume that, because of both the conservative politics of some states and the profit-driven nature of textbook publishing, largely conservative and "dumbed-down" textbooks will produce conservative and dumbed-down teaching. At times this may be the case, and just as certainly much of the current overemphasis on testing and reductive fact-based curricula can have very negative effects (McNeil, 2000). However, it is also possible—and I have witnessed this personally more than once—for teachers to use the text in ways undreamed-of by either the publishers or the state textbook adoption committees that provided the "avoid-controversy-at-all-costs" outline of the content to be covered. While we must not be romantic about this, texts can be and are subjected to oppositional readings. They can be and are made the subject of analyses in real classrooms of their silences, of whose stories are included and excluded, of their ways of looking at what counts as a "real-world problem," and many more (Apple, 2000; Apple & Beane, 1995). The same is true of all products.

Let me say a bit more about this, since its implications are profound both for this book and for our larger understanding of the limits and possibilities of counterhegemonic work in education. There is a *circuit of cultural production* with three moments: production, circulation, and reception or use. None of these is necessarily reducible to the others. Each can be the subject of concrete interventions and interruptions of its politics, processes, and commonsense assumptions (Johnson, 1983). Cultural commodities hence can be seen not only as products but as catalysts to action. Messages, in essence, are not simply sent and received but *made* at the point of reception. Commodities, whether they be textbooks or, say, computers (or things such as state sponsored subject positions), can either link one into a chain of dominant sets of social relations or provide an extension of collective cultural and political work (see, e.g., Willis, Jones, Canaan, & Hurd, 1990). Actually, this is *not* an either/or relation. It can be both at the same time—simultaneously a form of reproduction of dominant relations and an arena for counterhegemonic possibilities. The key is to recognize the possibilities of both without romanticizing the latter, since this is decidedly not a level playing field politically, culturally, or economically. Dominance does exist and cannot be wished away by calling it simply "discursive" and hence able to be deconstructed. Yet the possibility of difference is always there. We might say that—because all texts and commodities are "leaky"—there is always a surplus of meaning and interpretation that can lead to alternative or even oppositional uses. The real issue is *who* will use these alternative or oppositional meanings and practices for what social and ideological goals. The objective possibilities will always be there. How these possibilities will be organized and mobilized, for progressive or retrogressive purposes, is dependent on the balance of forces in each site.

If this sounds complicated and makes us a bit less romantic about the ease with which progressive educational movements might be formed, that may be because the real world is complicated. This paradoxical, or perhaps better *contradictory,* reality is built into the social and ideological fabric of this society. As social commentators have reminded us as far back as Durkheim, modern society is paradoxical. One side of this contradiction can be found in the fact that market societies like our own act to create and valorize the individual and, at the very same time, can actually work against that individual because of the society's lack of binding value commitments that might promote the ethical integrity of both the person and the social order. Modern and postmodern societies fragment personalities and solidarity (Slater & Tonkiss, 2001, p. 79). Slater and Tonkiss summarize these points well when they state that:

> The market is a strategic site for the creation and destruction of the modern individual. It presumes the autonomy of subjects who calculate courses of action in relation to their private desires and then enter into contracts to realize them. At the same time, their very ability to do so arises from the social conditions that destabilize the broader value commitments that would allow for a true autonomy and sociality. (p. 79)

However, the fact that market societies such as our own have a strong tendency to destabilize values that are productive of ethical commitments and a sense of collective participation does not mean that it is impossible to build such commitments and collectivities inside and/or outside education. Once again, remembering the circuit of production, the commodities that are the products of capital may have alternate or even oppositional uses. The question then becomes: Can they be used to support movements for a more socially just education? This will become evident in the discussion in this book, for example, of the use of computers and the Internet in the building of more democratic and socially critical educational practices in countries such as South Korea that have a history of authoritarian governments and centralized capitalist authority. Yes, the computer and the Internet were produced with profit (and in the United States, the defense of national interests and markets) in mind. But that does not fully determine the uses to which they may be put in the struggles by educators and activists to build a more just set of curriculum and teaching practices in schools. The contradictory ways in which, say, neoliberal policies are appropriated and reinterpreted in Scandinavia will also document why these issues must be taken seriously.

The Role of Theory

Because this introductory chapter has brought together a range of theoretical and political material to bear on the ways in which the state and knowledge are integrally connected with differential power relations, it is important that I say something about the uses of theory in this volume. The chapters in this book insist on working with and through theories (Clarke & Newman, 1997, p. xii). However, "with" and "through" are complicated words. The first signifies the importance of using conceptual/political lenses to make sense of the complex educational landscape one is investigating. This will certainly be evident in the chapters that follow. Yet, "with" also has another meaning. It signifies a connection, a relationship, as in "We are with them." This meaning points to a close relationship between theories and social movements and between the theories employed and the persons employing them. This second sense of "with" will be evident here, since all of us who have written this book are socially committed actors, people whose work is overtly committed both to what we believe are principles of social justice and to the social and cultural movements that are forming to transform the dominant institutions of this society in the direction of a thicker democracy. Many of us hence are not "simply" academics who write about these things but are also organically involved in practical activities to transform educational and cultural institutions and policies (see, e.g., Apple & Beane, 1995).

"Through" also has multiple senses to it. It not only embodies our need to use theories (e.g., I worked through the calculus problem and completed it) but also signifies another linguistic intuition in which we come out of the other side of a difficult problem (e.g., I tunneled through the snow to get to the other side). Our use here embodies both meanings. We employ theories to uncover and give meaning to realities; and in the process, we also go through them in such a way that the reality that is better understood enables us to look back on our theories to see where they are adequate or need to be reconstructed.

Our interest in reconstruction is not limited to the role of theories, however. As I just said, all of us are deeply committed to social transformation. That is, the chapters in this book are part of a larger project concerning the very possibility that the world and its educational and cultural institutions could be *different*. Because of this, among the most critical questions that need to be asked is this: What are the economic, social, political, and cultural possibilities and limits for the transformative power of agency? (Willis & Trondman, 2000, p. 11). In short, what can be done? This issue is forcefully put in the following:

> We must resolutely reject all discourses that try to convince us that we are powerless. How long can we go on listening to and speaking a language that contradicts what we feel and even what we do? How long are they going to go on telling us that we are subject to the absolute domination of the international economy, when we invent and defend ideals, discuss reforms and break the silence every day of our lives? (Touraine, 2001, p. 116)

Issues of subjectivity and identity once again become important here. Drawing on Salzinger's assertion that "Factories produce widgets, but they also produce people" (Salzinger, 2000, p. 87), we can say that the state produces policies but it, too, also "produces" people. How do we counter the identities being produced that are increasingly grounded in an understanding of the self as the possessive individual of the market, the very embodiment of thin—not thick—democracy? How can we produce new identities? What discourses can help us see ourselves as social actors who participate in national and international movements that are deeply committed to a politics of both redistribution and recognition? Who are the "we" and the "us" in the first place? Is it possible to build counterhegemonic movements across differences, what I have elsewhere called *decentered unities* (Apple, 2001a), in which various groups come together on those issues of pressing concern in education and the wider social reality? As a number of the chapters in *The State and the Politics of Knowledge* indicate, answers to these questions may not be easy. But as Raymond Williams, one of the wisest writers on the very possibility of a different and more equitable society and culture, wrote:

> It is only in the shared belief and insistence that there are practical alternatives that the balance of forces and chances begin to alter. Once the inevitabilities are challenged, we can begin gathering our resources for a journey of hope. If there are no easy answers, there are still available and discoverable hard answers, and it is these that we can now learn to make and to share. This has been, from the beginning, the sense and the impulse of the long revolution. (Williams, 1983, pp. 268–269)

Williams's words are powerful and they help to define this book's political and educational, as well as its academic, agenda. Such an agenda is grounded in what Eric Hobsbawm (1994) describes as the historian's and social critic's duty. For Hobsbawm, the task is to be the "professional remembrancers of what [our] fellow citizens wish to forget" (p. 3). By both examining a number of recent examples and restoring the memories of collective struggles over state policies and more specifically over educational reforms and over curricula, teaching, assessment, and language, the book's authors aim to demonstrate the power of social movements and organized groups of committed actors in building counterhegemonic tendencies. But we also aim to do this in such a way that readers are able to see the importance of the *specific* conditions that help determine the shape that these movements take. As I pointed out in the previous section of this chapter, we should not be sanguine about the possibility that counterhegemonic movements will in fact always be progressive. Thus these analyses of different nations teach us a good deal about the importance of paying close attention to specificity in our critical work on the relationship between education and power. Without such understanding, educational policy and practice are destined to remain a "hit or miss" process in which some of the most potent political realities continue to be ignored. There is too much at stake for that to happen.

Understanding the State/Knowledge Nexus

It should be clear, then, that this book has an ambitious agenda, at once academic and political. The chapters that follow are organized in the following way to meet this agenda.

"Becoming Right" by Anita Oliver and me illuminates the role of the state in creating the conditions for antistatist movements. It critically examines what seems like an "ordinary situation," a controversy over the adoption of a textbook, and shows how it is in such ordinary circumstances that rightist movements grow. As we demonstrate, they grow in halting, diffuse, and partly indeterminate ways that are located in an entire complex of economic, political, and cultural relations. In the process of our examination, we argue with much of the literature on conservative influences in education and the larger society, which sees such movements in relatively conspiratorial terms. Without denying the power of conservative forces outside education and the ways in which neoliberal and neoconservative discourses circulate so widely in this and other societies, we argue that much of this dynamic complexity will be missed if we focus on conservative movements only from the outside of the situations in which they are built. We suggest that a primary actor here is the bureaucratic state, which may have expanded its policing functions over knowledge for good reasons but which responds in ways that increase the potential for rightist movements to grow.

The chapter has an additional agenda, that of providing a concrete example of how multiple critical perspectives—neo-Gramscian and post-structural—can be employed to compliment each other so that we can more fully understand the political dynamics at work in the real world of education. Further, the chapter raises a question that lies at the heart of much of this book: How can we interrupt dominance in education?

In Chapter 2, our focus is on official knowledge, on the struggles that involved texts that have been declared legitimate for use in schools. Yet this does not exhaust the connections between the state and the production and reproduction of legitimate culture. In Chapter 3, Hannah Tavares demonstrates why it is equally crucial to direct our attention to popular culture. Tavares interrogates specific popular cultural forms and shows the ways in which they participate in a cultural politics of imperialism. She illuminates how the all-too-often taken-for-granted nature of such popular representations has major implications for the struggles over instituting changes in curriculum and teaching and over the ways the state represents "the other" in its own official documents and in its use of such representations in stimulating "development." In particular, "Reading *Polynesian Barbie*" examines a cultural icon and how it stands for a long history of colonial discourse and relations of dominance. The chapter provides a powerful example of the ways in which critical textual analysis can provide us with insightful analyses of the relationship among popular culture, the state, and economic and ideological relations, in this case tourist culture. In the process, Tavares is able to portray how domains conventionally regarded as "outside" the educational field can be treated as persuasive sites

of influence in the informal instruction and consolidation of the normative contents of curriculum and official knowledge.

With due recognition of the ways in which the popular and the official
interact and the struggles to make what some count as simply popular into
official knowledge, Chapter 4 returns us to the social context in which such
struggles go on. In "Rethinking the Education/State Formation Connection," Ting-Hong Wong and I place the state in motion and show how cultural and educational conflicts are actually closely connected to tensions
over what the state can legitimately do and what the state itself looks like.
This involves an understanding of the continual process of state formation.
In recent years, a growing number of scholars have examined the role of
education in state formation. State formation is generally understood as
the historical process through which ruling elites struggle to build a local
identity, amend or preempt social fragmentation, and win support from
the ruled. These analyses have deepened our understanding both of the
connections between political and educational changes and of the cultural
politics of education. Insightful though they are, many of these studies
treat the educational system only as a dependent variable influenced by the
dynamics of state formation. Schools are usually depicted as being
shaped—sometimes in an unmediated and mechanical manner—by the
emergence of the nation-state, new forms of citizenship, and the transformation of sovereignty. These works also often seem to assume that schools
always function to meet the demands of state formation. This formulation
neglects the relative autonomy of the educational system and overlooks the
possibility that schools themselves might generate profound effects that
may block or modify the course of state formation. A reformulated theory
of state formation is needed, one that shows the mediating effects of
schooling itself on the process of state-building.

To take the first steps toward the building of such a theory, Wong and I
undertake two tasks in the chapter. First, we strengthen the theory of state
formation and education by employing Basil Bernstein's notion of pedagogic device. This concept recovers the educational field as another moment of determination within a social formation by enabling us to detect
the incongruities, conflicts, and contradictions between educational development and the project of state building. Our second task is to demonstrate the effects of schooling itself on state formation. Thus we apply this
reformulated theory to one specific example—the conflicts over Chinese
school curriculum in Singapore from 1945 to 1965. This historical case
provides a concrete instance of the struggles and contradictory outcomes
in a situation where state-builders sought to reform one stream of schools

in multiracial societies. We show that because the pedagogic device in Singapore was fragmented and subject to strong influences from external pedagogic agents, the ruling power in Singapore was not fully successful in using the school curriculum to construct an integrated and local-centered Singapore nation. Social movements from below had real effects.

Chapter 5 brings us closer to the present. Like the analysis in which Wong and I engage, it examines the ongoing conflicts over state policy, once again with an eye to the subtle ways in which dominant international economic and ideological influences are mediated and partly transformed. The chapter is underpinned by a recognition that there have been attempts at least partly to interrupt some forms of dominance, especially within those nations that were guided by social-democratic policies in education and the larger society. Petter Aasen's analysis of the history and current status of such policies insightfully analyzes this tradition within the nations of Scandinavia, one of the areas in which social democracy has had its most powerful effects. Within social-democratic policy, the educational system was regarded as an instrument for individual and collective emancipation, social inclusion, social justice, and equality. Yet, as Aasen demonstrates, there have been major transformations in educational policy and practice in these nations. Within educational reform in Scandinavia, Aasen identifies tendencies that undoubtedly point toward a conservative restoration. Taking an insight from Foucault, Aasen stresses the importance of understanding objects for what they are within their particular location rather than as a symbol of some grand theory. Within the political and educational discourse in Scandinavia, neoconservative, neoliberal, and to a certain extent also authoritarian-populist positions and measures are definitively present. However, also following Foucault, Aasen suggests that we might not fully understand Scandinavian discourse over education in the 1990s as a practice if we isolate the different elements and simply interpret them as evidence of a universal conservative restoration. For this very reason, he identifies elements of the state/knowledge/education nexus that point in a quite different direction, one which also indicates a continuity and renewal of social-democratic progressivism.

In the process, at the same time as he offers a number of theoretical advances in our understanding of what is happening in the politics of knowledge and the politics of policy inside and outside education, Aasen insightfully shows the limits and possibilities of interrupting conservative modernization in those societies that have histories of social democracy. The detailed historical treatment of the ways in which neoliberal and neoconservative influences and policies are mediated and reconstructed once they enter into regions with different political and cultural traditions is important. But in order to see how these kinds of ideological effects are produced and disrupted, as we did in Chapter 2, we once again need to go to the most local level, the realities of schools, teachers, and students. This is where Chapter 6 enters. Most analyses of resistance, subjectivity, and identity formation have been developed out of research on predominantly "Western" industrialized nations. This research has been insightful, but it has limited our understanding of the importance of historical specificity, of conjunctural relations, and of the ways class, gender, and race/ethnic histories and experiences take on specific meanings in different contexts. In "Schooling, Work, and Subjectivity," Misook Kim Cho and I go beyond such limited perspectives. By focusing on one of these "different contexts"—South Korea and its recent moves to institute career education and to have more students identify as manual workers—we show how such specificities work to produce particular forms of resistance, subjectivity, and identity. In the Republic of Korea (South Korea), the dominant faction of the ruling power bloc has tried to reconstitute work subjectivity through education as part of its ongoing hegemonic project. This has been done in order to deal with economic stagnation and to recover the bloc's political and ideological power, which was seriously weakened by the democratic and labor movements of the 1980s. This chapter examines the ways in which administrators, teachers, and students in Korean commercial high schools responded to the policies and work subjectivities that were newly articulated by the dominant group. Like a number of the other chapters, it combines perspectives from both structural and poststructural theories to explore the complexities of these responses. The theoretical and political task of combining what are all too often seen as disparate traditions is an important part of our message in this chapter.

The complexities of the ways in which social actors such as teachers and students act in a time of ideological and political fluidity and the ensuing alterations in policies and power relations is the theme that is taken up in Chapter 7. In the chapter written by Youl-Kwan Sung and me, "Democracy, Technology, and Curriculum," we raise the question of whether technology can be employed to interrupt dominance in those nations that have a long history of centralized and authoritarian control. We examine the ways teachers in Korea have attempted to make use of technology to create partly counterhegemonic spaces to resist dominant forms of curriculum and teaching and the centralized modes of control that accompany them. We focus on the discourses expressed in an on-line communication group, socioedu.njoyschool.net, a forum for social studies teachers in Korea, and its accompanying off-line movement, which links teachers to progressive lesson plans, counterhegemonic discourses, the development of political issues for use in classrooms, and the discussion of a wide range of views and voices. As we show, while the use of on-line forms did create the conditions for serious political and educational work, it is also the case that a centrally controlled national curriculum and Korean students' obsession with college entrance exams both place major limits on what is possible for critical teachers to accomplish. Even with such limitations, however, the site and the voices represented in it did embody several important tenets of what Korean educators committed to social justice call "true education." Taken together, the site and the educators involved in it give evidence of the very real possibility of continued action. This is especially clear in the numerous discussions of actual critical practices and in the teachers' development and sharing of detailed lesson plans for critical curricula and teaching in classrooms. The fact that these teachers also employ recent government reforms in evaluation in complicated ways, ways that may be different from the interests of the government officials who instituted them, again reminds us that the politics of reception may be very different from the politics of production.

The contributions to *The State and the Politics of Knowledge* that I have just described devote a good deal of attention to the processes of mediation, resistance, and the contradictory results that may occur in times of transformation of state policies. In Chapter 8, we go considerably further. This chapter examines an instance in which there were major and lasting transformations of the relationship between the state and civil society and where the very nature of the state/knowledge nexus is radically altered in much more democratic and socially critical directions. As I mentioned earlier, our tasks as critical and public intellectuals include not only examining the forces that act against the formation of "thick" democracy; we need also to take responsibility for making public the successes of struggles against relations of dominance and subordination and the role that education can play in building and defending such successes. In "Educating the State, Democratizing Knowledge," Luís Armando Gandin and I demonstrate exactly this. We begin by situating the processes of educational policy and reform into their larger sociopolitical context. We describe the ways in which a set of policies has had what seem to be extensive and long-lasting effects *because* the policies are coherently linked to larger dynamics of social transformation and to a coherent strategy that aims to change the mechanisms of the state and the rules of participation in the formation of state policies. We describe and analyze the policies of the "Popular Administration" in

Porto Alegre, Brazil. We specifically focus on the "Citizen School" and on proposals that are explicitly designed to change radically both the municipal schools and the relationship between communities, the state, and education. This set of policies and the accompanying processes of implementation are constitutive parts of a clear and explicit project aimed at not only constructing a better school for the excluded but also a larger project of radical democracy where the subject positions "on offer" are very thick. The reforms being built in Porto Alegre are still in formation, but we argue that they have crucial implications for how we might think about the politics of education policy and its dialectical role in social transformation.

Finally, in the Afterword, I take the themes that have guided the chapters in this book and lay out what their implications are for more nuanced and socially committed critical analyses of the role that education plays in reproducing and transforming social and cultural relations of domination. I also suggest a way forward that goes beyond the unfortunate split among the various traditions in critical educational and sociocultural scholarship. As I argue, if our task is understanding both how domination works and the possibilities of interrupting it, then one of the things we can do is to learn from each other, to combine our critical efforts. Collective struggles need collective voices, but ones that do not silence the very real differences within and among the progressive communities whose lives and futures are at stake in the current situation. Let us begin our journey with an analysis of the growth of conservative movements and their roles in identity formation and in struggles over the state.

CHAPTER 2

Becoming Right: Education and the Formation of Conservative Movements

Michael W. Apple and Anita Oliver

Introduction

Throughout the United States, national organizations have been formed by conservatives to fight against what counts as "official knowledge" in schools. These organizations often reach out to local groups of "concerned citizens" and offer financial and legal assistance in their battles with school systems at state and local levels. Citizens for Excellence in Education, the Eagle Forum, the Western Center for Law and Religious Freedom, and Focus on the Family are among the most active. Mel and Norma Gabler, as well, have developed a system of opposition that aids parents and rightist groups throughout the country in their attempts to challenge educational policies and practices and either to change the content of books or to have them removed from schools. The "Christian Right" has become an increasingly powerful movement in the United States, one that has had major effects on educational policy deliberations, curriculum, and teaching (Apple, 2001; DelFattore, 1992; see also J.D. Hunter, 1983, 1987).

Yet it would be all too easy to read these organizations' imprint everywhere. Indeed, this would be a serious mistake not only empirically but conceptually and politically as well. While there is intentionality, too often we see rightist movements conspiratorially. In the process, we not only reduce the complexity that surrounds the politics of education but take refuge in binary oppositions of good and bad. We thereby ignore the elements of possible insight in some (even right-wing) oppositional groups and ignore the places where decisions could have been made that would not have contributed to the growth of these movements.

A basic question undergirding this inquiry is this: How does the religious right grow? Our claim is that this can be fully understood only by focusing on the interactions, those that often occur at a local level, between the state and the daily lives of ordinary people as they interact with institutions.

In no way do we wish to minimize the implications of the growth of rightist social movements. Indeed, the conservative restoration has had truly negative effects on the lives of millions of people in a number of countries (see Apple, 2000; Katz, 1989; Kozol, 1991). Rather, we want to provide a more dynamic view of how and why such movements are actually found to be attractive. Too often, current analyses not only assume what has to be explained but place all of the blame for the growth of rightist positions on the persons who "become right." No one focuses on the larger sets of relations that might push people toward a more aggressive right-wing stance. Yet this is exactly our point. People often "become right" due to their interactions with unresponsive institutions. Thus part of our argument is that there is a close connection between how the state is structured and acts and the formation of social movements and identities.

In what follows, we combine elements of neo-Gramscian and poststructural analysis. Our aim is partly to demonstrate how the former—with its focus on the state, on the formation of hegemonic blocs, on new social alliances, and on the generation of consent—and the latter—with its focus on the local, on the formation of subjectivity and identity, and on the creation of subject positions—can creatively work together to illuminate crucial parts of the politics of education (see Curtis, 1992, for an example of the integration of these often disparate programs of analysis). For the neo-Gramscian position, one of the major ways dominant groups exercise leadership in society is through the generation of consent. Thus people who may not totally agree with all of the ideological stances of powerful groups come under the "hegemonic umbrella" of the most powerful forces of a society through a process of the creation and re-creation of a new common sense. Dominant groups within the state, the economy, and other elements of civil society connect with the experiences, anxieties, and hopes of people and integrate these people under their leadership. For poststructural approaches, there is no essential social or personal identity in, say, class, race, or gender terms. Identity is socially produced, multiple, contradictory, and contingent. It is discursively constructed in real, local circumstances and often related to the ways in which powerful discourses are made available and circulate.[1]

Behind this analysis is a particular position on what critical research should do. In other publications, one of us has argued that in all too much of the current critically and oppositionally oriented literature in education, "our words have taken on wings." Theoretical layer upon theoretical layer is added without coming to grips with the real and existing complexities of schooling. This is *not* an argument against theory. Rather, it takes the position that our eloquent abstractions are weakened in the extreme if they are not formed in relationship to the supposed object of these abstractions—schooling and its economic, political, and cultural conditions of existence. Letting the daily life surrounding the politics of educational institutions rub against you is wholly salutary in this regard. In the absence of this, all-too-many "critical educational theorists" coin trendy neologisms but remain all too disconnected from the lives and struggles of real people in real institutions (Apple, 1986, 2000). We hope to overcome that here.

"Accidental" Formations

As Whitty, Edwards, and Gewirtz (1993) document in their analysis of the growth of conservative initiatives such as city technology colleges in England, rightist policies and their effects are not always the result of carefully planned initiatives. They often have an accidental quality to them. This is not to deny intentionality. Rather, the historical specificities of local situations and the complexities of multiple power relations in each site mean that conservative policies are highly mediated and have unforeseen consequences. If this is the case for many instances of overt attempts at moving educational policy and practice in a conservative direction, it is even more true when we examine how rightist sentiments grow among local actors. Most analyses of "the right" assume a number of things. They all too often assume a unitary ideological movement, seeing it as a relatively uncontradictory group rather than a complex assemblage of different tendencies, many of which are in a tense and unstable relationship to each other. Many analyses also take "the right" as a "fact," as a given. It already exists as a massive structuring force that is able to work its way into daily life and into our discourses in well-planned ways. This takes for granted one of the most important questions that needs investigation: How is the right *formed*?[2]

In previous work, it was argued that rightist policies are often compromises both between the right and other groups and among the various tendencies within the conservative alliance. Thus neoliberal, neoconservative, and authoritarian-populist-fundamentalist-religious groups and a particular fraction of the new middle class have all found a place under the ideo-logical umbrella provided by broad rightist tendencies. It was also shown how conservative discourses act in creative ways to disarticulate prior con-nections and rearticulate groups of people into this larger ideological movement by connecting to the real hopes, fears, and conditions of peo-ple's daily lives and by providing seemingly "sensible" explanations for the current troubles people are having (Apple, 1993, 2000, 2001). Yet this too gives the impression that the creative educational project that the right is engaged in—to convince considerable numbers of people to join the broader alliance—works its way to the local level in smooth, rational steps. This may not be the case.

We want to argue that much more mundane experiences and events often underlie the rightist turn at a local level in many cases. While the right *has* engaged in concerted efforts to move our discourse and practices in particular directions, its success in convincing people is dependent on those things that Whitty, Edwards, and Gewirtz (1993) have called "acci-dents." Of course, accidents are often patterned and are themselves the re-sults of complex relations of power. But the point is still a telling one. Ac-ceptance of conservative tendencies is *built* in ways that are not always planned and may involve tensions and contradictory sentiments among the people who ultimately "become right."

In illuminating this, we shall first describe the assemblage of cultural assumptions, fears, and tensions that underpin the cultural and religious right in the United States.[3] We shall then argue that the way the bureau-cratic state has developed is ideally suited to confirm these fears and ten-sions. Third, we shall instantiate these arguments by focusing on a specific case in which a textbook controversy led to the formation of rightist senti-ments in a local community. Finally, we want to suggest a number of im-portant implications of this analysis for the politics of education and for attempts at countering the growth of ultrarightist movements in educa-tion. We shall focus here on the ways in which one particular element of the right—authoritarian populism and the process of connecting it to other parts of the conservative alliance—is formed. Similar analyses are needed on the growth of acceptance of the neoliberal project—with its vi-sion of the weak state and the expansion of market relations into all spheres of society—and on the increasing visibility of neoconservative po-sitions—with their focus on a strong state and on control over "tradition," values, knowledge, and the body (see especially Apple, 1996, 2001). While we shall devote most of our attention to authoritarian-populist movements, we suspect that similar processes and experiences may underlie these other tendencies as well.

A World of Danger

There is a story told by a teacher about a discussion that arose in her elementary school classroom. A number of students were excitedly talking about some "dirty words" that had been scribbled on the side of a building during Halloween. Even as the teacher asked the children to get ready for their language arts lesson, most of them continued to talk about "those words." As often happens, the teacher sensed that this could not be totally ignored. She asked her students what *made* words "dirty." This provoked a long and productive discussion among these second-graders about how certain words were used to hurt people and how "this wasn't very nice."

Throughout it all, one child had not said a thing, but was clearly deeply involved in listening. Finally, he raised his hand and said that he knew "the dirtiest word in the world." He was too embarrassed to say the word out loud (and also knew that it would be inappropriate to even utter it in school). The teacher asked him to come up later and whisper it in her ear. During recess, he came over to the teacher, put his head close to hers, and quietly, secretly, said "the word." The teacher almost broke up with laughter. The dirty word, that word that could never be uttered, was *statistics.* One of the boy's parents worked for a local radio station and every time the ratings came out, the parent would angrily state: "Those damn statistics!" What could be dirtier?

For large numbers of parents and conservative activists, other things are a lot "dirtier." Discussions of the body, of sexuality, of politics and personal values, and of any of the social issues surrounding these topics are a danger zone. To deal with them in any way in school is not wise. But if they are going to be dealt with, these conservative activists demand that they be handled in the context of traditional gender relations, the nuclear family, and the "free-market" economy, and according to sacred texts such as the Bible.

Take sex education as a case in point. For cultural conservatives, sex education is one of the ultimate forms of "secular humanism" in schools. It is attacked by the New Right both as a major threat to parental control of schools and because of its teaching of "nontraditional" values. For the coalition of forces that make up the New Right, sex education can destroy the family and religious morality "by encouraging masturbation, premarital sex, lots of sex, sex without guilt, sex for fun, homosexual sex, sex" (Hunter, 1988, p. 63). These groups view it as education for—not about— sex, which will create an obsession that can override "Christian morality" and threaten God-given gender roles (Hunter, 1988). These were impor- tant elements in the intense controversy over the Rainbow Curriculum in New York City, for example, and certainly contributed to the successful moves to oust the city's school superintendent from his position.

The vision of gender roles that stands behind these attacks is striking. Allen Hunter, one of the most perceptive commentators on the conserva- tive agenda, argues that the New Right sees the family as an organic and di- vine unity that "resolves male egoism and female selflessness." He goes on to say:

> Since gender is divine and natural . . . there is [no] room for legiti- mate political conflict. . . . Within the family women and men— stability and dynamism—are harmoniously fused when undis- turbed by modernism, liberalism, feminism, [and] humanism which not only threaten masculinity and femininity directly, but also [do so] through their effects on children and youth. "Real women," i.e. women who know themselves to be wives *and* moth- ers, will not threaten the sanctity of the home by striving for self. When men or women challenge these gender roles they break with God and nature; when liberals, feminists, and secular humanists prevent them from fulfilling these roles they undermine the divine and natural supports upon which society rests. (Hunter, 1988, p. 15)[4]

All of this is connected to their view that public schooling *itself* is a site of immense danger (Apple, 2000, 2001). In the words of conservative activist Tim La Haye: "Modern public education is the most dangerous force in a child's life: religiously, sexually, economically, patriotically, and physically" (quoted in Hunter, 1988, p. 57). This is connected to the cultural conserva- tive's sense of loss surrounding schooling and community:

> Until recently, as the New Right sees it, schools were extensions of home and traditional morality. Parents could entrust their children to public schools because they were locally controlled and reflected Biblical and parental values. However, taken over by alien, elitist forces schools now interpose themselves between parents and chil- dren. Many people experience fragmentation of the unity between family, church, and school as a loss of control of daily life, one's

children, and America. Indeed, [the New Right] argues that parental control of education is Biblical, for "in God's plan, the primary responsibility for educating the young lies in the home and directly in the father." (Hunter, 1988, p. 57)

Here it is clearly possible to see why, say, sex education has become such a major issue for conservative movements. Its very existence, and especially its most progressive and honest moments, threaten crucial elements of the entire worldview of these parents and activists.

Of course, issues of sexuality, gender, and the body are not the only focus of attention of cultural conservatives. These concerns are linked to a much larger array of questions about what counts as "legitimate" content in schools. And in this larger arena of concern about the entire corpus of school knowledge, conservative activists have had no small measure of success in pressuring textbook publishers and in altering aspects of state educational policy as well. This is critical, since the text still remains the dominant definition of the curriculum in schools, not only in the United States but in many other nations as well (see Apple & Christian-Smith, 1991).

For example, the power of these groups can be seen in the "self-censorship" in which publishers engage. For instance, a number of publishers of high school literature anthologies have chosen to include Martin Luther King's "I Have a Dream" speech, but *only* after all references to the intense racism of the United States have been removed (DelFattore, 1992, p. 123). Another example is provided by the textbook law in Texas, which mandates texts that stress patriotism, authority, and the discouragement of "deviance." Since most textbook publishers aim the content and organization of their texts at what will be approved in a small number of populous states that in essence approve and purchase their texts *statewide,* this gives Texas (and California) immense power in determining what will count as legitimate knowledge throughout the entire country (see Apple, 1986, 2000; Apple & Christian-Smith, 1991).

Quoting from the Texas legislation on textbooks, the author of a recent study of textbook controversy describes it in this way:

"Textbook content shall promote citizenship and understanding of the essentials and benefits of the free enterprise system, emphasizing patriotism and respect for recognized authority, and promote respect for individual rights." Textbooks shall not "include selections or works which encourage or condone civil disobedience, social strife, or disregard of law," nor shall they "contain material which serves to undermine authority" or "which would cause em-

> barrassing situations or interference in the learning atmosphere of
> the classroom." Finally, textbooks approved for use in Texas "shall
> not encourage lifestyles deviating from generally accepted stan-
> dards of society." The Texas law's endorsement of free enterprise
> and traditional lifestyles and its prohibition of lawlessness and re-
> bellion are regularly cited by textbook activists to support their ef-
> forts to remove material which, in their view, promotes socialism,
> immorality or disobedience. (DelFattore, 1992, p. 139)

Clearly, here the "family" stands as the building block of society, "the foundation upon which all of culture is maintained." It provides civilization
with its moral foundation. The family's strength and stability, in essence,
determine the vitality and moral life of the larger society (Klatch, 1987, p.
23). One of the ways the family guarantees this is through its central place
in instilling in children the proper moral values and traits of character that
can withstand the "moral decay" seen all around us.

Yet it is not only the family's place as a source of moral authority that is
important here. The family and the "traditional" gender roles within it demand that "people act for the larger good" by taming the pursuit of self-
interest that is so powerful in the (supposedly) male public world (Klatch,
1987). Rebecca Klatch (1987) notes that:

> Implicit in this image of the family is the social conservative con-
> ception of human nature. Humans are creatures of unlimited ap-
> petites and instincts. Left on their own, they would turn the world
> into a chaos of seething passions, overrun by narrow self-interest.
> Only the moral authority of the family or the church restrains
> human passions, transforming self-interest into the larger good.
> The ideal society is one in which individuals are integrated into a
> moral community, bound together by faith, by common moral val-
> ues, and by obeying the dictates of the family, church, and God.
> (p. 24)

In this way of constructing the world, *all* of the nation's problems are attributed to moral decay. The signs of decay are everywhere: "sexual promiscuity, pornography, legalized abortion, and the displacement of marriage,
family, and motherhood" (Klatch, 1987, p. 26). Even widespread poverty is
at base a moral problem, but not in the way progressives might see this—as
the result of social policies that have little ethical concern for their effects
on the poor and the working class. Rather, as George Gilder put it in a
speech at the conservative activist Phyllis Schlafly's celebration of the ulti-

mate defeat of the Equal Rights Amendment: "The crucial problems of the poor in America are *not* material. This is something [we] must understand. The poor in America are richer than the upper fifth of all people during most of America's history. They are some of the richest people in the world. The crucial problems of the poor are not material but spiritual" (quoted in Klatch, 1987, pp. 28–29).

Given this definition of the problem, poverty and other aspects of moral decay so visible in our major institutions such as schools can be solved only through moral renewal, prayer, repentance, and a clear recognition of the centrality of religious belief, morality, and "decency" (Klatch, 1987, p. 29).

We should not take lightly the view of schooling—and the perception of reality that lies behind this view—that such movements espouse. Perhaps this can be best seen in a letter circulated to conservative parents and activists by the Eagle Forum, an active rightist group associated with Phyllis Schlafly. Such letters have been found throughout school systems in the United States. This one takes the form of a formal notification to school boards about parents' rights.

> To: School Board President
> Dear ———
>
> I am the parent of ——— who attends ——— School. Under U.S. legislation and court decisions, parents have the primary responsibility for their children's education, and pupils have certain rights which the schools may not deny. Parents have the right to assure that their children's beliefs and moral values are not undermined by the schools. Pupils have the right to have and to hold their values and moral standards without direct or indirect manipulation by the schools through curricula, textbooks, audio-visual materials, or supplementary assignments.
>
> Accordingly, I hereby request that my child be involved in NO school activities or materials listed below unless I have first reviewed all the relevant materials and have given my written consent for their use:
>
> • Psychological and psychiatric examinations, tests, or surveys that are designed to elicit information about attitudes, habits, traits, opinions, beliefs, or feelings of an individual or group;
>
> • Psychological and psychiatric treatment that is designed to affect behavioral, emotional, or attitudinal characteristics of an individual or group;

• Values clarification, use of moral dilemmas, discussion of religious or moral standards, role-playing or open-ended discussions of situations involving moral issues, and survival games including life/death decisions exercises;

• Death education, including abortion, euthanasia, suicide, use of violence, and discussions of death and dying;

• Curricula pertaining to alcohol and drugs;

• Instruction in nuclear war, nuclear policy, and nuclear classroom games;

• Anti-nationalistic, one-world government or globalism curricula;

• Discussion and testing on inter-personal relationships; discussions of attitudes toward parents and parenting;

• Education in human sexuality, including premarital sex, extramarital sex, contraception, abortion, homosexuality, group sex and marriages, prostitution, incest, masturbation, bestiality, divorce, population control, and roles of males and females; sex behavior and attitudes of student and family;

• Pornography and any materials containing profanity and/or sexual explicitness;

• Guided fantasy techniques; hypnotic techniques; imagery and suggestology;

• Organic evolution, including the idea that man has developed from previous or lower types of living things;

• Discussions of witchcraft and the occult, the supernatural, and Eastern mysticism;

• Political affiliations and beliefs of student and family; personal religious beliefs and practices;

• Mental and psychological problems and self-incriminating behavior potentially embarrassing to the student or family;

• Critical appraisals of other individuals with whom the child has family relationships;

• Legally recognized privileged and analogous relationships, such as those of lawyers, physicians and ministers;

• Income, including the student's role in family activities and finances;

• Non-academic personality tests; questionnaires on personal and family life and attitudes;

• Autobiography assignments; log books, diaries, and personal journals;

• Contrived incidents for self-revelation; sensitivity training, group encounter sessions, talk-ins, magic circle techniques, self-evaluation and auto-criticism; strategies designed for self-disclosure (e.g., zigzag);

• Sociograms; sociodrama; psychodrama; blindfold walks; isolation techniques.

The purpose of this letter is to preserve my child's rights under the Protection of Pupil Rights Amendment (the Hatch Amendment) to the General Education Provisions Act, and under its regulations as published in the *Federal Register* of Sept. 6, 1984, which became effective Nov. 12, 1984. These regulations provide a procedure for filing complaints first at the local level, and then with the U.S. Department of Education. If a voluntary remedy fails, federal funds can be withdrawn from those in violation of the law. I respectfully ask you to send me a substantive response to this letter attaching a copy of your policy statement on procedures for parental permission requirements, to notify all my child's teachers, and to keep a copy of this letter in my child's permanent file. Thank you for your cooperation.

Sincerely,

It is clear from this letter how much the state is distrusted. Here, schooling *is* a site of immense danger. The range of prohibitions covered documents the sense of alarm these parents and activists feel and indicates why they would closely examine what their children are supposedly experiencing in schools. In the minds of conservatives, raising these objections is not censorship; it is protecting the entire range of things that is at the center of their being.

State Formation and Bureaucratic Control

It is in the conflict over this range of issues that new parts of the state are formed. We have often employed a reified vision of the state. The state is seen as a thing. It is simply there. Yet, at all levels, the state is *in formation*. Not only is "it" an arena in which different groups struggle to legitimate and institute their own senses of needs and needs discourses (Fraser, 1989), but it also is itself formed and changed in both its content and form by these struggles.

Throughout the United States at local levels, school districts have established mechanisms to regulate conflict over official knowledge. As we

showed, rightist-populist social movements, especially Christian fundamentalist, have raised fundamental (no pun intended) objections to an extensive array of curricula, pedagogy, and evaluative procedures. Thus, for
example, textbooks in reading and literature have been challenged for their
"secular humanism," their sponsorship of "socialism" or occultism, their
"overemphasis" on minority culture, and even their supposedly veiled es-
pousal of vegetarianism (see DelFattore, 1992).

Focusing on textbook controversies is crucial in a number of ways.
First, in the absence of an overt and official national curriculum in the
United States, the standardized textbook that is partly regulated by and
aimed at widespread state adoption provides much of the framework for a
hidden national curriculum (see Apple, 2000; Apple & Christian-Smith,
1991). Second, even though many teachers use the textbook as a jumping-
off point rather than something one must always follow slavishly, it is the
case that teachers in the United States do in fact use the text as the fundamental curriculum artifact in classrooms to a remarkable degree. Third,
the absence of a codified national curriculum and the history of populist
sentiment here means that many of the most powerful protests over what
counts as official knowledge in schools have historically focused on the
textbook itself. It provides an ideal fulcrum to pry loose the lid from the
dynamics underlying the cultural politics of education and the social
movements that form it and are formed by it.

Given the power of these groups, many school districts have offices
and/or standardized procedures for dealing "efficiently and safely" with
these repeated challenges. One of the effects of such procedures has often
been that the institutions construe nearly all challenges to official knowledge in particular ways—as censorship, and as coming from organized
New Right groups. Thus the educational apparatus of the state expands as a
defensive mechanism to protect itself against such populist pressure. Yet
once this structure is established, its "gaze" defines social criticism in ways
it can both understand and deal with. This has crucial theoretical and political implications for how we see the role of the state in the politics of education. For it is in the growth of such bureaucratic procedures and the associated length of time that it takes to rule on challenges that the Right
often finds fertile soil. In order to understand this, we must say more about
how we should see the state.

"The state may best be studied as a *process* of rule" (Curtis, 1992, p. 9;
emphasis in original). In Bruce Curtis's words, state formation involves
"the centralization and concentration of relations of economic and political power and authority in society" (p. 5). State formation typically in-

volves the appearance or the reorganization of monopolies over the means of violence, taxation, and administration, and *over symbolic systems.* In essence, state formation is about the creation, stabilization, and normalization of relations of power and authority (p. 32).[5]

Education is not immune to this process. This is part of a much longer history in which the state, through its bureaucratic administration, seeks to keep the "interests of education" not only from the control of elites but also from the influence of populist impulses from below (Curtis, 1992, p. 172). This is crucial to the story we are telling here.

Bureaucratic systems have substance. Emile Durkheim recognized a century ago that efficiency "is an ethical construct, one whose adoption involves a moral and political choice" (quoted in Curtis, 1992, p. 175). The institutionalization of efficiency as a dominant bureaucratic norm is not a neutral technical matter. It is, profoundly, an instance of cultural power relations (Curtis, 1992).

No bureaucracy can function well unless those who interact with it "adopt specific attitudes, habits, beliefs, and orientations." "Proper" attitudes toward authority, "appropriate" beliefs about the legitimacy of expertise, willingness to follow all the "necessary" rules and procedures—these are crucial to the maintenance of power (Curtis, 1992, p. 174), even when such power is recognized as acceptable.

This process of freeing the interests of education from elite and popular control was and is a crucial element in state formation (see also Apple, 2000; Curtis, 1992). The state grows to protect itself and the self-proclaimed "democratic" interests it represents in response to such attempts at control. In the instance of Christian fundamentalists, insurgent cultural forces from below—the "censors"—have created a situation in which the state expands its policing function over knowledge and establishes new bureaucratic offices and procedures to channel dissent into "legitimate" channels.

Curtis puts it correctly when he states that the "standardization and neutralization of judgements [has] tended to make implicit, rather than explicit, the class-specific content of educational governance" (1992, p. 197). Bureaucratic procedures that have been established to promote "the public interest"—and that in some interpretations may do so—are there to try to forge a consensus around and an acceptance of cultural legitimacy that may be rooted in strikingly antagonistic perceptions of the world.

Yet what happens when these "appropriate" and "proper" beliefs and responses fracture? What happens when the state loses its hold on legitimate authority, when its clients—in interaction with it over a period of time—

come to refuse its monopoly over what counts as legitimate symbolic authority?

To answer these questions, we now want to turn to how this dynamic works in the real world by focusing on the conflict over a textbook series in a local school district where the parties in contention became polarized and where populist pressure from below increasingly turned actively conservative. In the process, we shall show how the workings of the bureaucratic state paradoxically provide fertile ground for parents to "become right."

Professionals and Censors[6]

The site of this study, Citrus Valley, is a semirural community of about thirty thousand people now within commuting distance of several larger Western cities because of the growth of the interstate highway system. It is in the midst of a building boom that is predicted almost to double the population of the area. This is likely to change the atmosphere from that of a quiet, slow-moving, rural community to one resembling a small, faster-paced city. Much of its growing population will probably consist of commuters.

The average household income in 1989 at the beginning of the controversy was estimated to be $23,500. Demographic data indicate that nearly one fourth of the current population is between the ages of sixty-five and seventy. The many "senior citizens" and the approximately fifty trailer parks suggest that Citrus Valley is seen by many people as an attractive place for retirement.

There are no large industries in Citrus Valley, but the city would certainly like some to move in. In fact, the largest single employer is the school district, with just under six hundred employees, of which half are teachers. In 1980, 72 percent of the adult residents over the age of twenty-five had a high school education or less. Approximately 10 percent had graduated from college. A significant portion of the residents with college degrees work for the school district. The population of Citrus Valley is 95 percent European-American, with a slowly growing Latino population. It is primarily a working-class community, but one with a clearly growing and increasingly visible commuter middle class.

Even with the growth of commuting, a large portion of the townspeople are lifetime residents. One person described the community as "people, it's a real ethic here. People believe in traditional values. And they believe in responsibility and working as a community."

Certain things are evident in this brief demographic description. One is the changing nature of class relations in the community. People are moving out of the large metropolitan area newly within commuting distance of Citrus Valley. Fear of violence, a search for "better schools," lower housing prices, and other elements are producing a situation in which members of the new middle class are becoming increasingly visible in the town. This class fraction is noted for its sympathy to child-centered pedagogy and for what Basil Bernstein has called loosely framed and loosely classified curriculum and teaching (Bernstein, 1977, 1990).[7] Thus a tension between "country" and "city" and between class-related educational visions may lie beneath the surface.

Second, the changing nature of the community is occurring at a time of perceived fears of downward mobility and a very real economic crisis in the United States in which many Western states—and the one in which Citrus Valley is located in particular—are experiencing economic dislocation and its attendant apprehensions about the future. Needless to say, farm economies are not immune to these fears and dislocations. For many individuals, this will have a profound impact on their sense of what schooling is for, what should and should not be taught, and who should control it. For many working-class women and men, economic anxieties and fears of cultural collapse are difficult to separate.

In the middle of these transformations and the possible tensions that underlie the town's outward tranquility and "tradition," the school district decided to move to a new orientation in its language-arts program. In this, it was following the guidelines and timetable laid out by the state's department of education for all school districts. The state guidelines strongly urged school districts to use a literature-based approach to teaching language arts, and in fact Citrus Valley had already begun employing such an approach, built on a core of books chosen by the teachers themselves. Both teachers and administrators were enthusiastic about what they perceived as the initial success of their literature/whole-language emphasis. The logical next step for them was to search for a textbook series that would complement the goals and practices already partly in place.

This particular state allocates funds for purchases of state-adopted material—largely textbooks that have passed through the complicated political and educational screening process necessary for winning approval as a recommended text by the state board. Seventy percent of these allocations must be spent on such recommended texts, while the majority of the remaining money may be used to purchase nonadopted supplementary material. School districts may use their own funds as well to buy unadopted material, but in a time of fiscal crisis this is considerably more difficult. Thus money is available largely for commercially produced and standardized textbooks. The task is to find textbooks that come closest to the approach you believe in.

There are many texts available. To make it more likely that a particular textbook will be chosen, inducements are often offered by publishers. The amount of "free" materials, for instance, given to school districts by a publisher is often considerable. This is common practice among publishers, since textbook publishing is a highly competitive enterprise (see Apple, 1986, especially pp. 81–105). In the case of Citrus Valley, the "gift" of such materials seemed to have an impact on the choice.

Citrus Valley began processing a new language-arts textbook series in the 1988-to-1989 school year. This was the year for changing reading/language-arts textbooks as school districts sought to accommodate revised state guidelines for introducing new series. The result of this process was the selection of the *Impressions* reading series, published by Holt, Rinehart, and Winston. The series uses a whole-language, literature-based methodology—one grounded in a loosely classified curriculum orientation—that this particular state strove to implement in all schools.

When school began in the fall of 1989, there was no reason to suspect that there would be any problems with *Impressions,* although it *had* been challenged in other districts in this state and in other states as well. After all, the steps for piloting and implementing a new series had been carefully followed. The district introduced the new series with confidence and enthusiasm. The memos circulated around the district after the selection of *Impressions* reflected the pleasure after much effort of finally having made a choice that seemed in tune with the district's goals. In June, after telling the teachers that close to a hundred and fifty boxes of the new books had arrived, one district administrator made a prophetic statement. She wrote: "Have a wonderful summer! We have an exciting next year in store for us." Truer words have never been spoken.

Within the first two months of the school year, some parents and teachers began to complain about the books. Parents became concerned about the content of the texts. Not only were the stories "scary," but there were concerns about the values that were in them and about mistakes in spelling and printing. The parents objected to a number of the selections in the textbook that the publisher had sent to the district. For example, one poem from a fifth-grade book was about pigs in a swamp near some houses (McGouch, 1989).[8] The pigs "live on dead fish and rotting things, drowned pets, plastic and assorted excreta." The poem ends with the pigs' having consumed the flesh in the pond, and now, having a taste for flesh, they look up toward the shore. The district explained that the poem carried an environmental message. For the parents, it was violent and fearful, a claim they made even more strongly about some of the other material in the books for even younger children.

Parents began talking to each other, and slowly a more organized sense began to emerge as community members went to school board meetings and had meetings in local churches. Ultimately, a group of parents formed Concerned Citizens of Citrus Valley (CCCV) in an effort to convince the school board to withdraw the textbook series. The board and the school administration acted in two paradoxical ways. They treated the challenge as nearly an act of aggression—in essence, they "geared up for war." At the same time, they slowed the process of challenge by channeling it through the bureaucratic procedures that had been developed—often for very good reasons in many districts so that teachers and administrators could be protected from outside attacks. In this way, "proper attitudes" and efficient procedures are wedded in the local state's response.

Nearly all the parents who were interviewed who opposed the books stated that their original introduction to the content of the textbooks began when their children came home upset by a particular selection in the texts. As they organized, CCCV parents were unwilling to be identified with outside groups. They felt that their intelligence was being questioned when supporters of the books accused the CCCV of being controlled by "outside forces." According to them, when their children brought home stories that disturbed them by, say, causing nightmares or frightening them, the parents' first reaction was disbelief. Textbooks were "innocuous." Thus they were more than a little surprised to read stories in their children's books that seemed inappropriate and were even more surprised and dismayed by what they felt was the board's and the administration's "heavy-handed" response.[9]

As the conflict grew, the CCCV organized a recall campaign against a number of board members. The school system dug in its heels against "far-right censors," and the community itself was badly split. For the board and the school administration, the CCCV was a symptom of a larger national censorious movement organized around a far-right agenda. "Giving in" meant surrendering professional expertise to the forces of political reaction. For the CCCV, the issue increasingly became one of parental power and of a school board and school bureaucracy that were arrogant and refused to take citizens' complaints seriously.

Crucial to understanding the situation here is the fact that the leadership of the CCCV began to form connections with the religious right only *after* confronting the district administration and the school board for a long period of time. In fact, the connections were never very strong between the CCCV and any outside group. Late in the controversy, one person did become a liaison between rightist groups, and that person is now firmly cemented within a national organization for "religious rights" and assists in rightist political campaigns. Yet even here, prior to this controversy this person was not only uninterested in such causes but was opposed to them.

When the CCCV parents were repeatedly rejected by the local school leadership, they were drawn into the rhetoric and views of the New Right. They felt, rightly or wrongly, that their concerns were minimized and trivialized by both the district administration and the school board. Since they were largely dismissed by the holders of educational authority, then and only then did they begin looking outside the community for groups to dialogue with that held views similar to their own about the nature of the textbooks that had been introduced into the schools. Organizationally, CCCV parents remained on their own, but the New Right increasingly came to be seen as a more attractive set of beliefs and as an ideological ally.

Thus, even when the district made limited attempts, as it did, to convince the protestors of the educational benefits of the new pedagogy and curricula, these efforts were dismissed. One is not likely to subscribe to the views of authorities who disparage you. The schools' immediate response, then—to treat these parents as far-right ideologues who were simply interested in censoring books and teachers—helped create the conditions for the growth of the ideological movements of which they were so frightened.

Let us examine this a bit more closely. It was the case that most members of the CCCV were what might best be called "traditionalists." They were indeed wary of change. They did like their community as it was (or at least as they perceived it to be). In their minds, they were opposed to the textbook series because of what they felt was its violence, its capacity to frighten children, and its negativity. By and large, the majority of the community seemed to lean in such a traditional direction. Yet the CCCV parents saw themselves as trying to find a middle ground between the right and what they considered the "liberal left." Most of them were quite surprised to find themselves identified as part of the right. Rather, their self-perception was as "hardworking citizens" who wanted to maintain positions that allowed them to conduct their lives as they had been doing in the past. Time and again they restated the position that they were just "ordinary people" who wanted the best for their children.[10]

The parent group that originally organized to oppose the textbooks was made up of people from a variety of religious and political persuasions.

There were Catholic, Jewish, "mainstream" Protestant, evangelical and fundamentalist Protestant, Mormon, and nonchurch and agnostic members. Also interesting is the fact that only a few church leaders became involved in the controversy in open support of the CCCV parents. There was little evidence that this was a "fundamentalist" religious issue organized initially either from the outside or by evangelical leaders eager to take on the schools as bastions of secular humanism. In fact, because of the religious diversity and a reluctance to be identified as New Right, many CCCV parents were quite hesitant to hold meetings in a church. However, given the paucity of buildings that were large enough to hold well-attended public meetings, when a local pastor volunteered his church for CCCV use, with some caution it was chosen as the meeting place.

There were other characteristics, however, that seemed to differentiate CCCV members from others in the community. While they were diverse religiously, in general they did not hold public office and they did not feel that they were part of a network that was central to the community's power relations and daily lives. Many expressed feelings that they were on the fringes of local power. Nor were they economically homogeneous; the group included some local business people and professional as well as working-class members.

At the first meeting of the CCCV about twenty-five to thirty people came. At the second meeting there were seventy-five. As the conflict intensified, seven hundred people packed into the local church that had been volunteered as a meeting place. The intensity is made evident by the fact that police were stationed at a school board meeting called to discuss the textbooks. Over 250 concerned community members jammed into the meeting room. The tension was visceral.

In many ways, then, most CCCV parents were in the beginning what might best be called "ordinary middle-of-the-road conservatives" without significant affiliations to rightist activist groups, people who did not have a larger ideological or religious agenda that they wished to foist on others. Certainly, they did not see themselves as censorious ideologues who wished to transform the United States into a "Christian nation" and who mistrusted anything that was public.

To reduce the conflict to one of relatively ignorant parents or simpleminded religious fundamentalists trying to use censorship to further the aims of a larger rightist movement is both to misconstrue the ways ordinary actors organize around local struggles and to underestimate these people themselves. Such a position sees "dupes"—puppets—in instances such as this and radically simplifies the complexities of such situations. In many ways, such simplifying views reproduce in our own analyses the stereotypes that were embodied in the school administration's and the school board's response to the issues raised by the parents.

The rapidity with which the district responded in such enormous proportions, as if it were in essence preparing for war, seemed to be the catalyst that actually drove the CCCV parents in the direction of rightist groups and caused them to take a stronger oppositional position than they might have otherwise taken. As soon as the parents challenged the district, the district immediately reduced the issue to one of "censorship." This very construction reduced the complexities to a form that both was familiar to the "professional" discourse of school administrators and teachers and enabled the district to respond in ways that did not leave open other interpretations of the motivations and concerns of the parents.

At the beginning of this controversy, information was shared by women talking to women in public places and in their homes. Mothers told each other about the contents of the books when they picked up their children after school, as they met for lunch, and while they visited their friends. As the controversy developed, however, more men became involved and exerted more leadership, thereby signaling once again the relationship between gender and the public sphere (see also Apple, 1994; Fraser, 1989). For some of the women who worked very hard in the CCCV group, it was the discounting of their concerns that led to even more persistence in getting answers to questions about the textbooks and about the process involved in their selection and in organizing activities against the books themselves. These women's response to the school's resistance and to the local state's definition of them as "irresponsible" was to become even more determined in their efforts to disseminate information about the books. Even though they were not visibly angry and confrontational and even though they became increasingly strong in their opposition to the series, they were *pushed* into resistance by not being taken seriously.

The women involved in the CCCV had initial political intuitions, but these were not fully formed in any oppositional sense. The group included both social/cultural conservatives and laissez-faire conservatives, with the former grounded in a belief in the importance of religiosity, "the family," and "tradition" and the latter grounded in ideas about "individual freedom," "American patriotism," and the "free market," thereby documenting the diversity within even the more moderate conservative positions held. Yet the most common themes of CCCV women were the sovereignty of the family and the perceived attack on their rights as parents to control their children's education. Added to this was their perception that *Impressions* did not represent America accurately or sufficiently. However, these women did not begin the controversy in previously defined conscious positions of conservatism. Rather, at the beginning they were startled that there was a problem with the textbooks in their community. Through the months of the conflict, their stances became *formed* and became more clear as a result of having to find a way of making sense out of the schools' response.

Thus, as the conflict deepened, one of the leaders of the CCCV became increasingly influenced by Francis Schaeffer, a conservative theologian who supported the idea of absolute truth. As this parent searched for ways of understanding her growing distress, she found Schaeffer's ideas more and more attractive. For Schaeffer (1990), there are "true truths." There are rights and wrongs, basic immutable values, that enable us to know with certainty that some things are absolutely right and other things are absolutely wrong. Without this, according to Schaeffer, there is no Christianity.

This becomes much clearer if we again take the example of one person deeply involved in the CCCV, the mother of a child in one of the schools that was using the textbook series. At the outset, she was not a deeply religious person. She rarely attended church, had no strong loyalties to any one organization, and would have rejected the label of "New Right." Her advice to others involved with her at the beginning was to work with the district and not to organize. As her views were directly confronted and challenged by the district and her position seemingly stereotyped, she began to look more closely at what she felt she had to do with her opposition to the books. Her views were repeatedly minimized and she was accused of being "right-wing." As a result of this, not only did she become a part of the development of the CCCV by parents, but at the end of the controversy she became deeply involved with Christian women's groups on national political issues. What began as a concern over the content of books ended with individuals like her becoming active members of right-wing national movements.

At the end of the conflict, the school district announced a "solution." It would continue to use *Impressions* and its core literature program. It would also continue the practice of allowing parents to request up to two alternative assignments to these materials each semester. It then went further. The district implemented alternative classes for those parents who had become totally opposed to *Impressions*. Parents were asked to return a letter in which they were asked if they wanted their children to be in a special non-*Impressions* class. They were told that "this may result in a classroom or school site change for your child. In the event a site change is necessary, you will need to provide transportation."

While this response does show some flexibility on the part of the school system, it immediately created a difficult situation for parents who worked outside the home or who were unable to provide transportation for their children. Work schedules, a lack of two cars (or even one), economic disadvantage, and other elements created a situation in which parents often had no alternative but to keep their children in the *Impressions* classrooms. Thus are the seeds of further alienation sowed.

As the next school year began, the district reported that 82 percent of the parents had chosen to put their children in *Impressions* classes. Whether this is evidence of choice or of having no real alternatives due to the conditions we mentioned above is unclear. Yet when nearly 20 percent of parents actively *choose* experiences different from officially defined knowledge for their children, it is clear that the controversy continues to simmer not too far below the surface.

There have been other changes in the openness of the school system concerning the processes by which official knowledge is chosen. For example, parents are now included in the early stages of textbook selection. The school district administrators and the school board are now much more aware of the complex politics surrounding parental concerns and the consequences of the "professional" decisions they make. Above all, however, there is a tense watchfulness on all sides and a polarization that is deeply cemented into the community. An active right now exists in powerful ways.

Conclusion

We have been not only interested here in illuminating the complex process through which people become rightist, though such analyses are crucial in understanding cultural politics in education; we also have a theoretical agenda. Too often, traditions talk past each other in critical educational studies. Neo-Gramscian, postmodern, and poststructural theories are seen as opposites. We reject these divisions for a more integrative approach. We have taken tools from the neo-Gramscian tradition—an emphasis on the power of the state and on the ideological currents within common sense and on the power of cultural movements from below—without ignoring the economic context of social action. We have complemented this with a focus on identity politics and the state's role in circulating subject positions, which are then reappropriated by real people in the complex politics of the local level. Behind this is a claim that the study of social movements and the condition of their generation, in a time of increasingly aggressive attacks on the school and on the very idea of "the public" by rightist groups, is essential. Integrating these various perspectives is an ambitious agenda, but the politics of education needs to be treated with the integrative seriousness its complexity deserves.

The implications of what we have described here are of great importance to any analysis of the formation of rightist movements and to the role
of the school in identity formation. Many writers have talked about the
school as a productive site. It is a site of the production of student identities
and of the production of a politics of identity formation (e.g., Wexler,
1992). Yet other identities are produced in interaction with state agencies
such as schools. Oppositional identities centered around conservative cultural politics are formed as well. This is clear in the instance—one of many,
we expect—that we have investigated here.

The subject positions made available by the state were only those of "responsible" parents, who basically supported "professional decision making," or "irresponsible" right-wing censors. The construction of this binary
opposition created a situation in which the only ways that parents and
other community members could be *heard* was to occupy the spaces provided by the state. These were expanded and partly transformed, of course,
but the only way in which attention was paid to these concerned individuals was for them to become increasingly aggressive about their claims and
increasingly organized around conservative cultural and religious themes.
Social identities are formed in this way. Thus moderately conservative and
"moderate" community members are slowly transformed into something
very different. The right *becomes* the right in a complex and dynamic set of
interactions with the state. (How the local state is itself transformed by this
is, of course, worthy of inquiry in this regard, but that will have to wait
until another investigation.)

At the outset of this analysis, we drew on the arguments of Whitty, Edwards, and Gewirtz (1993) in which they claimed that the right grows
through "accidents." It grows in halting, diffuse, and partly indeterminate
ways that are located in an entire complex of economic, political, and cultural relations. We shall miss much of this dynamic complexity if we focus
only on conservative movements from outside the situations in which they
are built. We have suggested that a primary actor here is the bureaucratic
state, which may have expanded its policing functions over knowledge for
good reasons but responds in ways that increase the potential for rightist
movements to grow.

One thing became clear during this study: the linkages between parents
who challenge textbooks and national "authoritarian-populist" groups
grow during a controversy and as a result of such a controversy, rather than
being driven by outside groups. In the case we have related here, a striking
change is evident. A number of CCCV parents have not only become part
of a larger network of New Right activists but are proud of making such
connections, connections that would have seemed impossible before. Here

we need to stress again that these are individuals who had no prior links with New Right organizations and who had no desire to have any connections with such conservative groups until well into the *Impressions* controversy. Equally important is the fact that these newly formed links are continuing to grow stronger as new conservative political identities—extensions of the subject positions originally offered by the local state—are taken on by these people.

Economic conservativism and populism become linked to religious fundamentalism in these local ways. "Concerned citizens," upset by what the schools have defined as official knowledge and (correctly) worried both about the downward economic mobility of their children and the values that they are being taught, put these two forms of conservatism together not through any natural process but in a manner that places the aspects of the state at the center of the formation of social allegiances and social movements.

Our points are not meant to imply that everyone has "free agency," that people "freely choose" to become rightist (or anything else) in a vacuum. Indeed, exactly the opposite is the case. The increasing dominance of conservative positions on the entire range of issues involving education, the economy, sexuality, welfare, "intelligence,"[11] and so on in the media and in public discussions means that people in cities such as Citrus Valley and elsewhere live in a world where rightist discourses constantly circulate. It is now increasingly hard *not* to hear such interpretations and even harder to hear positions opposed to them. However, there are multiple ways in which such discourses can be heard or read. Acceptance is but one of them (Apple, 2000, p. 58).

One is left here with many questions, but in our mind, among the most important is this: Could it have been *different?* If the school personnel had listened more carefully, had not positioned the parents as censorious right-wingers, would there have been a more progressive result? This is not "simply" a question about research. Given the right's hegemonic project and the success of its ideological transformations, if schools are one of the crucial sites where these transformations occur, then interruptions of the bureaucratic gaze of the school and concrete struggles at a local level may be more important than we realize, not only in the short term but in the long term as well.[12] In fact, it is just as crucial that schools focus their critical gaze on themselves and on how *they* may participate in creating the conditions in which ordinary citizens "become right."

Fears about a declining economy or concerns about what is taught to one's children do not necessarily have to be sutured into an authoritarian-populist attack on the state, nor do they necessarily have to be connected to the entire range of issues the right stands for. Moderate and moderately traditional positions may not be ones all of our readers believe in, but there is a world of difference between such positions and the aggressive campaign against all that is public and against the very idea of a truly public school that emanates from the far right. The widespread effects of such groups can be limited only if the larger number of the public who have populist concerns about schools are not pushed to the right.

There is evidence that a different response by schools to the politics of official knowledge can have very different results. Though this is discussed in much greater detail in *Democratic Schools* (Apple & Beane, 1995), it is worthwhile noting here the experiences of schools that deal with such possibly polarizing situations in more open ways. To take but one example: Fratney Street School in Milwaukee, a city that has suffered severely from the downturn in manufacturing jobs and from very real class and race antagonisms, faced a situation in which political conflicts around class and racial dynamics could have provided fertile ground for the growth of rightist sentiments. Here, too, the central administration was often highly bureaucratic. It too was originally suspicious of parental and community concerns about a curriculum that seemed out of touch with the values and anxieties of many community members. Stereotypes of parents and their concerns abounded, and there was a clear preference for the professional and the technical in making educational decisions.

Because the school is situated in a "border area" in which its student population is a combination of working-class European-Americans, African-Americans, and Latinos/Latinas, the issues of whose knowledge was represented in the texts, of what an appropriate pedagogy would be, and of whose voices within that tense and diverse makeup would be listened to could have been as explosive as those that surfaced in Citrus Valley. These issues could have instigated the development of movements similar to those found in the case we have analyzed here. Yet they did not lead to such development and in fact led to the formation of cross-class and -race coalitions for more progressive curricula and teaching and widespread support for the school.

In part this was due to a group of teachers and administrators who—as a group—opened up the discussion of curricula and pedagogy to the multiple voices with a stake in the school, including parents, community activists, and students. There was constant attention paid to this—not, as often happens in many school districts, as a form of "public relations," which is usually largely a form of the "engineering of consent," but as an ongoing and genuine attempt to relate both the content of the curriculum and the decisions over it to the lives of the people involved. In part it was the result of the immense amount of work done by the educators involved there to publicly justify what they thought was best for students and why, in words and in a style that could not be interpreted as arrogant, elitist, or distant, and to listen sympathetically and carefully to the fears, concerns, and hopes of the various voices in the community. Finally, it was due to a decidedly nonhierarchical set of beliefs about what happens both within the school and between the school and the wider community(ies) of which it is a part.

None of this guarantees that the right's restorational project will be transformed. Situations and their causes are indeed partly "accidental." Yet the experience at Fratney Street School and at other schools speaks to a very different articulation between the local state and its population, and it speaks to the very real possibility of interrupting a number of the conditions that lead to the growth of rightist social movements. There is work to be done.

Different kinds of "texts" are employed to legitimate an imperial and colonial state and to establish racial hierarchies. We turn to these issues in the next chapter.

Acknowledgments

A briefer version of this chapter appears in Michael W. Apple, *Cultural Politics and Education* (New York: Teachers College Press, 1996).

Reading Polynesian Barbie:
Iterations of Race, Nation, and State

Hannah Tavares

As a writer I have so many literary strait-jackets and myths about
the South Seas to break out of. . . . Still so much crap to unlearn!
——Albert Wendt, quoted in Tiffin, 1978, p. 6.

Introduction

In a book review concerning the American icon, Barbie, Claudia Mitchell
and Jacqueline Reid-Walsh (1995, p. 143) assert that Mattel's Barbie doll
"exists as a perfect cultural site" for interrogation. Their bid, informed by
analysis generated in the field of cultural studies, invites us to see how a
cultural text can be read to examine (and unsettle) our taken-for-granted
assumptions about the complex interplay between culture and power. Such
a query may not seem to impinge directly on educational concerns. Critical
educators, however, have argued otherwise, demonstrating the importance
of interrogating popular cultural forms in understanding the cultural politics of imperialism and in struggling to institute changes of curriculum
and teaching (Apple, 1993, 1996). Accordingly, domains conventionally regarded as "outside" the educational field are treated as persuasive sites of
influence in the informal instruction and consolidation of the normative
contents of curriculum and official knowledge (Apple, 2000). With respect
to the present chapter, this development has proven a valuable approach
for the study of the operation of colonialist discourse (see Spurr, 1993) and
its deployment in the management of neocolonial relationships. At its most
concrete, this development has advanced analysis of the ideological work-

ings of discourse, particularly in terms of the historically specific treatment of the procedures of ideological articulation and rearticulation (Hall, 1988). Above all, it has underscored the significance of making connections, in temporal terms, in spatial/geographical terms, in disciplinary terms, in intertextual terms, and in conceptual terms (Stam, 1995).

Although Mitchell's and Reid-Walsh's cultural interrogation is connected to how "Barbie-as-text" may bear on the dilemmas and contradictions of their lives as girls and women, here the analysis of the Polynesian version of Barbie treats the way the doll articulates a historical encoding of the *ideal* and *placid* Polynesian native. The ideal and placid Polynesian native is a surprisingly persistent image constituted in Euro-American written and visual representations of Polynesia, and yet each appropriation is historically specific. This is a pervasive figure in colonialist discourse, and I explore the sites of its emergence and the various ways in which it intersects with articulations of race, nation, and gender.

Methodologically speaking, I treat Polynesian Barbie as a cultural *text*, a complex web of signs drawn from the innumerable centers of culture, which is irreducible to a single signification (see Barthes, 1977a, p. 146). Cultural texts, as Roland Barthes (1972) has argued, are not innocent; rather, they are capable of producing supplementary meanings, or connotations. Thus, in reading Polynesian Barbie, I seek to grasp not only what is explicit and written but also what is unsaid or implied. Obviously "Polynesian" Barbie implies a *difference:* between "Barbie" and some other ethnic or racial kind. It is the figuring of this difference that concerns this inquiry. It should be emphasized that my reading seeks to map shifting power relations in the formation of officially sanctioned visions of Polynesia. I aim to put Mattel's Polynesian Barbie in the service of political analysis in order to consider the colonialist discourses that have coded Pacific cultures in infantile and idyllic ways and in allochronic time-space. Thus my reading of Polynesian Barbie is intended to politicize the way in which such representations work to reduce the historical Pacific—a Pacific of transcultural innovation, political discord, and heterogeneity—to a static space of childlike and placid bodies. If one objective as educators is to invest and valorize what colonialist discourses inscribe the primitive and provincial, it seems justifiable to proceed by identifying some of the sites and means through which historical and cultural coherencies are formed in the production of the colonial subject.

Polynesian Barbie's Debut

Polynesian Barbie is one of Mattel's many designated "ethnic" dolls. It is proudly marketed in Mattel's Dolls of the World Collection, a categorization which curiously echoes the freak show known in the United States during the nineteenth century in which "savage" or "primitive" peoples and "abnormal" human beings were contemplated with a mixture of horror and fascination. Polynesian Barbie, typified by the iconic representation of the "hula girl," an early Euro-American figure popularized on the continental United States connoting "a sexually attractive young woman," has all the familiar signifiers, such as long, luminous, dark hair, bandeau top and grass skirt, and lei.[1] Yet the doll remains a "Barbie," with long slender legs, stiletto-shaped feet, teeny-weeny waist and that much-discussed bosom.

Barbie has incited a range of responses from outright denouncements to the celebratory. As Mitchell and Reid-Walsh point out, adults, and particularly women and feminists, reject what Barbie dolls appear to stand for: standard beauty, the male gaze, femininity, materialism, big business, and mass marketing (1995, p. 143). Women's groups, for example, remind us that Barbie's insatiable material appetite perpetuates consumption while her anatomically impossible body is sexist and demeaning. Cultural critics have interrogated how Barbie is yoked to practices of consumerism, to debates over gender and race relations, and to changing notions of the body (Urla & Swedlund, 1995). Ann Ducille (1994) brings attention to the commodification of race and gender difference in her treatment of multicultural Barbie dolls. She has argued that:

> Regardless of what color dyes the dolls are dipped in or what costumes they are adorned with, the image they present is the same mythically thin, long-legged, luxuriously-haired, buxom beauty. And while Mattel and other toy manufacturers may claim to have the best interests of ethnic audiences in mind . . . profit remains the motivating factor behind this merchandising of difference. (p. 50)

Indeed, the clear profit motive, which required relocating to countries such as Indonesia, Thailand, and China, where Mattel and other companies produce the bulk of their trademark brands and where workers lack basic rights, has been good for those at the top of Mattel. In 1995, then Mattel C.E.O. John Amerman took in $7 million and held an additional $23 million in stock options, while workers molding Barbies in a China toy factory earned a meager 25 cents per hour (Press, 1996).

The more celebratory responses to Mattel's success include numerous articles in business magazines that praise its marketing strategies in achieving brand-name recognition and dominance (Morris, 1998). Jill Barad, who superseded Amerman as Mattel's CEO was featured in a cover story in the American magazine *Business Week*. Although no longer with Mattel, Barad built the Barbie brand from what was a $320 million U.S. business in

1985 to a $2 billion global brand by 1998. That successful recovery included Barad's execution of the idea of "roles"; her hit was the Day to Night Barbie. By day Barbie was a stylish executive, by night, a party girl. Another triumph for Barad involved her push to sell dolls for "play patterns," such as shopping, dating, and going to the beach, among others. Thanks to Barad, the average American little girl owns nine Barbie dolls (Morris, 1998).

Keeping Mattel a "success story" was Barad's (and the next CEO's) biggest challenge. It is no secret that Mattel's "success" relies on appropriating trends in popular culture, co-opting competing or opposing definitions of Barbie dolls, participating in persistent consumer research, and relocating to countries where workers, like those in Indonesia, have no right to organize independently and earn the insufficient wage of $2.25 per day (Press, 1996). The accomplishment of those tactics can be seen in the introduction of "ethnic" Barbie dolls, in the intense expansion into global markets (a move which required Mattel to "tailor" Barbie to "regional cultures"), and in the recent announcement to "redesign" Barbie; she will now sport a new smile and a belly button; however, the much-talked-about "makeover" that was supposed to result in a doll with a more realistic figure (i.e., wider waist, slimmer hips, smaller bust) curiously never materialized (Healy, 2000; Pollack, 1996).

But Barbie is not only on the minds of cultural critics and CEOs. Among Americans there is a more general fascination with the doll, or so it seems. When Barbie turned forty, the media covered Mattel's plan to release a Butterfly Art Barbie, a Barbie with a butterfly tattoo on her stomach, and a Working Woman Barbie equipped with a laptop and cell phone. In visual culture, there were two television programs that were aired in the summer of 1998, one by the network ABC, *The Secret Lives of Barbie* (1998), and the other by PBS, *Barbie Nation: An Unauthorized Tour* (1998). Incidentally, when the creator of Barbie, Ruth Handler died in April 2002, the *New York Times* saw fit to carry the obituary on the front page and the following day on its editorial page. Perhaps there is some truth to the assertion that Barbie is "a force to contend with," for Barbie is undoubtedly one of the toy phenomena of the second half of the twentieth century (Terry & Urla, 1995, p. 278).

Still, any discussion that attempts to dictate with certainty the force of Barbie on her playmates will quickly discover that there is quite a range of responses (not all negative) to Barbie dolls. A significant amount of work in feminist media theory and criticism and in popular culture and cultural studies has advanced more nuanced treatments of mass culture and its relation to cultural artifacts in the structuring of subjectivities and in the endorsing of prevailing cultural norms (Broude & Garrard, 1992; Donald, 1992; Giroux & Simon, 1989; McCarthy & Crichlow, 1993; Modleski, 1986; Schwoch, White, & Reilly, 1992). These works share a concern with elucidating how television, film, popular literature, and other mass culture media negotiate the cultural demands in the construction of subjectivities. Specifically related to analysis of popular cultures, educational theorists Giroux and Simon (1989) have stressed that "popular cultures are constituted not just by commodity forms but by practices which reflect a creative and sometimes innovative capacity of people" (p. 227). Their observation not only suggests the productive ways in which a cultural product is employed or taken up but also implies, and rightly so, that the self cannot be *perfectly* adapted to social norms.

Taken together, these perspectives are warnings against the cultural elitism so pervasive in cultural criticism. That Barbie dolls may be read and used in ways that are unintended is not an issue here; as my reading aims to show (and subsequent examples make evident), they certainly are. Herein, Polynesian Barbie is used in the theorization of the textual production of the colonial body. This involves an engagement with representations of Polynesia imparted by different genres (e.g., scientific, literary, educational, and popular) of writing on the Pacific.

Polynesian Barbie as Sign

Social semiotics provides a point of entry for introducing the subject of representation by its treatment of objects as participating in signifying systems.[2] The questions that guide semiotic inquiry are, generally speaking, concerned with meaning. With respect to an object, such as Polynesian Barbie, it may be said that it is not simply a "Barbie doll" but functions as a *sign* for a multicultural sensibility (the referent) deployed by Mattel to appropriate current political concerns over cultural diversity.[3] Polynesian Barbie, like many of Barbie's ethnic sisters—there are, for example, Hispanic Barbie, black Barbie, and Asian Barbie, among others—is, then, Mattel's response to the hitherto excluded (Berkwitz, 1990, p. 48). It is a gesture toward inclusion.

In his analysis of the advertising image, Barthes has elaborated the different messages it comprises (see Barthes, 1977b). To substitute Barthes's image for our object-as-cultural-text, let us consider the different messages Mattel's Polynesian Barbie stocks. The object at once yields a first message: a Barbie marked by a difference (an ethnic or racial difference is implied);

this is supported by the graphic vehicle "Polynesian Barbie" on its packaging. The first message, Barthes explains, can itself be broken down; thus Polynesian Barbie is not simply a name for Barbie but also, by an additional signified, that of "Polynesianicity." Barthes has repeatedly returned to the issue of connotation, which constitutes a central theme in such works as "The Rhetoric of the Image" (1977b) and, perhaps most important, *Mythologies* (1972). It is secondary meanings—or *connotations*, to use Barthes's preferred term—that he is interested in uncovering in *Mythologies*. Connotations, as Kaja Silverman (1983) explains, are understood as "second-order" signifying systems—systems that build on already existing ones (such as language). Furthermore, Barthes distinguishes them from "denotative" or "first-order" signifying systems (Silverman, 1983, p. 26). Elaborating Barthes's formulation still further, Silverman writes, "the connotative sign consists of both parts of the denotative sign [i.e., signifier and signified] as well as the additional meaning or meanings which they help to generate" (p. 27). The point to be emphasized here is that Barthes identifies connotation with the operation of ideology, or *mythic speech*. For Barthes, mythic speech consists of the deployment of signifiers for the purpose of expressing and surreptitiously justifying dominant values of a given historical period.

With respect to Barthes's formulation, the object—the Barbie doll—operates as the denotative signifier (that part that does the referring), while the conception of a "Polynesian" Barbie doll provides the denotative signified (that part that is referred to). The object and its corresponding concept are then seen as conjoining to form the denotative sign (a Barbie doll that is marked by difference). That sign becomes a signifier in a second signifying transaction, that of connotation. As Barthes writes: "we now know that the signifier can be looked at, in myth, from two points of view: as the final term of the linguistic system, or as the first term of the mythical system" (1972, pp. 116–117). Thus, as the first term of the mythical system, Polynesian Barbie constitutes in its entirety a signifier for such ideological signifieds as "multiculturalism" and racial and ethnic "inclusion." No doubt there are problems with this formulation which we will need to reassess if we are to hold on to connotation as an ideological event.[4] The two that concern us, which Silverman (1983) has outlined, consist in the assumption that connotation involves an ideological coercion, while denotation somehow engages on an ideologically innocent level. However, the theoretical work of Louis Althusser demonstrates otherwise. "Althusser," writes Silverman, "suggests that during a child's linguistic initiation, when he or she is ostensibly learning denotation rather than connotation, he or she is already positioned *within* ideology" (1983, p. 30; italics added). Secondly, in *Mythologies* Barthes suggests that ideology is a condition of false consciousness, which implies that there is a reality outside of ideology to which we would have direct access. Once again I will maintain, as Silverman (1983) does in her reference to Althusser where he demonstrates, in "Marxism and Humanism," that it is impossible to step outside ideology since it is only inside it that we find our subjectivity and our social reality. We must be mindful, therefore, of these reassessments if we are to hold onto to the notion of connotation as an ideological event.

Barthes's formulation suggests that the relationship between a connotative signifier and a connotative signified can be explained only through reference to a larger social field, a field that is structured in terms of values and interests. Since my concern is with Mattel's deployment of difference (i.e., Polynesianicity), let us consider the *codes* of the larger social field, which participate in the production and intelligibility of that difference. Polynesian Barbie is dressed not in an evening gown, a business suit, or any other contemporary outfit, but in a grass skirt costume. She has long, dark hair and a lei around her neck. The entirety of the costume is a cultural code for the enunciation of difference. But what permits the recognition of these details (e.g., grass-skirt costume, lei, long dark hair) and its association with "Polynesian"? This may be the place to introduce the *relational* status of the signifying instance. In *The Archaeology of Knowledge,* Michel Foucault (1972) indicates that the book is caught up in "a system of references to other books, other texts, other sentences: it is a node within a [discursive] network" (p. 23). His remarks encourage us to see how a work is only one component in a larger discursive network. This view of reading is suited to the project of uncovering the cultural and historical matrix within which a text is situated.

Polynesian Barbie's costume references an enduring image of the figure of the "hula girl," always alluring and hospitable, the iconic representation of the commercial production of "Hawaii." The creation of commercialism and popular culture, the hula girl is often clad in a native-style costume and depicted offering a lei, dancing the hula, serving exotic dishes, or simply gazing longingly out to sea (Brown, 1982). Jane Desmond (1999) asserts that "Polynesian looking hula girl" images surfaced on the U.S. continent around the decades of the turn of the twentieth century in the form of stereoscope pictures, postcards, and photographs, which "ran the gamut from beautiful to alluring, to sexual, to pornographic" (p. 48). Desmond indicates that in the following decades that look was altered, as a *hapa haole* or half-white look emerged as a dominant image of Hawaiian female beauty (p. 48).

Mainland venues depicting hula included live performances such as those at the Chicago World's Fair in 1893 and the 1915 Panama-Pacific International Exposition in San Francisco. Hula dancing was performed on the Midway Plaisance at the Chicago's World Fair in the ethnic village of South Sea islanders. In a study concerning the educational function of world's fairs in disseminating evolutionary theories about race and culture from academic circles to the space of popular consumption, Robert Rydell (1984) observes that the Midway, classified under the auspices of the exposition's Department of Ethnology, was seen as "a great object lesson in anthropology by leading anthropologists" (p. 40). The Midway, asserts Rydell, "provided visitors with ethnological" and "scientific sanction for the American view of the nonwhite world as barbaric and childlike" (p. 40). These ideas encountered at fairs were not sequestered from the formal domain of education, and indeed they were taught to young people in schools, as Steven Selden's (1999) telling study has shown.

The figure of the hula girl also surfaced in Hollywood South Seas films. These films often located the South Seas within a disjunctive space—a place of risk (i.e., moral corruption) and desire (i.e., hope of pleasure). Structured by and often adaptations of late-eighteenth- and nineteenth-century literary works, the South Pacific was "textualized" by numerous writings, such as those of John Hawkesworth, Herman Melville, and Pierre Loti. In a discussion of Hollywood images of the Pacific, Glenn Man (1991) points out that: "the Hollywood South Seas films offered the romantic myth of the noble savage in which the tropics were a pagan paradise where Anglo-Saxon customs and inhibitions could be shed along with Western clothes" (p. 17). Hollywood South Seas films often featured the hula girl and hula-style dancing. *Hula* (1927) starred the silent film actor Clara Bow, and *Bird of Paradise* (1932) featured Dolores del Rio as Luana, a native who performs two Hollywood-inflected hulas, one during a native dance sequence and the other for her wedding ceremony. As Man (1991) indicates, Hollywood's image of the South Seas as an idyll for the white man among people who are primitive but happy in their simplicity is but one aspect of the South Seas genre. Another version of the genre offers images of the destruction that the white man brings in his wake.

Concerning the image of the hula girl and the feminization of Hawaii, Desmond (1999) notes that the live performances of hula girls proliferated "from the most elite theaters on Broadway to tent shows and chautauquas in small towns" (p. 67). She points out that the dancers were "almost always female, often Caucasian, and rarely highly trained in hula" (p. 67). Most significantly, these performances from the mid-teens through the 1920s: "helped codify a vision of Hawaii as feminized, embodied, sensual, and *hapa haole*" (p. 67). The figure of the hula girl, not surprisingly then, has become the dominant visual image associated with Hawaii. But it is an affiliation that is more than ever in conflict with the neocolonial imaginings pursued by state officials and convention executives of the Hawaii Visitors and Convention Bureau who are intent in marketing Hawaii as a "business" destination—an international center for business and global exchange, a "Geneva of the Pacific" to use their official expression (Burris, 2001; Kayal, 2001). In their reassessment of the current destination image, officials are reacting with different campaigns to transform the dominant (feminized) image of a place of "leisure," a place to play in the sun and sand, to the (masculine) image of Hawaii as "a viable business destination" where serious work can be done. Although a destination image is largely shaped by media promotion of travel, it is also influenced by other circuits of representation in other times. Here Desmond is worth quoting at length:

> From the 1880s until the teens, Hawai'i's destination image was shaped mainly by visual and verbal representations. . . . Postcards, photographs, and stereoscope cards contributed to the circuit of images, as did sketches in advertisements. . . . Educational articles and documentary and scientific reports also circulated in public discourse . . . the outlines of which had been laid out during the preceding century by European explorers' reports, missionary diatribes, and writers' encomiums. (1999, p. 6)

It is precisely these ostensibly disparate modes of representation—literary, educational, visual, artistic, commercial—I would add, that are involved in the production and maintenance of the Pacific imaginary and the cultural screen of primitiveness. Moreover, it is this cultural matrix that the Polynesianness of Barbie, in the form of the hula girl, is situated. Thus Mattel's Polynesian Barbie does *not* simply enunciate a current enlightened sensibility toward the hitherto excluded; it also participates in the production of meaning and instructs in the hierarchies of race.

Barbie and the Indeterminancy of Meaning

But what of that nonbiodegradable plastic called "Barbie"? Barbie, so the story goes, was a knockoff off of the "*Bild* Lilli" doll, a plaything for adult men that was based on a post–World War II comic character in the *Bild Zeitung,* a downscale German newspaper similar to America's *National Enquirer* (Lord, 1994, p. 8). The doll sold principally in tobacco shops. "In her cartoon incarnation, Lilli," writes one biographer, is an "ice-blond, pixie-nosed specimen of an Aryan ideal" (Lord, 1994, p. 8). But Barbie was created by a woman, Mattel cofounder Ruth Handler. Jack Ryan, known for his work in designing the Hawk and Sparrow missiles for the Raytheon

Company, crafted her mold. Barbie made her debut in 1959 as Mattel's new teenage fashion doll. Urla and Swedlund relate the rise in popularity of the doll with the coinciding of the postwar creation of a distinctive teenage lifestyle (1995, p. 280). They note that: "teens, their tastes, and behaviors were becoming the object of both sociologists and criminologists as well as market survey researchers intent on capturing their discretionary dollars" (p. 280). Amidst the moral panic over juvenile delinquency, note Urla and Swedlund (1995, p. 280), Barbie was a reassuring symbol of middle-class values. Though Barbie started out looking like a vampy, "slightly Bardot-esque doll," she was gradually transformed into an "affluent, well-groomed, socially conservative" frat type (Urla & Swedlund, 1995, p. 280). Personifying the good girl who abstained from sex, Barbie had pajama parties, barbeques, and spending sprees. Barbie's appearance and packaging, furthermore, instill the dominant fictions about femininity.

Indicative is the pink-colored packaging along with the conventional somatic femininity (e.g., large and high breasts, narrow waist, madeup face, long legs, and stiletto-shaped feet). At the risk of stating the obvious, the pink packaging is a gendered code and serves to equate pinkness with girl/woman/feminine, while Barbie's large, high breasts and stiletto-shaped feet are drawn from an equally familiar prototype of the "pinup" photograph, an ensemble of codes associated with heterosexual male desire. Here stereotypical constructions about what constitutes femininity and a heterosexual male gaze are maintained.

Many cultural critics, however, insist that we treat Barbie as a site of struggle where meaning(s) are contested and dominant ideologies disturbed (Mitchell & Reid-Walsh, 1995). They warn that interpretations that assume meaning is fixed neglect the complex ways of consuming Barbie dolls, thereby casting those who play and consume them as cultural dupes and victims of false consciousness. This is not a trivial point. Cultural critic Stuart Hall (1992) asserts, and I agree, that: "there is always something decentered about the medium of culture, about language, textuality, and signification, which always escapes and evades the attempt to link it, directly and immediately, with other structures" (p. 284). To appreciate fully the politics implicit in Hall's remarks, we need to place it within a broader intellectual current on the problem of the determinacy or indeterminacy of meaning. This is an argument that has had theoretical and political implications in a range of disciplinary fields including education and cultural studies, but we are probably most familiar with its association with deconstruction and literary studies in America.

From a deconstructionist point of view, the question of indeterminate meaning is described in relation to the problematic of the linguistic sign and of writing, an engagement formulated systematically in the works of Jacques Derrida and others using deconstructive approaches more generally.[5] Derrida (1982) uses the neologism *différance* to suggest that meaning or signification, which the sign in classical semiology conveys, is at once differential *and* deferred (p. 9). For Derrida, signification is not simply the result of differentiation (as in Saussure), but is also the result of deferral, which implies that the sign is *deferred presence.* Deferred presence relates to the putting off of an encounter with a missing presence that the sign is presumed to be moving toward (Derrida, 1982). Politically speaking, because *différance* brings attention to the impossibility of ultimate closure of meaning, it can encourage a consideration of the exercise of power in naturalized meaning. In other words, it may bring our attention to how certain significations prevail over others.

The view that meaning is deferred gives concrete significance to the reappropriations of Barbie dolls and the potentially subversive commentary they manifest. The experimental installation "A Doll You Can Shave" by Zbigniew Libera at the Center for Contemporary Art in Poland some years ago is a mockery of contemporary society's drive for bodily perfection (Perlez, 1996). In Honolulu, a multimedia exhibit at Hawaii Pacific University entitled "Painted Virgins and Karma Babies," by artist and poet Alshaa T. Rayne, transforms Barbie dolls into images of dislocation, fear, and disaster, soliciting reflection on our vulnerabilities. The visual image of Rayne's work evokes discomfort as much as it provokes discussion. Other reappropriations include unauthorized versions of Barbie such as Trailer Trash Barbie, Hooker Barbie, and Drag Queen Barbie (see Ashley, 1996). Trailer Trash Barbie sports a cigarette in her mouth and black roots in her platinum-blond hair.

Along with the multimedia installations and the unauthorized versions of Barbie, there are also public performances and made-for-television programs, such as the satirical play *Plastica Fantastica,* which lampoons Barbie's anatomically impossible contours (Foley, 1997), and the PBS program *Barbie Nation: An Unauthorized Tour* (1998) by filmmaker Susan Stern. In *Barbie Nation,* Stern travels across the country collecting Barbie stories from people who have bought the doll. The stories, mostly from adults, give a wry glimpse into some of the attachments formed around the dolls, such as the fellowships formed around collecting Barbie dolls or the contemporary incarnation of Barbie as a favorite fetish object.

These rearticulations of Barbie not only illustrate some of the imaginative interpretive acts that enlist Barbies in interrupting the official reincarnations of the doll by Mattel, but also encourage more political commentary on the cultural matrix within which the doll is situated. They exist despite Mattel's vigilant management of their circulation, as, for example, withdrawing sponsorship of exhibitions, co-opting competing or opposing definitions of Barbie dolls, and threatening trademark infringement litigation.[6]

While the scope of signifying formations is tightly controlled so that a text is ostensibly made to express the dominant values of a given historical period, we have also followed interpretive strategies whereby the text is regarded as a node within a discursive network and discovered a variety of ways in which the meaning of a text has no necessary closure. With respect to Polynesian Barbie, we saw how its "Polynesianicity" was possible only on the basis of a complex field of discourse and prior representations. It is to this discursive field of Euro and Euro-American representations of Polynesia and the colonialist and imperialist ideologies embedded within them that I now turn. The written narrative that accompanies Polynesian Barbie will hereafter be the focus of my reading.

Modes of Colonialist Discourse: Exoticism and Primitivism

exoticism . . . , n. 1. Celebration of the culturally or geographically remote, together with more or less willful ignorance of historical particulars. 2. Sexual dalliance with difference and marriage to familiar. 3. A gustatory preference for rare condiments or pleasures: "Gauguin's . . . taste for the exotic" (F. Fénéon, La Cravache, July 6, 1889). *4. Fascination with non-natives (non-Europeans); fascination with natives (persons indigenous to a non-European land).*
——*Eisenman, 1996, p. 604.*

primitivism . . . , n. 1. Modern Western infatuation with the cultures of indigenous, tribal, and conquered peoples. 2. Belief in the superiority of early, remote, and technologically rudimentary cultures. 3. Assertion that people living in small-scale societies are backward, degenerate, or retarded. 4. The artistic use of forms derived from indigenous peoples. 5. Indulgence in sexual promiscuity or nudism: "a primitive stage when unrestricted sexual freedom prevailed within the tribe" (F. Engels, The Origin of the Family . . . *[1884], New York, 1990). 6. Antimodernism or anticapitalism.*
——*Eisenman, 1996, p. 607.*

The Polynesianicity of Polynesian Barbie is contingent on how the marks of difference do their magic. On the back of the package is an informative narrative that describes to young readers the place and customs of Polynesia. The narrative is supplemented with three sketches: one is of the Hawaiian archipelago, one of a thatched hut, and one of two hula girls and a young, presumably native male wearing a *malo*, or loincloth, holding fire torches. The narrative is written in the first-person voice of Polynesian Barbie, and it reads:

> Hello! Welcome to beautiful *Polynesia*, which means many islands. All together there are 13 groups of tropical islands included in this vast South Pacific paradise. They form what is called *The Polynesian Triangle*.
>
> Some well-known locations in the triangle include *New Zealand, Tahiti* and the *Hawaiian Islands*, which is the largest group. There are also many volcanic islands made of solid black lava rock, and surrounded by beaches of beautiful black sand!

Following the geographical and topological information, the manners and customs of Polynesians are introduced:

> I live with my family in a thatched hut made from bamboo and woven palm branches. . . . Throughout the many islands of Polynesia, large families of grandparents, aunts, uncles and cousins all live and work together, building huts, gathering food, and caring for children. To preserve peace and happiness among our people, it is our custom to speak only kind words to one another.

In order to authenticate the information and give it a greater sense of reality, playmates of Polynesian Barbie are taught some Polynesian words and their English translations:

> In the Hawaiian Islands especially, everyone looks forward to a feast called a *luau*, where the finest *ia* (fish), roasted pig, *poi* (taro root paste), coconuts and bananas are served with great delight. The luau is also a time for dancing! Women dance in traditional grass skirts, like the one I'm wearing. Men perform, too, often juggling torches of fire!

And finally, young readers are invited to partake in contemporary tourist activities of leisure:

> As the sun passes across the tropics, it gently heats the water, making the ocean a wonderful spot for canoeing, fishing and surfing.

On many levels Mattel's narrative is a troubling representation of Polynesia, especially for those who appreciate and value the diversity of Polynesian cultures. The narrative recuperates a familiar picture of Polynesia, one which trivializes its forms of sociality. Perhaps most disquieting is the persistence of colonialist discourse that inscribes Maori, Tahitian, and Hawaiian subjects as infantile and ideal and the ideological production of these heterogeneous islands as a "South Pacific Paradise," which echoes an all-too-familiar Euro-American representation of exotic surplus.

The simple/ideal/exotic encoding of cultural others has a long and intertextual history; its dissemination and the variety of its incarnations require discussion of it with historical specificity. A way to approach these associations and their deployment in the context of the South Pacific (even though Hawaii is actually located north of the equator, it is attached to the web of associations with the South Pacific) is offered by James Knapp (1989) and Abigail Solomon-Godeau (1992) in their discussions of primitivism as a discourse. To be sure, the fascination with the "primitive" has a long and contradictory trajectory. Its existence at various times and in various contexts may be characterized by combinations of desire and repulsion, rejection and incorporation, exploitation and idealization (Solomon-Godeau, 1991).

The word *primitive*, writes Stephen Eisenman (1996), acquired "its modern English and French significance in the fifteenth and sixteenth centuries, when it came to mean 'earliest,' 'first,' 'originary' and 'basic'" (p. 607). The concept surfaced in early accounts of the "New World," Montaigne's essay "Of the Cannibals," Rousseau's critique of civilized life in the eighteenth century, and the exhibitions of primitive art and culture staged by the colonial powers in the last half of the nineteenth century (Knapp, 1989; Solomon-Godeau, 1991). There is, then, no continuity in its usage or meaning; as a discourse, says Knapp, it is capable of traversing the boundaries of culture, language, and genre (1989, p. 53). Its deployment is ecumenical; it can be found worldwide in philosophical, literary, artistic, and popular representations, to name a few, but it is *not* independent of historical time or from the shifting contexts of power to which it is often adapted. By the eighteenth century the concept of the primitive had become a ground for debates about progress and civilization (Eisenman, 1996).

The published accounts of the various voyages to the Pacific is one domain for considering the specific valency of primitivism as it relates to the European encoding of Polynesia and Polynesian bodies. Louis de Bougainville, the French colonel of the 1768 voyage to the South Seas, on seeing Tahiti, addressed the island initially as "la *nouvelle Cythère*" and referenced his observations of Tahitian life to the "Golden Age" and the "Elysian Fields," myths that are associated with Western antiquity but were refashioned in the eighteenth century as a general discourse of the superiority of "primitive man"—the belief that the earliest condition of humankind, or humans in their original and natural state, was the best condition. In our time we are most familiar with these myths as literary devices. For example, reference to the "Golden Age" is often used to signify peoples who lived in happier times than we do, while "Elysium" in its variations frequently implies a mythical land located somewhere at the world's end. These classical myths are often used by themselves or combined with other ones. In either case, they operate by designating distances between self and other.

The primitivist representation of Pacific peoples followed two forms.[7] As Bernard Smith remarks in his pioneering work *European Vision and the South Pacific,* there was: "a soft primitivism, applied mainly to the inhabitants of the Society Islands, and a hard primitivism, applied to such peoples as the Fuegians, the Maoris, and the Australian aborigines" (1985, p. 5). In European representations, Tahitians in particular became identified with the inhabitants of Elysium, an association that secured itself, according to Smith, "permanently upon the imagination of Europe" (p. 42). The parallels drawn between Polynesia and classical antiquity that Europeans projected onto non-European bodies articulate one component of what Henri Baudet has defined as "the mythical element in the European conception of itself and of the outside world" (1965, p. 59). Bougainville, for example, by means of analogies with legendary literary topoi, materializes a prelapsarian figure in the South Pacific. It is a figure that was first projected, according to Baudet, "onto the European and his past," then later "it was projected onto non-Western peoples who, 'not-yet' corrupt like the European, were 'still' in the practically paradisiacal state [that] we may . . . have lost forever" (p. 59).

But Bougainville's Tahiti not only evoked nostalgia for Western fantasies of a space that stood outside time, static, unchanging, and not-yet corrupt; it also aroused fantasies of plenitude which was often sexually coded. Here is as an illustrative passage from Bougainville's *Voyage.* Upon anchoring at Tahiti, Bougainville made the following observation:

> The periaguas were full of females; who, for agreeable features, are not inferior to most European women; and who in point of beauty of the body might, with much reason, vie with them all. Most of these fair females were naked. . . . The glances which they gave us . . . seemed to discover some degree of uneasiness, notwithstanding the innocent manner in which they were given; perhaps, because nature has every where embellished their sex with a natural timidity; or because even in those countries, where the ease of the golden age is still in use, women seem least to desire what they most wish for. (Bougainville, 1967, p. 218)

Bougainville's observation is pregnant with associations. One image that certainly stands out is the aesthetic positioning of the Tahitian body. Bougainville clearly makes the body of Tahitian women tantamount to the beauty of "most" European women. In this equalizing gesture, he also, intentionally or not, codes Tahitian bodies with a sexual freedom that European women supposedly lack. It has been said that Bougainville's classical training mediated much of what he saw and wrote (Smith, 1985). It can also be said that his appellations of Tahitian life in terms of the "Golden Age" code that living in ways that deny it historical time. Tahitian life is rhetorically wiped clean of history and constitutes a space that renders it not only static but natural as well. The striking constellation of native woman/naked/nature/Golden Age in Bougainville's report is also suggestive of how an entire people is allegorized by the figure of the female body onto which images of fantasies of seduction and the fulfillment of sexual desire are projected. Bougainville's description of Tahitian life encapsulates the "exoticized" primitivism ascribed to Polynesia that will become so central to a Euro-American Pacific imaginary.

The Western literary imaginary of the Pacific is yet another space of entanglement with primitivism. Recent discussions of Western literature on the Pacific, for example, have brought attention to the way in which the South Pacific was textualized, often by conflicting motifs, in the literary modes of representation. Rod Edmond (1997) has charted the recurrent literary forms and motifs that shaped European representations of the South Pacific. These literary constructs lent themselves to the perception of the Pacific as an area for settlement and commerce. In the British context, William Dampier's books, published in the last years of the seventeenth century, reveal the interplay between the literary and imperial designs. Dampier's books were considered "spectacular literary successes"; his influence can be discerned not only in the publication and translation of several essays of Pacific geography but also in the inception of a national plan for the occupation of the South Seas (Leon, 1994, p. 19).

The literary influence, however, is not the only form of writing folded into Mattel's narrative. There are traces of other kinds of writing, too. Paul Carter maintains that most histories of Pacific places deny "the plural nature of historical space" (1987, p. 303). Carter's insight is invaluable in making apparent the process of discursive territorialization, the inscription of names on presumably amorphous space. The information in Mattel's narrative describing Polynesian islands as "tropical" and "volcanic" and their geographical location as being in the "South Pacific" or in the "Polynesian Triangle" disregards the multiple versions, stories, myths, and histories enunciated by indigenous peoples. The orders of topography and geography appear universal and natural rather than revealing that they are products of a culturally specific classificatory practice, one that is implicated in the project of scientific and cultural imperialism.

Mattel's narrative provides information on the type of dwellings that Polynesians live in and the kinds of materials used in building them. Playmates of Polynesian Barbie learn that Polynesians come from a place where people live in "thatched huts" made from "bamboo and palm branches." It is worth noting that in the writings by British evangelical missionary scholars during the early nineteenth century, the dwelling-house index was often deployed as a moral code for justifying distinctions that located Polynesians in a lesser moral space and an anachronistic historical time.[8] As one of the first annual reports of mission work in Tahiti dated September 1819, informs:

> Several of the natives have made neat dwelling-houses, and plastered them inside and out. We hope to make them utterly ashamed of their continual practices of sleeping together as a flock of sheep; and we are determinately desirous of introducing among them those habits which will contribute to their temporal felicity and prepare them for domestic life. (quoted in Lovett, 1899, p. 246)

The dwelling-house index, as it was used in missionary accounts, was not simply a way to describe a living space; it was a code for moral progress. For these evangelists it mattered whether the dwelling was "neat" and "plastered" and whether families slept together or in separate rooms, because these taken together served as signs of the moral condition of subjects. But what is obscured here is the arbitrary (culturally specific, not universal) moral value imputed to the "neat" and "plastered" dwelling-house. And while the dwelling-house category functioned in the nineteenth century as a moral code for the social development and moral progress of natives, here, in Mattel's picture of Polynesia, it operates to deny the coevality of Polynesians.

Mattel's narrative also furnishes information about the manners and customs of Polynesians. Children learn how Polynesians supposedly interact with each other—"it is our custom to speak only kind words to one another." This figure of the agreeable and untroubled native invoked in Mattel's narrative is a persistent stereotype that is repeated in a variety of media from late-nineteenth-century educational books to contemporary journalism. An illustration of the persistence of this trope in the present time is the nationwide airing of a *60 Minutes* CBS TV investigative program that featured the inquiry surrounding the mismanagement of the Bishop Estate.[9] The reporter of the story remarked that "Hawaiians" put up with the

trustees' behavior for years because "traditionally they tend to be noncon-
frontational and slow to anger" ("The Bishop Estate," *60 Minutes,* 2000).
This observation recuperates an image, so ingrained in Euro-American
imaginary of the Pacific, of the Hawaiian subject as placid and gullible. Not
only are *kanaka maoli* (indigenous Hawaiians) hailed to identify with this
placid subject, but mainland audiences of the program do not get any sense
of the history of Hawaiian agency, a history well documented by activists,
scholars, and intellectuals (McGregor-Alegado, 1980; Silva, 1998; Trask,
1987).

The other "customs" that Polynesians share, according to Mattel's
account, include building huts and gathering food. These purported
"customs" sustain an already sedimented cultural screen. Polynesians are
located outside historical time and are consequently inscribed with an unchanging essence. Insofar as contemporary urban life no longer involves
"building huts" or requires "gathering food"—in truth, Hawaiians never
adhered to the latter for they were remarkably good farmers and especially
skillful in the cultivation of wet taro (Kirch & Sahlins, 1992)—these descriptions of Polynesian life are codes for a past time, not a now-time. In effect, Mattel's narrative reinscribes colonialist discourse by rearticulating
some of the most insidious tropes in European observations and writings
that textualized Polynesians as infantile and idyllic and in allochronic time-
space.

Representations of Imperial America: Educational Texts, Commercial Advertising, and Guidebooks

Mattel's narrative relies on a repertoire of visual images affiliated with the
commercial production of Hawaii as a feminized site of placid but exotic
bodies. Central to this construction is the images of the "hula girl" and natives entertaining or engaged in presumably authentic cultural activities,
for example, women dancing in traditional *ti* skirts and native men in *malo*
juggling fire torches at a *luau.* Speaking about the indigenous dance of the
Hawaiian Islands, Hawaiian activist and scholar, Haunani-Kay Trask
(2000) calls the appropriation of hula for the entertainment of tourists an
"insidious form of cultural prostitution" (p. 9). Trask insists that, "the
hula . . . an ancient form of dance with deep spiritual meaning, has been
made ornamental" (p. 9).

The representation of the contemporary Hawaiian Islands in Mattel's
narrative as an "exotic destination" and the image-repertoire that it relies
on and refers to are authorized not by adventurers, explorers, or mission-

ary scholars, although many of the tropes that actively constructed Polynesia in various modes of representation from these encounters certainly lay the groundwork. Rather the representation is ordered by a neocolonial imaginary manifested in the tourist field. The screen of primitiveness deriving from colonialist discourse constituted in the Western European encounter with Polynesia is not obliterated, and with respect to Honolulu, it is what fuels the emerging tourist industry at the turn of the twentieth century.

Before the turn of the century, well-off Euro-Americans visited Hawaii on pleasure trips, but the development of organized tourism as a commercial venture was new and coincided with several important political events and shifts in power (Desmond, 1999). Significant was the overthrow of the Hawaiian monarchy in the person of by Queen Lili'uokalani in 1893 by American-backed businessmen, many of whom were plantation owners and descendants of missionaries. In 1898 Hawaii was annexed to the United States despite protests by native Hawaiians (see Silva, 1998), and in 1900 it became a territory of the United States. These interventions, asserts Desmond (1999), "echoe[d] that in Guam, Cuba, the Philippines, and Puerto Rico and was part of the same expansionist policy that fed the Spanish-American War in 1898 and established the new U.S. 'imperial archipelago'" (1999, p. 35). After the war, Desmond notes, public discourse would locate Hawaii both in relation to these other new colonies and in relation to mainland populations as part of a renegotiated U.S. national imaginary (p. 35).

Educational Texts

This rearticulated national imaginary found expression in illustrated compendiums and in educational and scientific pamphlets and books that portrayed the newly annexed territories as America's "possessions." The common feature of these books was the "feminization" of these possessions (Desmond, 1999, p. 49). The visual representational strategy, says Desmond, utilized the female figure as a metaphor for the "the people," while the narrative served to inventory the resources and people newly available to the United States (pp. 49–50). Here it is sufficient to mention the theorization of governmentality and its relation to the mapping of the nation-state. Matthew Hannah's (2000) study of governmentality in nineteenth-century America, for example, maintains that census-taking be placed alongside land surveys and treated as a spatially organized epistemological tool with political implications. The narrative in *Our New Possessions:*

Cuba, Puerto Rico, Hawaii, Philippines (Baldwin, 1899), which was designed as a geographical aid for instruction, imparts a "scientific" mode of writing that connotes objectivity toward its subject matter. It presents a list of information-oriented classifications for each "possession." That its objectivity should break down the moment an element of difference is introduced is most apparent in its inventory of the "People," as this example on Hawaii illustrates:

> People.—The latest census returns, taken in 1896, give the total population of the islands as 109,020. . . . The Kanakas, as the natives are called, are noted for their gentleness and intelligence. Although individually brave and tenacious . . . they are a peaceloving race and easily governed. No other people have so readily adopted civilization, or become so soon and so thoroughly Americanized . . . the English language is very generally spoke in preference to the mother tongue. Since the introduction of modern civilization upon the islands the native population has steadily decreased. . . . The immediate cause of this reduction is probably due in a large measure to the radical changes which civilization has made in the manners and customs of the people, depriving them of that lightheartedness and freedom from care which characterized their former life. (Baldwin, 1899, p. 23)

The inventory of the people is far from an objective observation. The information presented on *kanaka* relies heavily on prior representations and discourses, namely the primitivist representations of Polynesians found in European voyage accounts since the eighteenth century. While this mode of representation—"educational"—pretends to be distributing disinterested knowledge, it is clearly involved in the production of difference and in the affirmation of a specific addressee, the sovereign "American." Its narrative articulates what David Spurr calls "the rhetoric of affirmation," which he explicates as an element in colonialist discourse that is "deployed on behalf of a collective subjectivity which idealizes itself variously in the name of civilization, humanity, science, progress, etc., so that the repeated affirmation of such values becomes in itself a means of gaining power and mastery" (1993, p. 110). What is being affirmed in this allegedly objective teaching tool is the representation of "American civilization" through implicit demonstrations of its superiority. This superiority is conveyed through seemingly trivial or unmotivated remarks about its form of governance, its language, and its overall civility.

The imagery invoked in the narrative intimates that Hawaii is in need of what Desmond calls "the masculine dynamism of U.S. colonial administration" (1999, p. 50). And while the invisible voice of the narrative expresses some ambivalence toward the civilizing assault on the indigenous population, it forms no hindrance to the epistemological and economic exploitation that is taking place. In truth, the assumptions about American civilization that the inventory iterates carry more direct pedagogical implications. It need not be said that the geographical aid has a crucial educational function—it does not simply provide disinterested knowledge; it is also involved in upholding and preserving the dominant fiction of the nation-state.

There is still another component to the rhetoric of affirmation that needs to be underscored. It includes the articulation of material prosperity and its linkage with moral progress (Spurr, 1993). This combination, moral goodness and material wealth, is expressed in the books and pamphlets on America's possessions. In the same instructional guide discussed above, under the inventory of "Resources and Industry," the observation is made that: "Large amounts of American capital have been invested in this industry [sugar cane], and to it the present prosperity of the islands is to a large extent due" (Baldwin, 1899, p. 20). The positing of American capital with material prosperity of the islands not only performs the ideological work of affirming a capitalist economy but also operates to sanitize its economic and social relations. Writing a year earlier, the journalist, author, and historian Trumbull White asserted a similar view about the effect American investment would have on moral development in America's new possessions. Still uncertain of the kind of American political involvement in these territories, White is content with economic domination with a moral purpose. "To dominate in commercial influence and in all things for the uplifting of a swarming population of alien races," wrote White, "is a function as worthy and of more interest and consequence to most of our people, than the mere detail of official sway" (1898, p. 16).

These publications, used for educating young Americans about their new possessions, not only involved the production of difference, they also involved the production of a collective national consciousness through a rhetoric of affirmation. The perpetual need for self-affirmation, Spurr notes, "is essential to all [Western] language as a symbolic activity which validates the presence, that is, the symbolizing power, of a speaking or writing subject" (1993, p. 109). But this narcissism in writing, Spurr remarks, also involves subordination (p. 110). Concerning Hawaii and the Hawaiian subject, that asymmetrical relation is most pronounced in the inscribing of the *kanaka* body as essentially placid and ideal. The observations made about their readiness to adopt civilization, about enthusiastically absorbing "American" manners and preferring those ways to their own, as well as the construction of *kanaka* as easily governed and nondisruptive ultimately deprive Hawaiian subjects of the status of political subjects and symbolically strip them of their agency. In the subsequent sections it will be shown that the educational domain is not the only site where race, nation, and gender fictions underwrite the Western representation of the ideal and placid native. This interface has also featured prominently in the advertisements for commercial tourism.

Commercial Advertising

Following the overthrow of Queen Lili'uokalani in 1893, the commercial prospects of U.S. tourism seemed to offer new opportunities for business expansion. In 1901 the Merchants Association in Honolulu began discussing tourism possibilities, and by 1903 the Hawaiian Promotion Committee had been created.[10] After World War I, tourism was fed by an increase in advertising by steamship companies such as Matson Line and Oceanic Line and by the Hawaii Tourist Bureau (Desmond, 1999). At this time photography also began to replace drawing as the primary medium for advertising, and by the 1930s almost 80 percent of illustrated advertisements employed photographs (Johnston, 1997). The difference in these two media can be seen in the advertisements for travel to Hawaii that were carried in the upper-bourgeois magazine *Vanity Fair* during the early 1930s.

In early illustrated advertisements, Hawaii was portrayed as a South Seas playground for well-off urban whites, whose visual presence dominated the advertisements (Desmond, 1999). In 1933, for example, a series of full-page drawn illustrations displayed a sophisticated and wealthy class of white travelers in settings of leisure—dining, dancing, sipping cocktails, relaxing near the pool—aboard the steamships that departed from the ports of San Francisco and Los Angeles to Honolulu. Illustrated advertisements by the steamship companies and the Hawaii Tourist Bureau presented Hawaii as an American holiday destination that was safe, "exotic yet comfortingly familiar, unspoiled, yet with all the modern conveniences one might need" (Desmond, 1999, p. 79). In these advertisements, America's relation to the Hawaiian Islands, or more specifically Honolulu, was ambiguously articulated moving between the terms identification and difference. This view toward the other is expressed not only in visual images but in written representations as well.

"Hawaiian Medly" (Granger, 1934), an article featured in *Vanity Fair,* illustrates this tension. It is a story of the islands that, as the secondary title suggests, "are of the United States and yet not in it." The article begins with an anecdote about President Roosevelt's visit to Hawaii and a remark made while he was there. "Your Administration in Washington," Roosevelt said, "will not forget that you are in very truth an integral part of the nation" (quoted in Granger, 1934, p. 42). From this assertion of identification, that is to say, the rhetorical gesture that the "Islands are American," the writer shifts to affirming difference by inviting his readers to seek "pure pleasure" in Hawaii. It appears that the securing of a pleasure that is pure—not yet corrupt—is an experience only Hawaii can supply. But what is this untainted and unmediated pleasure that America presumably lacks? The rendering of difference involves not just a catalogue of weather, flora, and fauna but also of customs and traditions.

"Despite the American flag," the writer notes, "despite reality, despite the pronouncements of the sugar factors [American sugar plantations], Hawaii is a *foreign* land" (Granger, 1934, p. 42; italics added). But what is the basis for its "foreignness"? The writer repeats several already recited observations. Chief among these is the alleged "ease and leisure" of mid-Pacific islanders. "[T]he citizens," Granger observed, "go about their business with what seems to be more ease and leisure than they would in the same jobs back on the mainland" (p. 42). There are other seemingly trivial observations which we read in no order of importance, for instance reports of the marvelous climate and unbelievable scenery, of surfing and paddling, of the extraordinarily hospitable people, of the brown bodies, of *hapa haole* hula girls wearing real grass skirts made of *ti*, and of the fantasy of paid sex.

The written representation of difference is reinforced with visual images as well. In conjunction with the written representation are four photographs. On the first page of the article are two photographs; one is of a *hapa haole* hula girl, and the other of four dancers performing "gourd-hula," according to the caption. On the next page are two more photographs, one of modern-looking tourists leisurely enjoying their meal at the Royal Hawaiian Hotel with Diamond Head in the background and the other of six presumably native men climbing a coconut tree.

The visual and written representations in *Vanity Fair* produce a text of the Hawaiian Islands that is no different from Mattel's production of Polynesia, where the tourist is coded in historical time and the Polynesian in a static time. The seemingly trivial and mundane themes and observations reported in "Hawaiian Medley" foster the illusion that "reality" precedes enunciation. However, these "trifling data," to use Barthes's expression, are not only woven from other texts and other sentences from other times, they are also the result of intense cultural coding (1974, p. 22). The "ease and leisure" attributed to the people of Hawaii are a persistent symbolic code that operate to assert gender-coded oppositions. For example, the conventional connections between passive and female and active and male are played out and maintained in the text through connotation. America(n) is inscribed as active and masculine, while Hawaii, by the association made to leisure (not work), is inscribed as passive and therefore feminine.

"Hawaiian Medley" dramatizes some of the tensions within the larger cultural order and preserves some of the symbolic value of those differences. In addition to the gendered differences that are maintained, it also asserts racial difference in its references to the "brown" bodies that scatter Honolulu. Skin color, as it is produced in "Hawaiian Medley," is "fetishized" as if it contained the truth of a people's identity (Ahmed, 1998). And half-white, or *hapa haole*, bodies, such as the hula girl in the photograph, get a very special look from Granger, one that confers aesthetic status, as his reference to her as "the prettiest" of the hula girls suggests. Written representations, as I noted earlier, were not the only modes of representation by which America's relation to the Hawaiian Islands was staged; visual representations in the mode of photography also expressed this cultural anxiety.

The shift from drawn illustrations to photography in commercial advertising rendered images with a realism that illustrations could not achieve. As Patricia Johnston points out in her book *Real Fantasies*, which treats the American photographer Edward Steichen's advertising photographs, the photograph's power lies in its "ability to obscure its artistic construction with accurate renderings of detail and thus to present emotional appeals in a seemingly objective style" (1997, p. 1). Edward Steichen ostensibly played a pioneering role in advertising photography, and his commercial photography developed at a critical moment in the history of American capitalism. His photographs, as Johnston notes, "helped to transform brand name products made by small family operations— Welch's grape juice, Fleischman's yeast, Jergen's lotion, and Woodbury's facial soap—into household names across the country" (p. 3). My concern here is with his well-known advertising photographs for the steamship company Matson Line that focused on Hawaii as an "exotic destination."

A few of these photographs circulated in 1934 and 1935, but it is a series of color photographs for the cruise line from 1940 and 1941 that are especially notable, for they depict what Johnston calls "pensive native women in exotic settings" (1997, p. 249). Johnston discusses one of these images, which appeared in the magazines *House and Garden* and *Vogue*, this way:

> The model wears a hibiscus flower in her hair, an emblem of
> Hawaii. . . . She perches high atop the rugged volcanic outcrop,

overlooking a picturesque lighthouse, with the wide stretch of sea beyond. The text of the advertisement reinforces the exoticism of the location by warning readers to "prepare to be captivated by the isles of unparalleled charm" but also reassures them that they would "sail in *safe* American ships, across *peaceful* seas." (p. 249; italics added)

This particular photograph won an Art Directors' Club medal for color photography in 1941, and the image was reproduced in the Art Directors' annual, which credited Steichen with "a truthful spiritual interpretation" that "embodies amazing fidelity to Hawaii's restful, Polynesian simplicity" (quoted in Johnston 1997, p. 249). Steichen's image, but to a greater extent the commentary on it in the annual, rearticulates and reinforces the trope of the ease and passivity of Pacific peoples. This is a productive discourse that encodes Polynesians outside historical time and outside the adult and "grown-up" world and struggles of which history is understood to consist (Knapp, 1989, p. 59).

The text accompanying the photograph that is discussed by Johnson, in asserting the exoticism of the location also maintains, through reassurances of safety in American ships and the rendering of the Pacific ocean as "peaceful," the production of America as masculine. As noted earlier, in educational writing this paternalism asserted itself in the representations of Hawaii as a U.S. "possession." This colonialist discourse and the feminization of Hawaii are articulated in another Steichen image of a Euro-American tourist and a native woman. The native woman is leaning against what appears to be a trunk of a tree, her head resting on her hand, a hibiscus placed in her dark, long hair; she has a look that suggests longing, and her position in the photograph hints that she is fixed in nature, for she is cautiously placed as part of the natural background. The Euro-American tourist is wearing modern vacationer's attire. She, too, is wearing a hibiscus in her hair and a lei, and she is surrounded by selected cultural items presumably there to provide authenticity, or possibly enchantment. The caption of the advertisement reads: "Among the important forces, working for the Nation, are Matson ships—carrying American citizens and American products between mainland U.S.A. and Hawaii, U.S.A."

The photograph of the Euro-American tourist once again reiterates the production of Hawaii as in need of U.S. protection, but it also proffers a certain susceptibility to study on the part of the native woman or to American command and possession. Johnston has indicated that cross-cultural advertising photographs such as Steichen's and their accompanying texts are an "index of American imperialistic sentiment" (1997, p. 252). At the same time, the image also involves a complex coding of what constitutes "American" identity. The Euro-American tourist in the photograph ostensibly represents the collective "American," which is concomitant to the "nation" that is coded as "white."

Guidebooks

Guidebooks to the Hawaiian Islands have also played a significant role in the production of the Pacific imaginary and the screen of primitiveness. Although they are often interpreted as superficial sources of information, David Gilbert argues that: "guidebooks must be seen as 'transcultural texts,' as writings which help to establish popular understandings of the meanings of other cultures" (1999, p. 281). The guidebook is also one of the means in which colonialist discourses inscribe the Hawaiian Islands and render it intelligible in particular ways. In 1875, Henry M. Whitney, publisher and bookseller, published *The Hawaiian Guide Book,* a guidebook aimed at supplying information and facts not just to travelers but for settlers as well: "[The] object has been to present in it such information as travelers require in a hand-book of this description, and at the same time to supply all the facts which intelligent settlers may wish to know" (Whitney, 1970, Preface). Whitney's guidebook consisted of sketches (some brief) of all the islands. *The Hawaiian Guide Book* is a tour first through Honolulu, "the commercial emporium of the Hawaiian Islands," where the traveler lands and receives "his first impressions of Hawaii and Hawaiians," which then proceeds through the rest of the archipelago, pointing out noteworthy places and sites to visit and suggesting itineraries and excursions to take connecting those sites (Whitney, 1970, p. 6). But Whitney's guidebook is also intended for settlers, so advice related to those concerns is also covered. Whitney addresses what he says are common inquiries of those who are disposed to settling permanently. The settlers he imagines, though, are of a particular kind. Questions considered include whether foreigners can endure the tropical heat, whether men of little capital have a chance for establishing enterprise, whether the islands are well adapted to raising cane, rice, coffee, and tobacco, and, most important, whether field labor is available.

A reading of the knowledge presented in guidebooks suggest that they are not merely a source of disinterested advice and information but rather an agent of ideological production. In *Mythologies* (1972), Barthes's essay on the "Blue Guides" insists that the guidebook information mystifies social and political realities by its obsession with monuments and picturesque landscapes. Whitney's guidebook, for example, not only directs our looking but mediates what is seen. His seemingly singular voice acts as both interpreter and guide. The tour of the islands is taken from aboard the deck of a steamer, where the traveler glides smoothly along the shores of the twelve islands that make up the Hawaiian archipelago. From the deck, when Whitney looks, he sees the picturesque scenery—the enormous gulches, the richest foliage, sparkling and shining waterfalls and streamlets, what he describes as the "most delightful picture imaginable" (1970, p. 4). Approaching nearer to the land, he makes visible the "plantations of golden sugar-cane" (p. 4). The appearance of Hawaiians—that is to say, their becoming visible in the narrative—is through the figure of "simple natives," themselves relaxing under the shade of coconut palms in primitive dwellings or "strolling on the beach, fishing in the sea, or sporting in the surf" (p. 4). Readers are not encouraged to see the political reality of many Hawaiians, such as the appropriation of their land or the attempts to control their labor. The struggles taking place over land, labor, and water resources between sugar interests and the Hawaiian local economies are reduced to picturesque landscapes and simple, nondisruptive natives (see also Maclennan, 1995).

Once again, a familiar text emerges. What we find is the "disease," as Barthes (1972) called it, of thinking in essences. As should be clear by now, there is more history and textuality to be observed in the making of Whitney's guidebook. Indeed, Whitney's guidebook reaches its audience by means of a range of already available discourses, of inherited myths, and from fragments of events that have already been read, seen, and experienced in another time. Significant is that the addressee of Whitney's guidebook is the Euro-American settler. Only empty spaces can be settled, and the space is made empty in the guidebook by acknowledging the indigenous population but relegating them to the category of children. Whitney's guidebook, distributed in the latter part of the nineteenth century, illustrates that imperialist ideology not only underwrites its depiction but extends those operations that work to fetishize the representation of the other.

Guidebooks published almost a century later than *The Hawaiian Guide Book* recuperate the trope of the ideal and placid native, though its ideological production is underwritten by a very different set of events. *Hawaii 1961* (Fodor, 1961) illustrates this shift. The guidebook is one of the titles introduced in Fodor's Modern Guides series. It was written for the most part by William W. Davenport, professor of English and journalism at the University of Hawaii, but it also included vignettes of the islands and people by the novelist James A. Michener and by A. Grove Day, the author of numerous books on Hawaii. Published a couple of years after statehood, the guidebook expresses some of the anxieties over the Americanization of people of non-European ancestry. Such anxieties as they were played out in the islands during that time were directed mainly at Americans of Japanese ancestry, a xenophobic response to the 1941 Pacific war, but they were also part of a more historically specific development expressed by Euro-Americans of the supposed danger posed by foreigners to the presumed coherence of American identity, values, and institutions. The fear of foreigners commenced with the forging of the new republic, the task of nation-building, and the desire to create a distinct American nationality. The Chinese Exclusion Act of 1882, which excluded Chinese immigrants from acquiring citizenship, illustrates the force of such xenophobic campaigns on American policy. While the anxieties expressed in the guidebook reverberate through that history, it is also prompted by the historical specificity of the 1960s. Hawaii as presented by these writers was unique not only because it was "America's most newest and exotic state," as the editor put it, but because of its polyracial citizenry (Fodor, 1961, p. 9).

On one level the polyracial citizenry and interracial harmony of Hawaii were viewed as America's answer to its history of racial prejudice, and on another they were the cause of concern, for it was possible that such heterogeneity was an impediment to Americanization. What we discover in this seemingly innocuous guidebook is that desire and threat coalesce in the formations of cultural projections. These anxieties were expressed and managed in different ways. One strategy was to contain the heterogeneity by mystifying it or treating it as amusement, thereby undermining its potential and ultimately making it politically and socially insignificant. In one vignette, for example, titled "Above All Nations: Integration without Tears," the writer asserts that "the most interesting scenery" in the islands is the "still-evolving human product of the crucible, America's newest citizens" (Fodor, 1961, p. 61). It is then remarked that there are "no less than 64 possible racial combinations" and that a "bewildering variety of races get along harmoniously in a society which is the best example anywhere of unity amidst diversity" (p. 61).

Another strategy involved translating heterogeneity into terms that were manageable. This was achieved by marking difference through codes of American paternalism. In one sketch the writer portrays the Hawaiian Islands as "allergic to thought" and "anti-idea" (Fodor, 1961, p. 46). It is followed by the observation that "there have been no Hawaiian intellectuals," and "there may never be" (p. 46). In all accounts this is a remarkably ethnocentric mode of seeing for its time, given the backdrop of the Civil Rights movement. Yet framing heterogeneity in this way does not cease. Indeed the writer inserts the authorizing voice of an English professor at the University of Hawaii who complained that "this island is like the womb," where "the Pacific Ocean is the amniotic fluid in which all our students are immersed. They're so secure they don't have to think" (p. 46). Those who are educated in the islands, "especially largely those of Oriental background," continues the writer, are characterized by having a "massive, immovable literal-mindedness" (p. 46). As an illustration of this characterization, it is observed that "irony, metaphor, poetry . . . are almost incomprehensible to local college students, to the great despair of their teachers" (p. 46).

Continuing the strategy of managing heterogeneity, an anecdote of the improper (a reference to the use of pidgin) but nonetheless charming use of the English language is recounted. The writer reasons that the "atmosphere of aloha" is what brings about these conditions, and he then goes on to say that: "the virtues of Hawaii are the virtues of love and not of syntax. That's one reason it's so restful to go there. The fires of the intellect are banked. They become as dormant as the crater of Haleakala" (p. 47). This representation not only effaces the conditions of plantation labor that introduced pidgin, but obliterates the eighteenth-century literary predecessors that produced the image-repertoire of lustful but ultimately placid bodies.

Because of the cultural premium placed on the thinking and speaking subject (a subject with its own conditions of production), subjects who are coded as falling short or without these capacities are not only obliged to identify with an image that is inimical to the rational and speaking subject but are also embroiled in dispelling an infantilizing imago. Jerry Phillips has asserted that the idea of infancy carries great significance for the imperialist: "Infants are dependent, powerless, and speechless; they are paradigms for cultures that cannot represent themselves. Infants are particularly receptive to the example of their elders; they can be made to imitate their parents. Infants are a model for all pupils" (1993, p. 26). So at the same moment that Hawaii is seen in ways that extol its interracial society and culture of understanding and mutual respect, it is also made to be seen in the preordained chronotope. It is a way to stabilize the other. Thus, rather than directing its reader's look to a renegotiation of the relation between the Western (adult) self and the Pacific Islander and Asian (infant) other, we are encouraged to see in ways dictated in advance by a colonialist gaze. The seeing that is encouraged in the guidebook affirms rather than displaces the dominant elements of the cultural screen.

Conclusion

This chapter has not only explored the many ways in which Mattel's Polynesian Barbie-as-text iterates photography and guidebooks; I have also
traced the rearticulation of the trope of the placid and ideal native, a figure
of colonialist discourse that has coded Polynesian cultures in infantile and
idyllic ways and in allochronic time-space. I both traced the emergence of
this figure and outlined its persistence and resilience in various modes of
representation and in various times. I have also witnessed how this figure is
recuperated and refashioned to accommodate historically specific processes of ideological articulation. I have suggested that while this figure is a
Euro-American invention—that is to say, compiled from specific cultural
anxieties, numerous anecdotes, stories, fragments, and texts—it is a powerful construction of Polynesia, one that inevitably articulates power relations. It is significant that of the many ways to *imagine* Polynesia, this one
has been the most persistent.

Equally important to the aim of this chapter was to show the potentiality that the method of reading offered here might have in the analysis of the
production of colonialist discourse and the colonial subject. For this reason
I do not approach Barbie from the angle of the ultimate signifier of femininity and consumerism, preferring instead to locate its specifically "Polynesian" ideological articulation as the instantiating of temporal, spatial,
and conceptual boundaries. This approach invites us to consider the distances we place between self and other and the practical pedagogical work
needed to address those distances. To be sure, this approach builds on a
critical tradition in the field of education that interrogates popular cultural
forms in understanding the cultural politics of imperialism. It also regards
domains conventionally regarded as "outside" the educational field as persuasive sites of influence in the informal instruction of knowledge, suggesting just how contested is our knowledge—our official knowledge (Apple,
2000)—of the Pacific. This tradition has, above all, underscored the importance of making connections and, in the context of this reading, it has
brought attention to the various ways in which the figure of the ideal and
placid Polynesian native unavoidably intersects with articulations of race,
nation, and gender. As we shall see in the next chapter, imperialism, race,
and nation are crucial to understanding official knowledge as well as popular culture.

Rethinking the Education–State Formation Connection: The State, Cultural Struggles, and Changing the School

Ting-Hong Wong and Michael W. Apple

In recent years, a growing number of scholars have examined the role of education in state formation. State formation is generally understood as the historical process through which ruling elites struggle to build a local identity, amend or preempt social fragmentation, and win support from the ruled (Green, 1990, 1994). These analyses have deepened our understanding of both the connections between political and educational changes and the cultural politics of education. However, insightful though they are, many of these studies treat the educational system only as a dependent variable influenced by the dynamics of state formation. Schools are usually depicted as being shaped—sometimes in an unmediated and mechanical manner—by the emergence of the nation-state, new forms of citizenship, and the transformation of sovereignty (Boli, 1989; Curtis, 1988; Green, 1990, 1997; Harp, 1998; Melton, 1988). These works also often seem to assume that schools always function to meet the demands of state formation. This formulation neglects the relative autonomy of the educational system and overlooks the possibility that schools themselves might generate profound effects that may block or modify the course of state formation. We believe that such tacit assumptions within most existing theories of state formation and education can cause us to lose a number of important insights about the complicated and subtle dynamics surrounding the relationship between state-making and education. A reformulated theory of state formation is needed, one that shows the mediating effects of schooling itself on the process of state-building.

To take the first steps toward the building of such a theory, we undertake two tasks in this chapter. First, we will strengthen theories of state formation and education by employing Basil Bernstein's notion of pedagogic device. Given the fact that Bernstein developed this conceptual tool as a corrective to the mistaken assumption that school pedagogy is a neutral carrier or relay for external power relations (Bernstein, 1996, p. 39), our position is that this concept can also advance our understanding of the complicated dynamics between state formation and education. This is the case because rather than assuming a correspondence between the political and educational fields, the idea of pedagogic device directs us both to anatomize the *specific* rules, practices, and social relations regulating pedagogic transmission and to examine their effects on the production and reproduction of consciousness in schools (Bernstein, 1996). Thus this concept recovers the educational field as another moment of determination within a social formation. It enables us to detect the incongruities, conflicts, and contradictions between educational development and the project of state-building.[1]

Because we do not want to leave our theoretical argument in this chapter at an abstract level, our second task will be to demonstrate the effects of schooling itself on state formation. Thus we shall apply this reformulated theory to one specific example—the conflicts over Chinese school curriculum in Singapore from 1945 to 1965. Given the fact that most existing works on state formation and education focus on monoracial settings, this historical case will provide a concrete instance of the struggles and contradictory outcomes in a situation where state-builders sought to reform one stream of schools in multiracial societies. We will show that because the pedagogic device in Singapore was fragmented and subject to strong influences from external pedagogic agents, the ruling power in Singapore was not fully successful in using the school curriculum to construct an integrated and locally centered Singapore nation.

The use of Singapore is important because it provides a set of counterfactuals that "troubles" accepted theories in a number of ways. In the two decades after World War II, Singapore went through the turbulence of decolonization. It first became a completely self-governing state in 1959, then got independence from Britain by joining Malaysia in 1963, and finally became an independent nation itself in 1965. In the process, the ruling regimes sought to build a new, coherent, and independent nation.[2] One of the key goals was to transform the curriculum of Chinese schools. Since historically this curriculum was used to transmit a China-centered—not a Singapore-centered—consciousness, the task was to change the China-centered focus. While we shall direct our attention primarily to the struggles over Chinese schools, it is crucial to realize that the effort to enlist schools for state formation encountered a great deal of difficulty because the educational system inherited from the prewar era was deeply fragmented by four discrete streams—English, Chinese, Malay, and Tamil schools. Each of these different types of institutions was subject to respective influences from pedagogic agents in Britain, China, Malaysia, and India. As we shall demonstrate, the postwar ruling regimes failed to overcome the fragmented and dependent nature of the pedagogic device. The ideology advanced by the school curriculum was often unable to contribute more than very weakly to the formation of a unified and Singapore-centered nation. For these very reasons, Singapore and the struggles over Chinese schooling provide an appropriate example of the arguments we wish to make.

In the following sections, we will first unpack Bernstein's concept of pedagogic device and discuss its implications for a more nuanced theory of state formation. We are mindful of the fact that Bernstein's theory was formulated out of the contexts of Britain and Western Europe (Archer, 1995) and thus should not be applied mechanically to other sociohistorical settings. Yet, when used appropriately, it does provide a way of examining smaller, multiracial, and postcolonial settings, all crucial characteristics of postwar Singapore. Then, to contextualize curriculum politics in Singapore, we will discuss the problem of Chinese schools in the prewar era. Finally, we will analyze reforms carried out by the three postwar ruling regimes, namely the British (1945 to 1955) and the two publicly elected governments—the Labour Front (1955 to 1959) and the People's Action Party (1959 to 1965). In the process, our investigation will show why a much more nuanced and dynamic approach to the role of schooling in state formation is necessary.[3]

State Formation and Pedagogic Device

As we noted, state formation is the historical trajectory through which the ruling power struggles to build a local identity, amend or preempt social fragmentation, and win support from the ruled. These tasks of state building necessitate the transformation of social relations and ideology of the dominated groups (Corrigan & Sayer, 1985). Since schools are widely con-

sidered as essential in "shaping" people's hearts and minds (Meyer, Kamens, & Benavot, 1992), almost all ruling regimes have sought to ensure
that the school knowledge transmitted by the educational system advances
their interests in state formation. However, it is dangerous to assume that
schools in general and the curriculum in particular serve the dominant
group in a mechanical and unmediated manner (see Apple, 2000; Cho &
Apple, this volume; Dale, 1989). Doing so mistakenly portrays the education field as merely an instrument that carries ideological messages determined by external power relations (Bernstein, 1986, 1990). Precisely because we seek to avoid this mistake, we enlist Bernstein's notion of pedagogic
device to strengthen existing theories of state formation.

According to Bernstein (Bernstein & Solomon, 1999, p. 269), the pedagogic device regulates the production of the school curriculum and its
transmission through three types of hierarchically related rules: *distributive rules, recontextualizing rules,* and *evaluation rules.* The distributive
principles mediate the social order through distributing different forms of
knowledge and consciousness to diverse social groups. While in many ways
these rules—being "the expression of the dominant political party of the
state" (Bernstein, 1990, p. 199)—stand for the guiding principles for state
formation, they are not solely determined by the ruling regime because
these principles are always challenged by other contesting forces.

The recontextualizing rules are the pedagogic discourse. These principles constitute school curriculum by selectively dislocating discourses from
the primary contexts—the site where knowledge is originally produced—
and then relocating and refocusing them in the secondary context to form
the pedagogic text. When such a recontextualization takes place, the discourses concerned will be transformed by the rules in the secondary context—the site where the moved discourse is reconstituted as a pedagogic
text. In this sense, then, the pedagogic text will never be identical with the
discourses from which it is produced (Bernstein, 1996, pp. 46–47). The
movements of discourse from the primary to the secondary context are
regulated by the recontextualizing context—named by Bernstein as the
third context. There are two major fields within the third context, namely
the official recontextualizing field (ORF), which produces the official pedagogic discourse, and the pedagogic recontextualizing field (PRF), which
creates the nonofficial pedagogic discourse (Bernstein, 1986, p. 216; 1990,
pp. 191–193). The existence of the PRF as well as the unofficial elements
within the ORF strongly suggest that the state can never monopolize power
in curriculum production.

Bernstein hints that, at the level of recontextualizing rules, many con-
frontations may emerge that may hamper the use of pedagogic reform for

state formation. First, when the PRF is strong and has a certain level of autonomy from the state, the discourse it creates can impede official pedagogic discourse (Bernstein, 1996, p. 48). Second, because of the manifold agents within the ORF and PRF—the former includes a core consisting of officials from state pedagogic agencies and consultants from the educational system and the fields of economy and symbolic control, whereas the latter comprises agents and practices drawn from universities, colleges of education, schools, foundations, journals and publishing houses, and so on—there is the potential for conflict, resistance, and inertia both within and between these two fields (Bernstein, 1990, pp. 191–193, 199).

What does this mean for Singapore? As we shall soon demonstrate, in small, multiracial, and postcolonial settings like Singapore, the pedagogic device can also be fragmented by several other contradictions or ruptures. It can be disrupted by some external pedagogic agents, particularly those from the metropolis. The governments of small territories may have to share the curriculum, textbooks, and public examination systems with other countries and consequently may have less freedom actually to regulate the pedagogic text. State pedagogic reforms can also be blocked because in postcolonial societies the fields producing knowledge about the local settings have been fragmented by diverse ethnic groups and dominated by some externally oriented agencies of cultural production. When this problem exists, the ruling regime will not have an appropriate primary field to extract discursive materials for producing a common and locally centered curriculum.

Finally, the evaluation rules are the lowest level of principles within the pedagogic device. These principles specify the transmission of suitable contents under proper time and context and perform the significant function of monitoring the adequate realization of the pedagogic discourse (Bernstein, 1986, p. 211). Here again, ruptures and cleavages at this level impede the effectiveness of education in state formation. For instance, when the evaluation rules are not tightly linked up with the rewards of higher-education opportunities, materials, political power, and social status, these principles are ineffective in ensuring the implementation of state pedagogic reform. Also, when the evaluation rules have strong ties with external pedagogic agents, they can become a weak tool for the local state authorities to discipline pedagogic practices. All of these problems characterized the situation in Singapore.

While the points we make above are rather abstract, their implications are profound if we wish to understand the complex sets of dynamic relations that connect schooling and state formation. In order to see how this works in practice, we need to give a sense of the history of the conflicts over what counts as and who has the power to define "official knowledge" (Apple, 1990, 1995, 2000) in Singapore. The next section will outline how the confrontation over Chinese school curriculum developed out of a complicated constellation of historical factors, including British colonialism, demography, racial relations, the overseas Chinese policies of the Chinese government, and the often tense connections between Singapore and the neighboring Malay Peninsula.

Colonialism, Racial Relations, and the Problems of Chinese Schools

Singapore is a small island adjoining the southern tip of the Malay Peninsula. In 1824, an Anglo-Dutch agreement made Singapore and the peninsula the exclusive preserve of the British. Two years later, the British combined Singapore with Penang and Malacca—two cities on the western coast of the peninsula—into one administrative unit known as the Straits Settlements (SS) (Bedlington, 1978, p. 31; Yeo, 1973b, p. 1). On the peninsula, the British combined four states into the Federated Malay States (FMS) and another five into the Unfederated Malay States (UMS) from the 1870s to 1910s by signing treaties with the Malay sultans of the nine states concerned (Bedlington, 1978, pp. 33–34). These agreements confirmed the Malay sultans as the ruling partners of the British and upheld Malays as the only indigenous group (Lau, 1991, p. 8; E. Lee, 1991, pp. 3–19). This Malay-biased constitution was not extended to Singapore. However, as the SS, the FMS, and the UMS (together known as British Malaya) shared a framework of administration, the special relation between the British and Malays in the peninsula did spill over to the island and tilted the colonial authorities there toward the Malays (Yeo, 1973b, pp. 1–13, 69). This background of colonialism and racial relation had far-reaching effects on the politics of Chinese education in Singapore.

By the mid-nineteenth century, the Malays enjoyed unquestionable numerical superiority on the Malay Peninsula (Khoo, 1981, p. 93; Purcell, 1966, p. 234). But with the consolidation of the British rule, burgeoning tin and rubber industries in the peninsula attracted a continuous flow of immigrants, mainly from China though also from India (Ee, 1961, pp. 33–35). These successive tides of immigration changed the demographic composition of British Malaya. In 1931, census data revealed that on the peninsula the Malays still outnumbered the Chinese. However, if the peninsula and Singapore, where 70 percent of the population were Chinese, were put together, the Chinese population—1,709,392—would have exceeded that of the Malays—1,644,173 (Vlieland, 1932). These demographic features were basically unchanged in the postwar decade. Since Singapore had the potential of upsetting the numerical prominence of the Malays, the Malays viewed the island with suspicion.

Notwithstanding this demographic change, the Anglo-Malay pacts, which recognized only the position of Malays, consigned the Chinese to the status of aliens (Lau, 1989, pp. 216–217; 1991, pp. 6–7). Without a definite status in the local setting, the Chinese residents were very susceptible to influences from China. Since the late nineteenth century, successive Chinese regimes had actively sought to solicit the support of overseas Chinese for their campaigns to strengthen the nation of China (Fitzgerald, 1972; Yen, 1982, 1984). Recognizing that education was essential in winning people's hearts and minds, the Chinese authorities appointed inspectors, decreed rules, and promulgated curricula to regulate schools maintained by the large population of Chinese living abroad (Fitzgerald, 1972; Ng-Lun & Chang, 1989). These policies transformed Chinese schools in Malaya, which before the twentieth century were only *sishu,* or old-style schools teaching predominantly Confucian classics, into modern institutions transmitting Chinese patriotism and anti-imperial sentiment (T.H. Lee, 1987; Loh, 1975).

Given their position that their responsibility was toward the Malays only, the British colonial regime supported basically English and Malay schools and were relatively indifferent toward Chinese and Tamil institutions. Without substantial financial sponsorship and curriculum guidance from the British authorities, Chinese schools in Singapore by default followed curriculum and instructional materials from China (Gopinathan, 1974; Tan, 1997). In the 1920s and 1930s, when Chinese schools were deeply involved in political activism, the colonial authorities realized that these institutions could be subversive and sought to control the knowledge taught in Chinese schools by providing financial assistance, screening textbooks, and prohibiting "undesirable" materials (Gopinathan, 1974, pp. 4–5; Tan, 1997, pp. 19–20; T.-H. Wong, 2002). These actions were ineffective, however, both because the financial support given was extremely small and because the colonial regime had an insufficient administrative capacity to monitor these institutions closely. Furthermore, the policy of the prewar colonial regime was based in essence on what might be called negative selection—to exclude "objectionable" elements from school curriculum. It did not attempt to integrate Chinese institutions into the local educational system (Tan, 1997, p. 28). This practice of negative exclusion (Liston, 1988; Offe & Keane, 1984) might have been appropriate for the demands of state formation in the prewar colonial era, when the ruling regime did not need to win the active consent of the ruled, integrate the various ethnic groups

into a national whole, or create a locally centered identity. However, it became completely obsolete when Singapore underwent decolonization in
the postwar era.

State Formation in the Immediate Postwar Period

In September 1945, Singapore was recovered by the British after more than
three years of Japanese occupation. The British faced a number of entirely
new challenges of state formation in the postwar era. The humiliating defeat by the Japanese shattered the myth of British invincibility. Compounded with pressure from the United States and the rapid decline of
Britain as a global power, this military debacle bred movements for decolonization in Singapore and elsewhere (Louis, 1985; Tarling, 1993). To prepare the island for self-government and ultimately independence, the
British had to cultivate people's loyalty to Singapore and unify its several
racial groups. This new scenario for state formation propelled the British
to resolve three core problems, or to realize three distributive principles, in
curriculum policy. First, to stop the Chinese residents from identifying
themselves with China, the British had to *de-Sinicize,* or minimize the elements of Chinese culture and China-centered content in the Chinese
school curriculum. Second, the state needed to *localize,* or transform the
Chinese school curriculum into a Singapore- or Malaya-centered one. Finally, the state needed to pursue *unification.* It had to make the curriculum
of Chinese schools similar to those of other institutions.

At the same time as the agenda of decolonization was pressing the colonial state to promote racial integration, relations between the Chinese and
Malays were deteriorating rapidly. During the Japanese occupation, for
complicated historical reasons, many Malays were used by the Japanese as
collaborators in carrying out anti-Chinese measures. Immediately after the
Japanese surrendered, interracial conflict escalated as the Chinese retali-
ated ruthlessly against the Malays (Cheah, 1981, 1983). More fuel was
added to the flame later on when in 1946 the British advanced a plan to
combine Malacca, Penang, and the nine states in the peninsula into the
Malayan Union, leaving Singapore as a separate Crown Colony. This plan
also withdrew many of the special privileges enjoyed by Malays and gave
the Chinese in the union local citizenship under very lenient terms. The
Malays regarded their interests as having been sold out and strongly opposed these measures.[4] Finally, the British were forced to replace the union
with another political and geographic plan. This plan, the Federation of
Malaya, preserved most of the prerogatives of the Malays and required the
Chinese to fulfill more stringent requirements for citizenship (Yeo, 1973a,

pp. 43–44). This then provided the Malays with an opportunity to use their position in the federation to advance many anti-Chinese policies in citizenship, language, and education. Alarmed, the Chinese in both the federation and Singapore campaigned strongly for both political rights and official recognition of Chinese language and education (Yeo, 1973b, pp. 144–149).

Such interracial conflict placed the colonial authorities under contradictory pressures in terms of state formation and pedagogic reform. To deal with the increasingly tense relations between the Chinese and the Malays, the British were now more eager to desegregate Chinese schools and bring them into line with other schools. These tasks both presupposed and required the realization of the principles of de-Sinicization, localization, and unification we focused on before. However, since the Chinese were deeply committed to safeguarding their culture and language, any attempt to dislodge Chinese culture from the school curriculum would put the colonial government and the Chinese community on a collision course.

Curriculum Reform under the British, 1945 to 1955

Although the demands for state formation had changed remarkably since the war ended, the British once again adopted the prewar practice of textbook screening. In September 1946, the colonial state inaugurated two pan-Malayan bodies, namely, the Chinese School Textbook Committee and the Chinese Education Technical Advisory Committee. Composed of both education officers and representatives from Chinese schools, these bodies were employed to vet textbooks used in Chinese schools and to recommend necessary changes to the publishers (*Straits Budget* [SB], September 12, 1946; and CO 825/90/7). Unsurprisingly, this practice failed to realize the three distributive rules. Thus five years later, in 1951, materials used by Chinese schools still abounded with China-centered content, addressed China as "our country," and devoted a "disproportionally" large number of chapters to China (CO, 825/90/7).

In response to this, in the early 1950s the British decided to replace the imported textbooks. After the Chinese Communist Party came into power in 1949, new textbooks from mainland China displayed strong procommunist tendencies. These tendencies were extremely worrisome to the state authorities since they were inimical both to the fight against the Malayan Communist Party (MCP), which had launched a military insurrection against the colonial state in 1948, and to Britain's maneuvers against communism in the context of the Cold War. There were additional difficulties that mitigated against the use of, say, textbooks from the anticommunist forces now in control in Taiwan. Textbooks from Taiwan were undesirable as well since they, too, were dominated by China-centered content which would impede the development of the locally centered consciousness sought by the British. Knowing that Chinese schools would keep using those undesirable materials unless something else became available, the British decided to institute a set of policies (in effect, a stronger pedagogic device) that would produce "suitable" Chinese books (CO, 825/90/7).

In 1951, the Fenn-Wu Committee, an advisory body appointed by Kuala Lumpur to recommend policies for Chinese schools, released its report. It proposed making Chinese schools contribute to the building of a common Malayan culture. To achieve this goal, the report upheld de-Sinicization, localization, and unification as the distributive rules. It suggested elimination of the separateness of and foreign politics in Chinese schools. It also proposed the Malayanization of their curriculum and the unification of their curriculum with the syllabi of other institutions (Fenn-Wu Report, 1951, pp. 12–15). Having accepted these recommendations, the governments in the federation and Singapore assigned E.C.S. Adkins, the secretary of Chinese Affairs in Singapore, to translate the recommendations of the Fenn-Wu Report into a workable policy. Like many British colonial bureaucrats in Malaya, Adkins was strongly distrustful of the Chinese. Thus even more emphasis on de-Sinicization was added at this stage of policy-making.[5]

In early 1952, the colonial authorities moved to reshuffle the official recontextualizing field (ORF). On the advice of Adkins, they installed a General Textbook Committee (GTC) and a Teachers Advisory Committee (TAC) to draft a curriculum outline for textbook production. The GTC was made up mainly of government officers, although it also had some representatives from Chinese education. The members of the TAC were largely teachers and principals from Chinese schools (*Sin Chew Jit Poh* [SCJP], March 18 and April 16, 1952). To circumscribe the influence of the Chinese educators within the ORF, the British also consigned the TAC to being a purely advisory body (SCJP, April 11 and 17, 1952).

The British authorities took several steps to limit the autonomy of the pedagogic recontextualizing field (PRF). They signed a pact with the United Publishing House Limited (UPHL), an amalgam of four major Chinese publishing firms. This agreement bound the UPHL to follow the government's instructions when compiling textbooks. In return, Britain promised to grant its imprimatur solely to the UPHL. The colonial authorities hoped this pact would ensure that the books compiled under their tutelage had the strongest possible position in the market and that this would also give all Chinese schools little choice but to use these state-preferred materials (CO 1022/285).

These actions by the British provoked determined resistance since they were perceived by the Chinese as a conspiracy to eliminate their culture. Chinese educators challenged all three of the distributive principles. For example, the United Chinese School Teachers Association (UCSTA), the most prominent teacher organization in the federation, opposed de-Sinicization and unification. They argued that because Chinese people bore a distinct cultural heritage, the new curriculum should not be identical with those of other institutions (SCJP, April 24, 1952). In late May 1952, an editorial in a leading vernacular newspaper in Singapore disputed the localization rule. It countered the claim of E.M. Payne, the chairman of the GTC, that the new syllabi should "start from proximity" and include more topics about Malaya. Having delineated the concept of proximity into two aspects—geographical and cultural—the editorial maintained that because cultural proximity meant more to Chinese students, the new curriculum should give considerably more attention to China (SCJP, April 27, 1952). Chinese educators also struggled against the de-Sinicization and localization rules at the level of individual subjects. For instance, before being scrutinized by the TAC, the textbook guidelines for Civics addressed Singapore and the federation as "nations," advised that the textbooks should cover the British Commonwealth, and undermined the importance of China. But after TAC scrutiny, the same document classified Singapore and the Federation of Malaya as "places" and suggested that new textbooks have more topics about China and reduce those for Malaya (SCJP, June 20 and 21, 1952).

To strengthen their position in this campaign, the Chinese educators also struggled to augment their power inside the ORF and to recover the autonomy of the publishing sectors within the PRF. In April 1952, the UCSTA disputed both the accord between the colonial state and the UPHL and the procedures for textbook vetting. The teachers' association asserted that the TAC should have the final say on all textbook manuscripts (SCJP, April 24, 1952). The Singapore Chinese School Conference (SCSC) opposed the special privileges given to the UPHL and insisted that the government should encourage free competition for textbook publication (SCJP, April 27, 1952). Later, the SCSC asked the British authorities either to withdraw the privilege bestowed on the UPHL or to confer the same right on all publishers (SCJP, June 25, 1952). In October 1952, the SCSC also escalated its protest by convening a meeting attended by representatives from some forty-six Chinese schools (SCJP, October 13, 1952).

Because of such opposition, the colonial regime was forced to adopt a more conciliatory position on a number of issues. In late May 1952, GTC chairman Payne accepted the position that the new syllabi should preserve the essence of Chinese culture. Equally important, he agreed that all publishers were free to publish textbooks written according to the official syllabi (SCJP, May 23 and 24, 1952). In October, the colonial authorities allowed the Chinese community more influence on the final form of textbooks by promising that all manuscripts would be finalized by a joint meeting of the GTC and TAC (SCJP, October 31, 1952). Notwithstanding these concessions, the colonial state failed to reduce the autonomy of the pedagogic recontextualizing field. Chinese educators now had strong leverage to challenge the state pedagogic discourse. Finally, in late 1953, when some Chinese schools were determined to use the old China-centered textbooks despite the fact that the UPHL series had already been published (SCJP, December 12, 1953), the Department of Education in Singapore yielded by reaffirming the discretion of Chinese schools in textbook selection (SCJP, December 23, 1953). Although they averted further agitation from the Chinese community, these concessions ultimately had very real effects. They clearly perpetuated the China-centered tendency of the Chinese school curriculum and slowed the formation of a locally centered and integrated Singapore.

Pedagogic Reform under the Labour Front, 1955 to 1959

In 1955, the Labour Front (LF) won the first general election in Singapore. Under the new constitution, the British transferred most of the power for internal affairs to the Legislative Assembly, of which most members were popularly elected. The new practice of automatic registration of voters also turned the Chinese into the predominant majority among the electorate.[6] However, getting only 26 percent of the total vote, the LF won the election mainly because the more established political powers, such as the Progressive Party, were formed by English-speaking elites without strong connections with the Chinese masses, and the fledgling People's Action Party entered only a small number of candidates (Yeo & Lau, 1991, pp. 132–133). To generate more popular support, the LF pressed London for immediate complete self-government (Lau, 1994; Yeo, 1973b, pp. 149–150). This demand for faster decolonization put the LF under even more pressure to constitute a common and Singapore-centered identity.

In May 1955, a committee was appointed by the LF government after the involvement of Chinese school students in an industrial conflict brought about serious riots (Wilson, 1978). Members of this committee, whose charge was to investigate the situation of Chinese schools and give suggestions to make Chinese education contribute to self-government and ultimately independence, were from the political parties holding seats in the Legislative Assembly (All-Party Report, 1956, p. 1). In early 1956, the Report of the All-Party Committee on Chinese Education (hereafter, the All-Party Report) was released. It recommended that Chinese schools be transformed into local institutions by granting them treatment equal to other schools. As in the previous reform, the committee upheld the de-Sinicization, localization, and unification rules. It responded negatively to the China-oriented nature of the Chinese textbooks and took the position that: "The Malayan background must be stressed from the very beginning." It further advocated that: "All textbooks in all schools should therefore be reviewed at an early day" and that there should be "standardization of textbooks" (pp. 13–14). Even though the report clearly took what could be seen as an anti-Chinese position, this proposed curriculum policy did not elicit strong opposition from the Chinese for a variety of reasons.

First, unlike previous pedagogic reforms initiated by bureaucrats within the colonial government, the policy in 1956 was recommended by the elected members in the Legislative Assembly, a body that seemed to have a more locally oriented and anti-British attitude. Thus, compared to past reports, the committee put less blame on Chinese schools. For example, it also stated that the textbooks in *English schools* were unsuitable to Singapore as they were not much different from those used in schools in the United Kingdom (p. 13). In saying this, it noted that the problem of Chinese education could not be resolved if no corresponding action was taken in other schools (p. 7). By connecting its position with the theme of anticolonialism, therefore, the report struck a responsive chord. Hence the distributive rules of the LF elicited less resistance from the Chinese (T.-H. Wong, 2002).

In addition, the reactions of the Chinese community were mediated by other recommendations within the All-Party Report. Some suggestions in the document, such as increasing both financial subsidies and teacher salaries, were received favorably by a considerable number of Chinese educators. They softened the Chinese community's reaction to the report as a whole and, indirectly, to the proposed curriculum reform as well. This was accompanied by the fact that a number of other proposals, such as the tightening of control over the management of Chinese schools and the strengthening of teaching of English, were perceived as more consequential for the future of Chinese education. They drew the Chinese people's attention away from the matter of curriculum.[7] Furthermore, after a decade of often successful campaigns for local citizenship and political rights, more Singaporean Chinese now considered the local society as their permanent home (Chui, 1989). In essence, because of changes in identity over time, they had become more receptive to the localization and unification principles.

The LF realigned the recontextualizing field before the publication of the All-Party Report. After January 1956, the Singapore Textbooks and Syllabi Committee (STSC) functioned to design syllabi and make recommendations for textbook production for all schools (*Singapore Legislative Assembly Debate*, p. 30). Unlike the GTC and TAC in the previous reform, which incorporated only Chinese educators, the STSC General Coordinating Committee also included representatives from English and Malay schools. Also, five out of a total of eleven STSC subcommittees, whose charge was to design common syllabi for all schools, had delegates from all four types of schools (*Singapore Legislative Assembly Debate*, p. 30; SCJP, July 17, 1956).

Perhaps learning a lesson from the early 1950s, when the resistance of Chinese educators within the TAC paralyzed the state curriculum reform, the LF tried to keep social movements out of the ORF. It stipulated that all representatives of Chinese and Malay schools in the STSC committees should be appointed by the Department of Education. The LF also required that the STSC members keep all meetings and documents from the committees strictly confidential (SCJP, July 17, 1956). These moves seemed to have further deactivated the Chinese community in terms of curriculum reform. Evidence of such deactivation can be found in the fact that from 1956 to 1958, there was only one report documenting the reaction of the Chinese community to the STSC in *Sin Chew Jit Poh,* a leading Chinese newspaper in Singapore (SCJP, May 6, 1957).

Given this set of circumstances, the proposed curriculum policy moved forward more easily than in the past. By April 1958, the guidelines for civics, geography, physical education, and English language (for English schools) were done (SCJP, April 28, 1958). In July and August, the STSC completed the History and Science syllabi (SCJP, July 17, and August 6, 1958). When Singapore began using the new curriculum in early 1959, textbooks for primary school history and geography were made available by Educational Suppliers, Ltd., an amalgamation of several Chinese publishers (SCJP, January 11, 1959).

The Inadequate Realization of the De-Sinicization and Unification Rules

Our last section demonstrated some of the social conditions that enabled the LF to realize both the unification and de-Sinicization principles at the level of *official* syllabi. The new curricula were officially proclaimed as common syllabi for use in all schools. The guidelines of geography and history for the primary level contained very few topics on China. While the syllabus for history at the secondary level committed marginally more space to Chinese history, its world-history approach decentered China by placing it within the context of Western history (*Syllabus for Geography, 1957* and *Syllabus for History, 1957*). If smoothly implemented, these syllabi would make it much more difficult for Chinese schools to cultivate a China-centered ideology.

However, as we know from a considerable number of studies, there are often striking differences between official curricula and what actually happens in schools or in the creation of texts to meet official guidelines (Apple, 1986, 1996, 2000; Cho & Apple, this volume). Therefore, it would be unwise to conclude that these common syllabi had the effect of standardizing and de-Sinicizing pedagogic practices in all schools. This is especially the case because their execution could be crippled by nonstandardized textbooks emanating from a divided PRF. For instance, in the late 1950s instructional materials used by English schools were produced by Western publishers, such as Longman and Macmillan, whereas the books for Chinese schools were compiled by local or Hong Kong–based Chinese publishers. Because of their diverse orientations, backgrounds, and PRFs from which the discursive resources were extracted for text configuration, even though they were formally guided by common syllabi, these publishers created distinctly *different* sets of teaching materials (L.K. Wong, 1971, pp. 18–19).

Just as importantly, the LF's common and de-Sinicized curriculum also suffered from the disunity of the evaluation rules. There were no common evaluation rules for different streams of schools. When the LF ended its term of office in 1959, the Primary School Leaving Examination, a test to allocate places in secondary schools, still *excluded* pupils from the vernacular institutions. Consequently, Chinese primary schools were not motivated to comply with the common official syllabi. In addition, students completing secondary education in English schools sat for the Cambridge Overseas School Certificate Examination (COSCE) conducted by the University of Cambridge Local Examinations Syndicate (UCLES) in cooperation with the local Ministry of Education. Pupils graduating from Chinese middle schools entered the Senior Middle III Examination, conducted solely by the Ministry of Education in Singapore (FETS, 1955–1957, p. 37). The requirements of these two examinations differed widely.[8]

The distinctions and differences did not end there. The Senior Middle III Examination had limited power in shaping pedagogic practices in Chinese schools because the University of Malaya generally did not accept students from Chinese institutions. Diploma holders from this exam could apply only for the Teachers Training College and for some low-level positions in the government.[9] Thus the most important higher-education opportunity for pupils from Chinese middle schools was then provided by Nanyang University, a private college inaugurated by the local Chinese in the mid-1950s to safeguard the tradition of Chinese education in Southeast Asia. Most professors of this China-centered university were born in China, and a substantial part of their careers were spent there.[10] Conducting its own entrance examination and accepting applicants without any certificates from examinations held by the Singapore government, Nanyang University operated as an autonomous PRF, one that provided countervailing content that acted against the de-Sinicization, localization, and unification principles.

The Inadequate Actualization of the Localization Principle

The new curriculum of the LF government was also unsuccessful in realizing the localization rule. Throughout the entire syllabi of history, topics on Singapore and Malaya were given very limited space in the curriculum. Also, when the history syllabus proposed content for the study of local history, the guidelines were much briefer, vaguer, and less substantial than those for Europe, America, and other Asian countries. The geography syllabus fared only marginally better. It did propose some rudimentary topics on Singapore and Malaya at the primary level. However, it suggested an extremely unlocal curriculum for the secondary level by advocating the study of Australia and New Zealand at Secondary I; America, Europe, and Africa at Secondary II; and Asia (excluding Singapore and Malaya) at Secondary III. The same syllabus only recommended that pupils spend part of the first semester of Secondary IV in the study of Singapore and Malaya (*Syllabus for Geography, 1957* and *Syllabus for History, 1957*).[11]

Even when such localized content did appear, the localization principle was betrayed by what might best be called pseudo-Singaporean or -Malayan sections. For example, the history syllabus had a section on the "Cultural Background of All Races in Malaya" for Secondary III and IV. Apparently Malayanized, this section only remotely pertained to the local circumstances. Its five subsections, namely "Islam," "Indian Culture," "Buddhism," "Chinese Culture," and "Western Civilization," were basically organized around the histories of these traditions in their places of origins—India, China, Greece, Rome, and England (*Syllabus for History, 1957*, pp. 26–27). The construction of the "local" here is more than a little interesting; its pseudolocalized nature created a centrifugal, rather than centripetal, tendency.

The realization of the localization principle also suffered from the British nature of the model taken for curriculum making. For instance, among the five sections proposed by the history syllabus for Secondary III and IV, two of them—"Commonwealth History" and "The Development of Freedom and Responsibility"—were British-centered. "Commonwealth History" covered many British colonies, including India, Pakistan, Ceylon, Hong Kong, Borneo, Australia, and New Zealand. Its proposed outline was double the length of that of "Malaya History." "Development of Freedom and Responsibility" was not only about the political systems in England and its colonies; it also attempted to induce a positive appraisal of those institutions (pp. 21–28). In reality, then, this recontextualizing practice imposed an alien, British-centered worldview on Chinese schools and once again interrupted the official focus of localization.

How can this be understood? Why did the Singapore state successfully de-Sinicize the official syllabi but fail to localize or Singaporeanize it? Even though it proclaimed itself to be anticolonial, why couldn't the LF government de-Anglicize school syllabi and achieve genuine localization? In the following section, we will argue that answers to these questions lay in the dependent and fragmented nature of the pedagogic device in Singapore.

Fragmenting the Pedagogic Device

The LF failed to dislodge these Anglicized elements in part because of the very nature of the persons who populated the educational apparatus of the state. It still relied on expatriates and English-educated locals for curriculum-making. For example, the General Coordinating Committee of the STSC in 1956 had fifteen members. Among them were four education officers who were definitely English-educated. At that time, the state recruited only graduates from the University of Malaya and British and Commonwealth universities for executive and administrative posts. In addition, there were one professor nominated by the University of Malaya, one delegate from the Teachers Training College (basically an institute producing teachers for English schools), one representative from the Methodist Church, and three English school principals (*Singapore Legislative Assembly Debate*, pp. 30–31). The predominance of the English-educated members who were trained in and comfortable with the curriculum framework of English schools prolonged the state's dependence on the British model.

It is important not to reduce one's explanation only to the individual, however. Other elements played a large role as well. The dearth of suitable pedagogic alternatives perpetuated the state's dependence on the British model. There were three other curriculum paradigms in Singapore at that time. The Chinese school curriculum, which the state was so desperate to depose, was simply out of the question. The Malay model was not a good candidate either, both because the Chinese would reject it and because it did not fit the needs of the modern state. For example, in the colonial era the British, fearing that an overexpansion of Western education would upset the stability of Malay society, gave the majority of school-going Malay "commoners" a maximum of four years of rural-biased education to prepare them for agricultural life. The British had operated a small number of special schools to groom the sons of traditional Malay elites and some promising Malay commoners as future Malay administrators. However, these more prestigious schools used English as the medium of teaching and fashioned themselves after institutions in England. Consequently, Malay schools had been confined to the primary level before World War II (Loh, 1974a; 1974b, pp. 225–229; Stevenson, 1975; Watson, 1993, pp. 156–161). The unsuitability of Malay primary school curriculum and the absence of Malay secondary curriculum further limited the choices that the state could make. Furthermore, other ethnic alternatives had similar problems. For instance, the curriculum of Tamil schools could not be a foundation to build a common Singapore-centered curriculum. Most of these institutions were estate schools providing rudimentary instruction, and the textbooks they used were published in South India.[12]

Just as crucial, the localization rule was also undermined by the absence of a strong indigenous intellectual tradition. A good deal of the "local" knowledge production activities were conducted by people whose outlooks were hardly locally oriented. Thus most English works on Malayan literature and history were written by colonial officers and foreign journalists (Cheah, 1997, pp. 41–42; Lau, 1992, pp. 46–48). Those written in Chinese were mostly produced by intellectuals from China or under inspiration of their motherland (Lin, 1992). Hence the structures and histories of the actual production of what was seen as important "local knowledge" resulted in a nonlocal orientation of the primary field of cultural production. This poverty of local intellectual discourse was vividly revealed by the difficulty encountered by the History Department of the University of Malaya in the 1950s. Its faculty embarked on the teaching of Malayan history, but found that suitable materials were simply insufficient (Tregonning, 1990, p. 8). The *underdevelopment of local studies* deprived the state of a substantial primary field of discourse production from which the agents in the recontextualizing field could appropriate discursive resources for the production of local and common curricula.

The localization principle was also thwarted because of the complicity of external pedagogic authorities in the evaluation rules. In the late 1950s, the school-leaving examination for English secondary schools was the Cambridge Overseas School Certificate Examination (COSCE), which was conducted by the University of Cambridge Local Examinations Syndicate (UCLES) in cooperation with the local Ministry of Education.[13] The LF government preserved this imperial linkage to assure the international recognition of local diplomas. This decision maintained the leverage of the imperial power on local school knowledge. As we shall see in the final historical period we analyze here, all of these factors that created difficulties for the realization of the state pedagogic discourse remained and haunted the next ruling regime, the People's Action Party (PAP).

Further Partition of the Pedagogic Device under the People's Action Party

After a landslide victory in the general election in May 1959, the People's Action Party became the new ruling power in the now completely self-governing Singapore. After assuming office, the PAP continued to forge a common and locally centered curriculum for all schools. The PAP nevertheless was also unsuccessful in realizing these recontextualizing rules, for it failed to deal adequately with the incoherence and dependent nature of the pedagogic device. Worse still, the pedagogic device suffered further fragmentation when the PAP sought to merge with the Malay Peninsula and win popular support from all races in Singapore.

The PAP swiftly instituted a new framework to transform teaching syllabi after winning the election. In June 1957, the Ministry of Education asked various educational associations to nominate representatives to the Educational Advisory Council (EAC), a body formed to advise the Ministry of Education on educational issues (SCJP, June 9, 1959). In October, the EAC was founded with eight representatives from four streams of schools and six nominees of the Minister of Education (SCJP, October 29, 1959; ST, October 29, 1959). At its inaugural meeting, a Committee on Syllabi and Textbooks (CST) was formed to revise syllabi and encourage the production of Malayanized textbooks. Shortly afterward, fourteen subject committees were installed, consisting of members from all streams (MEAR, 1959, p. 2). By the end of 1960, the Ministry of Education had approved thirty-three new syllabi (SCJP, October 13, and December 11, 1960). The government then decreed that from early 1961 on, all schools would adopt the new common curriculum (SCJP, December 20, 1960).

Like the LF, the People's Action Party was successful in promoting the principles of de-Sinicization and unification at the level of syllabi, since the official curricula were for the use of all schools and only a very small amount of their content was about China. However, the PAP did not actualize the official pedagogic discourse beyond that level. First, the teaching materials utilized by Chinese and English schools continued to be produced by writers from diverse backgrounds. This disunity continued to create the conditions for the production of distinct sets of instructional materials and consequently undermined unification and localization (L.K. Wong, 1971, pp. 18–19). For instance, the history series produced by the World Bookstore, a Chinese publisher, devoted four out of a total of six volumes to Chinese history. This Sinocentric approach deviated from the world-history approach recommended by the official history syllabus.[14] The PAP nevertheless permitted Chinese schools to use these materials, in large part because, as in earlier periods, the ruling group had no better option.

Moreover, the unification rule was continuously weakened by the incoherence of the evaluation rules. Under the PAP, students from all types of schools were now allowed to sit for the Primary School Leaving Examination, which was previously limited to only candidates from English institutions (MEAR, 1960, p. 6). However, it is doubtful that this examination provided a standardized evaluation for the four streams. The government claimed only that this exam was "conducted in four languages" and was "participated in by all types of schools." It avoided suggesting that the contents and the evaluative criteria of this examination were identical for all students. More vitally, the school-leaving exam for Chinese middle schools still differed from that for English secondary schools. Students from the English stream took the COSCE after finishing the fourth year and then the Cambridge Higher School Examination (CHSE), which was jointly held by the UCLES and the University of Malaya and Singapore after two years of sixth form.[15] Their Chinese school counterparts sat for the Secondary IV and Upper Secondary II examinations, which were administered entirely by the Ministry of Education in Singapore.[16] The contents of these two sets of examinations were not similar. These issues are not only visible in the examinations but are clear in the syllabi themselves.

Although the PAP alleged that all of its thirty-seven approved syllabi were Malayanized in content (MEAR, 1960, p. 6), closer scrutiny of the geography and history curricula hints otherwise. The new geography syllabus did suggest some topics on Malaya and Singapore for Primary IV and VI. However, the curriculum suggested for the secondary level was not very local. It proposed the study of Australia, New Zealand, America, Europe, Africa, and other parts of Asia from the first to the third year of secondary education, and recommended committing only the first term of the fourth secondary year to local geography (*Syllabus for Geography, 1961*). The history curriculum fared no better. Following a world-history approach, it covered too many countries and as a result left very limited curriculum space for Singapore and Malaya (*Syllabus for History, 1961*).

Admittedly, the 1961 history syllabus had made progress in eliminating some explicitly colonial elements. For example, it deleted two sections on imperial history—"Commonwealth History" and "The Development of Freedom and Responsibility"—from the curriculum for Secondary III and IV. The syllabus also incorporated "disturbances" and independence movements as minor topics of India, Ceylon, and Malaya histories (*Syllabus for History, 1961*, pp. 9, 11). These changes were not unimpressive given that Secondary III and IV were the two years for preparing pupils of English schools for the COSCE. The UCLES granted these concessions in part because in an era of decolonization it was more willing to accommodate the local state in order to preserve the cultural ties between Britain and its former territories and protect the imperial interests of Britain (Stockwell, 1990).[17]

The new curriculum nevertheless failed to exorcise the more subtle influences of colonialism. This problem concerning localization reflected the predicaments of the Singapore state. It had inherited a long colonial past, a blurred identity, a small territory, a civil society partitioned by several relatively new immigrant groups, and a weak local intellectual discourse. In the history syllabus, topics on Singapore and Malaya were always entwined with those of their neighboring areas, such as Siam, Annam, Cambodia, Burma, Philippines, and India. This curriculum was outsider-centered in other ways as well. Many of its suggested contents on local regions were about the activities of the Portuguese, Dutch, British, Spanish, French, American, and nonimmigrant Chinese in Southeast Asia (*Syllabus for History, 1961*, pp. 3–4). Moreover, the curriculum defined the local territories using the categorization of Western imperialism. This is clearly seen in the following proposed outline for the section on "Europeans Territories in Southeast Asia":

4. European Territories in Southeast Asia:
   a. The British East India Company.
      1. In India and Burma.
      2. In Malaya.
         (1) The Strait Settlement.
         (2) The Federated Malay States.
         (3) The Unfederated Malay States
   b. French Revolution and Napoleon, the French in SE Asia.
   c. Americans in the Philippines. (p. 4)

Added to this was the fact that the state was unable to define the local setting historically without referring substantially to external historical events and cultural traditions. For example, the new history syllabus preserved the section on "Culture Background of Malayan People" from the 1957 curriculum for Secondary IV. Yet once again this section was merely an amalgamation of topics about five external cultural traditions, namely Hinduism, Islam, Buddhism, and Chinese and Western civilizations (pp. 11–12). More tellingly, the proposed section on "Modern Malaya" for Primary VI contained the following topics:

(a) Chinese Nationalist Movement (including the Taiping Movement) and the Establishment of Republicanism in China.
(b) The First World War and the Depression Aftermath.
(c) The Marco Polo Bridge Incident and China's Anti-Japanese War.
(d) The Second World War and the Nationalist Movement Aftermath.
(e) Independence of the Federation of Malaya and Self-Governing in Singapore.
(f) Scientific Invention and Modernization of Malaya. (p. 4)

Among these six items, two (a and c) were historical affairs of China, and two (b and d) were events originating in the external global settings. Also, item f was constructed around the impact of Western forms of modernization on the local society. Since five out of the total of six topics it introduced as local history were basically external or externally generated events, it is clear that the state simply had a severe identity crisis.

In sum, the PAP's policy of transforming the curriculum of Chinese schools was only partly successful at best. At the level of the syllabus, the PAP created some common curriculum guidelines shared by all schools. These new syllabi had removed a considerable amount of Chinese content and overtly British imperial elements. However, the reformed curriculum could hardly construct a Singapore identity. It failed both to rid itself of the subtle influences of colonialism and to provide a substantial set of guidelines for learning coherently about the local society. Since the PAP failed to establish a standardized and locally grounded field of textbook production and evaluation, the considerable gap that existed between the official syllabi and the actual realization of the state pedagogic discourse in Chinese schools did not get any narrower.

Further Struggles to Unify and Localize the Pedagogic Device

The People's Action Party was not unaware of these problems. It struggled to unify and localize the pedagogic device. These attempts were never fully successful, however. The PAP first of all tried in vain to delink English schools from the recontextualizing field in Britain. In July 1959, two months after winning the General Election, Yong Nyuk Lin, the Minister of Education, announced that in 1964 the government would scrap the Cambridge exams and set up a Singapore Examination Syndicate to conduct public examinations for all pupils (*Standard*, July 10, 1959). One year later, probably after realizing the severe consequences of severing the external ties, the government sought to preserve the bond. For instance, the PAP allowed the establishment of the Singapore Advisory Committee of the UCLES, a coordinating body between the Ministry of Education of Singapore and the UCLES in 1960 (MEAR, 1960, p. 7; SCJP, May 19, 1960). Further, when setting 1963 as the earliest date for a local secondary school-leaving exam, Yong praised the contributions of the UCLES in the past and stressed that the Singapore government hoped to maintain a "close relation" with Cambridge after the local exam was established (ST, May 19, 1960). In 1964, after Singapore joined Malaysia, Toh Chin Chye, the vice-minister of the island, disclosed that the PAP government had decided to keep the COSCE and the CHSE. Toh explained that the exams conducted solely by the Singapore government would have only local recognition, while those given by the UCLES enjoyed worldwide acceptance. He also argued that although the government valued autonomy in education, these Cambridge exams were needed as common currencies of qualification in the three regions in Malaysia, namely the Borneo territories, the peninsula, and Singapore (SCJP, May 17, 1964).

In the early 1960s, the PAP also found its pedagogic device being divided by more external forces. Ironically, these external pedagogic elements served to disintegrate further the pedagogic discourse of Singapore. The PAP sought further integration between the island and the peninsula and wanted to win support from all racial groups within the local setting. Previously, the Singapore government had aimed chiefly at winning the support of the Chinese when they advocated "equal treatments for all streams." However, since the late 1950s this direction needed to be modified because when the PAP pursued merger with the peninsula, its policies toward the local Malays had to be more acceptable from the peninsula's viewpoint. The demands surrounding state formation, therefore, prompted the PAP to improve the position of Malay education. The effects were not only felt on Malay education. The policies also opened space for Indian groups to argue for improved state support of their schools.

In August 1959, the Malay Education Advisory Committee was appointed by the Minister of Education. Several months later, it recommended the establishment of a complete system of Malay education embracing six years of primary education and four years of secondary (MEAR, 1959, p. 2; SCJP, January 19, 1960). In 1960, Singapore had its first Malay secondary institution when the Kallang Secondary Malay School was opened (ST, January 12, 1960). In the same year, the state also started the Umar Pulavar School, the first secondary class in the Tamil medium (Ponniah, 1968, p. 103). These developments exposed the local pedagogic device to more external recontextualizing fields. In 1962, because of the inadequacies of Malay textbooks, the Singapore Trade and Cultural Representatives in Jakarta, Indonesia, purchased and then distributed textbooks to Malay medium secondary classes in Singapore (MEAR, 1962, p. 4). Later, the state imported teachers and textbooks from India and Ceylon to relieve the shortage of suitable teaching staff and instructional materials in the Tamil stream (MEAR, 1964, p. 5). These moves further defied unification by *enlarging* the gap between the teaching materials used by Chinese and other vernacular schools.

Furthermore, the growth of Malay and Tamil education created an ever greater division in the evaluation rules. At the end of 1963, when the Malay schools in Singapore produced their first batch of Secondary IV pupils, the government entered all of these 210 students for the Federation of Malaya Certificate of Education Examination, which was conducted by the Federal Examinations Syndicate in conjunction with the UCLES (MEAR, 1963, p. 4). This practice continued even after Singapore withdrew from Malaysia. For example, in 1967—two years after the separation—pupils completing four years of education in Malay secondary schools on the island still sat for that exam on the peninsula (MEAR, 1967, p. 7). Also, in 1963, the Singapore state installed the School Certificate (Tamil) Exam (MEAR, 1963, p. 8). From then on, pupils from four streams took four different secondary school-leaving exams sponsored by institutions or pedagogic agents from diverse territories.

The educational policies proposed by the People's Action Party did not focus only on Malay and Tamil education. The politics surrounding Chinese schools was also a central focus in the PAP's attempt to structure a locally oriented pedagogic device. For instance, the regime attempted to integrate the pedagogic device by offsetting the counterhegemonic effects of Nanyang University, among the most powerful agents within the PRF that interrupted official pedagogic discourse. Through a prolonged and complicated process, the government reformed the university by channeling financial subsidies in particular directions, planting progovernment forces in Nanyang University, and forming a series of committees to review various aspects of the university. These state actions culminated in an agreement between the government and the university authorities to reform Nanyang University in 1964. After that, a committee headed by Professor Wang Gungwu from the History Department at the University of Singapore was appointed to review the curriculum of Nanyang University. In May 1965, the report completed by the committee judged that the curriculum of Nanyang University was too China-oriented and not relevant to the development of the new nation of Malaysia and gave a number of suggestions for "correcting" this situation (Wang Gungwu Report, 1965, p. 1). In the same year, the state took one more step to weaken the disruptive effect of Nanyang University on the official pedagogic discourse. The PAP allowed 331 (out of a total of 549) new students to enter the university without taking its admission exam. All these new students were certificate-holders of the government's Upper Secondary II (Chinese) Exam (MEAR, 1965, p. 18).

Although the PAP finally put Nanyang University under its grip, it was not at all certain that the reconstituted institution from then on actually cultivated local consciousness and served the state-formation project of the PAP. This was because a successful realization of official pedagogic discourse demanded much more than the colonization of the nonofficial pedagogic field. It needed a strong and solid primary contextualizing field in which the primary discourse about local society was produced and from which agents from the recontextualizing field could selectively appropriate discursive resources to create a local and common curriculum as well. The development of such a primary context took time. However, under a highly pragmatic government prioritizing science and technology disciplines over arts and humanities, the primary context of Singapore needed to surmount more obstacles if it was ever to be built. In the *absence* of such a primary context, once again the PAP's policies on using Malay, Tamil, and Chinese education continually faced contradictory pressures and had contradictory results.

Conclusion

By employing and expanding Bernstein's concept of pedagogic device, we have attempted to strengthen the theory of state formation and education by bringing back the relative autonomy of the school system. Our major contention is that the educational field has its own rules, practices, and social relations that are not necessarily reducible to the status of "dependent variable" (see also Cho & Apple, this volume). Because of the specific conjunctural configuration of the educational system, schools may at times generate profound effects that may block or modify the process of state-building. To concretize this theoretical claim, we applied our reformulated theory of state formation and education to state reforms of Chinese curriculum in Singapore from 1945 to 1965. Rather than a story of the role of education in state formation, we have told a more dynamic and much "messier" story. During the period concerned, the ruling regimes in Singapore sought to build an independent and unified nation. To achieve this goal, the ruling powers toiled to realize the de-Sinicization, localization, and unification rules in Chinese school curriculum reform. Nevertheless, since all three successive governments in Singapore failed to overcome the fragmented and externally oriented nature of the pedagogic device, reforms in Chinese school curricula were largely unsuccessful.

From 1945 to around 1955, when Singapore was still a British possession, the pedagogic reform initiated by the colonial authorities was perceived by the Chinese community as a conspiracy to eliminate Chinese culture. The Chinese educators, both inside and outside of the official recontextualizing field, strongly resisted the three distributive rules. They also struggled for more control over the examination and publication of textbooks. Finally, the British were forced to both grant the Chinese community a great deal of control over the content of the textbooks and compromise their pedagogic reform.

From 1955 to 1965, when Singapore was governed by the first popularly elected government, the Labour Front, the ruling regime again sought to realize the de-Sinicization, localization, and unification principles. Although members of the Chinese community now tended to consider Singapore as their permanent home and did not resist state reforms as strongly as before, the LF still failed to localize the Chinese school curriculum and unify it with the pedagogic model of other schools. This was largely due to the fact that all of the existing pedagogic models in Singapore, namely those of the English, Chinese, Malay, and Tamil schools, were fashioned after the curriculum paradigms in England, China, the Federation of Malaya, and India. Without a suitable local pedagogic model, the LF, whose state bureaucrats were mainly English-educated, imposed the curriculum of English institutions as the model for all schools. This defied the rule of localization. Moreover, without a standardized framework for textbook publication and evaluation, the state was not able to discipline the pedagogic activities of Chinese schools and unify them with those in other institutions.

After 1959, when Singapore became a completely self-governing state ruled by the People's Action Party, the state became even more eager to develop a common and locally centered consciousness. Ironically, the developments in state formation further fragmented the pedagogic device and exposed it to more external forces. As a result, the contradictory pressures pushed the school system and its curricula in ways which partly undercut the demands of state-building. After assuming office, the PAP actively sought to merge with the Federation of Malaya and to win popular support from all the local racial communities. To achieve these goals, the PAP had to win the goodwill of the Malay and Indian communities by supporting their schools. As the Malay and Tamil schools had been by and large neglected before, Singapore had a very poor infrastructure for operating these two types of schools. As a result, the PAP was forced to rely on the Federation of Malaya, Indonesia, Ceylon, and India for teaching materials, teachers, and evaluations. These actions of the state further fragmented the recontextualizing field and evaluation rules within the pedagogic device and extended the gap between Chinese and other schools in terms of both their pedagogic activities and the consciousness these materials produced.

The historical case of Singapore clearly demonstrates that in racially tense colonial and postcolonial contexts, the constant tension between the educational system and the project of state formation can mediate and compromise the process of state-building. Our analysis also suggests that when we study state formation and education, we need to anatomize the rules, practices, and social relations embedded in the educational field. In doing so, schooling and the struggles over it lose their dependent character and take their place as an active site, as a distinctive moment of determination within the social formation. Recognition of this is central to the development of critically oriented approaches to the role that education has played and can play in societies structured around relations of differential power.

The ways in which state sponsored educational reforms are mediated and play an active role in social change in other areas of the world is what we examine in our next chapter. As we shall see, issues of particular views of knowledge, of identity, and the state's place in creating subject positions will play key roles.

What Happened to Social-Democratic Progressivism in Scandinavia? Restructuring Education in Sweden and Norway in the 1990s

Petter Aasen

Introduction

To many observers from the outside, the Scandinavian countries of Denmark, Sweden, and Norway appear rather similar. And, although in terms of their natural conditions and their economic, social, and cultural histories they are quite different, there can be no doubt that with reference to social structure, forms of government, and predominant attitudes toward society, the Scandinavian countries have many common features. To a great extent, the similarities stem from political thinking and actions, which in the latter part of the twentieth century were characterized as an attempt to create social democratic welfare societies. This commitment to welfare policy was clearly reflected in the education policies of the three countries. In spite of differences, something that might be called a *Scandinavian educational model*, with Sweden in particular as a role model, was developed during a period of thirty to forty years after World War II. In the first part of this chapter, I give a general presentation of this educational model as it was developed in Sweden and Norway.

A series of volumes on educational policy have examined the international tendencies of restructuring in education during the 1990s and the struggle over and contradictory effects of the neoliberal and neoconservative policies that have been influential in many regions of the world. In the second part of the chapter, I analyze how this restructuring has been affecting educational policy in Sweden and Norway.

Educational Reforms from 1945 to 1975

The interwar years brought labor-party, or social-democrat, governments to power in all three Scandinavian countries. These governments established a political order that retained its hegemony from the 1930s until the early 1970s. Political opinion and the dominant political beliefs were strongly oriented toward the political ideas and principles of the labor movement, toward a planned economy and state regulations, toward evening out differences and increasing equality and social inclusion. A reform model based on collaboration between capital and labor was introduced. The Social Democrats, as the political force of the labor movement, held political power for decades in an economy based to a great extent on private ownership.

Within the framework of a strong apparatus of central government, conflicts of interest would be handled as political issues that could be resolved through expansion of the public sector. The big and powerful state was understood as an active state, a regulatory power concerned not only with merely redistributing income, but also—and this was a central tenet of social democratic ideology—with a duty to ensure that all citizens enjoyed a minimum set of rights. On the other hand, the state was also understood as negotiation-oriented and committed to a corporative type of governance: employer federations, labor unions, farmers' associations, and so on were seen as partners with whom agreements could be reached. The development resulted in an extensive public sector and a number of reforms in different sectors of society. The reform processes can be characterized through concepts such as centralism, universalism, social engineering, standardized solutions, and consensus.

For the whole of the Western world, the first decades after World War II were marked by economic growth and great confidence in the state as the instrument of government. Thus a policy of state intervention with considerable growth in public responsibilities and expenses was an international trend. It was a time of what has been referred to as *the social democratic accord,* in which government increasingly became an arena for a focus on the conditions required for equality of opportunity (Aasen, 1994, 1997, 1999; Apple, 2000; Furre, 1991; Hall, 1988; Telhaug, 1992, 1997b).

In this endeavor to create societies characterized by equality and equity, the collectivist democratic ideal of the Scandinavian model and the unity of state and society, as expressed in terms of the Swedish *Folkhem,* was an inspiration for reform policies in other countries. In Scandinavia, however, the attempts to implement welfare societies were in many ways more ambitious and the consequences were wider than in most other countries, where more often this was seen solely as a matter of income redistribution or just adopted as convenient political rhetoric. Within the Scandinavian social-democratic model, an individual possessed a set of minimum rights simply by the fact of citizenship. These included state-supported services in the areas of health, education, social security, consumer protection laws, life-line utility guaranties, occupational safety and health regulations, workplace democracy, democratic control over investment decisions, and extensions of the norms of reciprocity and mutual participation and control in most areas of social life.

Within this model of democracy, a more or less coherent philosophy of education was formed. Education was regarded as an important contributing factor in the process of replacing the bourgeois society by the social-democratic welfare state. Powerful state control was to promote the development of education in the direction of a common school for all children where everyone would have equal possibilities for education independent of their geographical or cultural background and parents' social and economic standing.

The social-democratic movement regarded education as a social and citizenship right promoting public and collective good. It was a prerequisite for equality and equity, an essential preparation for social inclusion and democratic participation. Formulated by liberal and social-democratic political forces in the first part of the century, these political and educational visions were implemented through the extensive educational reforms from the end of World War II until the late 1970s and early eighties. During this reform period, an egalitarian, compulsory, comprehensive school system was implemented (Slagstad, 1994).

In the 1950s and early 1960s, educational policy in Scandinavia, as in the rest of the Western world, was marked by the "discovery" of education as an essential factor behind national economic performance. In other words, it was pushed by research findings that had a serious impact on policy. This, however, occurred in a situation in which politicians in Scandinavia as well as in other countries despaired that traditional investments in physical capital yielded little in terms of increased productivity in the economy. Thus there also existed a "pull" on economic research, and this combined "push" and "pull" undoubtedly had a real impact on the political will in the Western countries to favor educational expansion. Thus, in the transition from education for the elite to education for the masses, political authorities wished to employ the educational system as an active means of stimulating economic growth. A connection was seen between a generally high level of education in a country and its economic situation. The education budget was not seen as an expense but as a general investment that improved the economy, living conditions, and quality of life for the individual and society. Education was regarded as one of the most important means the state possessed to create economic development and growth for both the individual and the nation (Eide, 1995b).

Educational reforms were, however, linked to the modernization of Scandinavian societies in several ways. In education in general, there is always a tension between, on the one hand, a moral and identity-oriented dimension, a cultural dimension expressed by the German term *Bildung*, and, on the other hand, an instrumental, technological, and utility-oriented dimension. Within the social-democratic reform movement in Scandinavia, the cultural arguments were in many ways stronger than the conception of school as an instrumental agency. Education was viewed as a cultivating agency, and enlightenment was seen as an essential prerequisite in the democratization of the society. Indeed, the social-democratic progressivism in the 1950s, sixties, and seventies was continually seeking the opportunity to reduce external pressure for achievement on students, no doubt based on the wish to protect children against the brutality of the economic system and capitalism. In general, the Scandinavian model was based on a genuine respect for childhood and a child-centered perspective. Social-democratic progressivism tried to turn receptive and reproductive student activity into productive activity. It also offered greater influence for students on their learning situation. In the words of the Norwegian sociologist Rune Slagstad (1996a): "The democratic conception of folk cultivation is the Scandinavian gift to the modern world" (p. 308).

Within social-democratic policy, the educational system was regarded as an instrument for individual and collective emancipation, social inclusion, social justice, and equality. For the social-democratic political parties and the labor movement in the Scandinavian countries, the public educational system was fundamental in the reconstruction of the bourgeois class society and in the struggle to create a classless participatory democracy based on solidarity. Education was fundamental to the redistribution of wealth through not only equality of opportunity but also equality of results. Social-democratic educational policy promoted equal preparation through unequal treatment (more resources to the disadvantaged regions and individuals) to achieve equality of learning opportunities and equality of results in terms of competent participatory citizens collectively discussing and making decisions in a democratic society. The national funding system was a system of detailed earmarking of grants and was based on strong positive discrimination. This made it possible to transfer substantial funds to rural and peripheral areas. The objective of this funding policy was to avoid differences in the quality of schooling. The participation perspective, the effort to make education accessible to the largest possible number of people, was dominant in the heyday of social democracy (Telhaug, 1997a).

These school reforms ran fairly parallel in Norway and Sweden, directed mainly toward the establishment of a fully comprehensive school system for children up to the age of sixteen and later toward an integration of and extended access to upper secondary education. In the 1970s and eighties, public institutions to take care of children below school age expanded. For quite some time, the upper secondary school remained the exclusive preserve of upper-middle-class children. During the 1970s and eighties, it became a general arena for development and qualification for all Scandinavian youth, in part as a result of working-class and rural youth loosing their foothold in the labor market. During three decades, the educational system in Scandinavia was continuously reformed from a system of parallel schools to a comprehensive school system based on three main principles: uniformity of school structure, equality in educational opportunities, and, to a certain extent, inequality in distribution of resources and treatment to obtain equality of results (Telhaug, 1994).

An educational system based on "hierarchical steering" developed and resulted in a centralized infrastructure and an expanded educational administration. Historically, however, local authorities have a stronger tradition in Norway than in Sweden, particularly regarding the running of schools at the compulsory level. The machinery for educational policymaking and implementation of reforms at the central level was stronger in Sweden. The Swedish reform strategy was accordingly more top-down-oriented. Central directives and innovations were implemented from the top to an undifferentiated periphery. In Norway, a law on innovation in education was passed in 1954. This law allowed the Ministry of Education to exempt any municipality, school, or teacher from the general legal regulations of the school system and thus allowed them to try out educational innovations beyond what normal legislation and regulations permitted. More and more municipalities were gradually brought under the innovation law, up to a point where a majority of Norwegian schools were taken out of the general educational legislation. In this way, the social-democratic reforms were gradually introduced. Accordingly, when legislation on compulsory comprehensive education and on reforms in upper secondary education was passed later, this was to a great extent just a formal political confirmation of an existing situation (Eide, 1995a).

The process toward major reforms both in Sweden and Norway was based on government-appointed commissions, often working for several years. Commission reports were then subject to broad hearings and negotiations at the political level, leading toward propositions securing a safe majority in Parliament. The production of formal national curricula texts both in Sweden and Norway was also the result of the work of government-appointed committees preceding decisions in Parliament. In Norway as in Sweden, representatives with educational expertise were appointed to these committees. The final decisions taken by Parliament were broadly anchored and supported by all, or nearly all, political parties (Eliason, 1989; Husén, 1988; Husén & Kogan, 1984).

Characteristics of the Educational System

In spite of some differences in strategy, the policy interaction between Norway and Sweden was considerable. Norway had already introduced comprehensive education up to the age of fourteen in 1920, probably the first country in Europe to do so. The apparently effective functioning of this system clearly influenced the Swedish Social Democrats and served as an argument when, after World War II, they introduced comprehensive education up to the age of sixteen. This political move, backed by extensive research arguments, clearly inspired the Norwegian Labor Party to start working on a similar reform in the 1950s. When comprehensive education in Norway was finally made compulsory for the country as a whole in 1969, practical experience from experiments all over the country had demonstrated that the Swedish system of junior secondary schools with three ability-based streams could be avoided. A few years afterwards, Sweden followed the same pattern, abandoning organized streaming in the upper stages of compulsory education. In general, the objectives of the educational reforms in all Scandinavian countries were the same, and with certain differences in strategy and time lags in the implementation process, an educational system emerged with common features representing a specific model of educational philosophy and policy. Furthermore, educational policy-making was well integrated with government policies in other sectors. The reforms of the educational system were introduced through coordination between educational policy on the one hand, and cultural policy, social policy, manpower policy, and regional policy on the other, all initiatives and innovations being taken within the framework of general welfare policies.

Within the Scandinavian model, children started school relatively late, around the age of seven. This had a historical explanation in scattered habitation and long distances to school. The school units were mostly small. This was the situation in Norway even in the 1990s, where the average size of a school for grades 1 to 6 was about 150 students, and of schools for grades 7 to 9 about 250. This was not only a consequence of scattered populations but also the result of deliberate policy. The policy was based on the belief that a good school should have close contacts with parents and with the local community. Furthermore, schools were seen as essential to the life of the local community.

The Scandinavian educational system was characterized by late differentiation with an increasingly higher level of general education for all and national curricula for compulsory education (grades 1 to 9) and upper secondary school. Within schools and classrooms, social integration ("mainstreaming") and community replaced segregation and organizational differentiation/organized streaming. Thus this comprehensive organization through the first nine years made it possible for small schools to operate. Students of different abilities were kept together in the same classroom, and during the 1970s this also included the integration of handicapped or disabled children. In the area of teaching methods, the individual school and teacher experienced extensive freedom.

The system of central government financial support was aimed at securing equal quality all over the country, often through highly unequal resource input. In Norway, poor municipalities with scattered populations spent twice as much per child in compulsory education compared to the national average. As a consequence, parents tended to regard the nearest school as equal in quality terms to any other school.

The questions both of what should be taught in school and of teaching methods were not political issues in the early stages of the reform. National curricula, inspired by the ideas of progressive education, identified a common frame of reference, which was considered important for the development of equality and democracy. The curricula defined how to organize what was regarded as an unproblematic knowledge base within the school.

Even though national curricula, specifically the Norwegian national curriculum of 1939, were influenced by American progressivism and the German *Arbeitsschule,* promoting learning by discovery and productive student activity, classroom activities in the 1950s and sixties were characterized by authoritarian strictness, inscrutable and unalterable teaching material, and traditional teacher instruction focusing on basic skills and factual information. Students' activities were dominated by memorization exercises, reproduction, and self-discipline in daily conduct.

The school was seen as imparting a generally accepted molding ideal. The school was to impart ideas—values and knowledge—to the next generation. It was considered a particularly valuable foundation on which to develop the general culture. Attending school was the initiation into a common national culture. Individuals came to school with their local perspectives, and they were then molded into citizens of society. The knowledge and values that were taught were believed to be absolute and necessary for becoming a citizen. Neither parents nor students showed much doubt in school.

The traditional molding ideal and the understanding of school knowledge as given maintained a learning-by-rote school, which at times was literally meaningless. But on the other hand, a meaning was tied to school as an institution, which made the student feel that she or he took part in something significant and important. Teachers brought general culture into the classroom, and students struggled to emulate this. The meanings given to schooling made students feel significant.

In the first decades after World War II, schooling in Scandinavia was able to benefit from the fact that the relation between the generations was firmly established. There was a high and solid wall between the worlds of the child and of the adult. The school possessed almost exclusive rights to act as guide for young people on their journey into the adult world. Entrance to the adult world was gained through the portal of school. This lent importance and status to teachers. The school was freely able to build on a culturally conditioned motivation basis, which meant that self-discipline was given a positive subjective value. Self-discipline was taken as given. The conviction that life is hard to bear and mainly consists of gritting your teeth and tolerating its hardships was relayed from generation to generation. Thus the school was able to take for granted a utilitarian motivation basis as well as values such as self-discipline, obedience, order, subjugation, diligence, modesty, precision, and stamina.

The school appeared as a neutral provider of services for everybody. It was considered a fair tool for selection of talents from any social stratum. It gave equal opportunities to all. Schooling was part of shaping a collective identity and was not concerned with individual identity in relation to gender or one's historic and social roots. The school was primarily a tool for social mobility and was the ticket to the privileges of work and social life. In this light, schooling could be uninteresting without being indifferent. Knowledge was seen as a tool, and motivation was based on the utilitarian ideal. Schooling served long-term interests; it was primarily defined as a public good and used and created a utilitarian but often self-denying consciousness of self.

In other words, the Scandinavian educational policy regarded education as a source of social mobility but was rather uncritical of curricular content. The educational content was defined by two dominating curriculum codes: a national essentialist code in which emphasis was placed on religion, humanities, and cultural heritage, and a realistic curriculum code focusing on the scientific disciplines and at the same time creating a link between education and working life outside school. Within this latter code, educational content was regarded as a simplification of scientific progress and adjustments of curriculum to scientifically investigated demands arising from the needs of a technological society.

Educational policy-makers and researchers were concerned with the problem of increasing access to schooling without examining the nature of the education that they sought to distribute more widely. There was a confident assumption that what we took for granted as education was good in itself and that it was in the interest of both individuals and the national economy that they should receive more of it. The curriculum policy perspective was uncritical in the sense that it did not seem to take into consideration that inequality and the reproduction of power are connected not only to limited access to education and biased distribution of economic capital but also to the cultural capital of the school and to whose knowledge is taught in schools.

A number of factors reinforced the central political control of the compulsory school of this period. For many years before the war, private school enrollment had declined, and the decline continued after the war. Both Norway and Sweden had developed a system of government with three levels: the national or central level, the regional level, and the municipal level. The central level directed developments toward greater equality between town and country and between social classes. Partly, this was effected through *earmarked funding,* which did not allow local units much latitude in their spending, though public investments in education increased. Later, central authorities increasingly applied *legislative* means of governance in the form of detailed regulations.

The Swedes were in the vanguard in this respect. Their School Act of 1842 for the seven-year primary school introduced a regulation with only fourteen sections. By 1882 and again in 1897, the regulation had ten chapters with sixty-eight and seventy sections respectively; the 1962 regulation had twenty-nine chapters with a total of 701 sections, of which 354 sections related to primary schools. The 1969-to-1970 official compilation of regulations published by the National Swedish Board of Education filled almost fifteen hundred pages, and it was no exaggeration when, in 1973, a public report (SOU 1973:48) claimed that "state control is now almost 100% percent effective."

Redefining the Reform Agenda in the 1970s and 1980s

The Norwegian and Swedish educational reforms from 1945 to 1975 were aimed at making education more accessible to all children, regardless of social class, gender, and economic and geographic background. A general faith in individual emancipation and social justice through enlightenment and knowledge was pursued through the principle of participation and the concept of unified schooling. All children should obtain education of good and equal quality. The reforms essentially concerned the organization and structure of the school system. They were initiated from the central level, and their implementation and local schoolwork were governed by the state through a number of different mechanisms.

During the 1970s, country after country in the Western world found that enormous investments in education for everybody did not yield the expected economic results. Quite to the contrary, it was recorded that economic growth was flagging in the Western world. In Scandinavia, productivity also sank and unemployment started to climb. Moreover, new research conducted by social scientists confirmed that investment in schooling had not yielded any particular gain in the shape of increased social, economic, political, and gender equality. In contrast, "the new education society" brought new social and conduct problems into the school, and these became increasingly more visible in the seventies. Thus growing economic crises and social science research findings gave rise to questions about education as an investment factor and initiator of change in society. In Scandinavia, the welfare state faced a number of problems that could not be treated with old solutions. The founders of the old reform ideology had apparent problems formulating new ideas and visions. The strong belief in state planning characterizing the postwar period was infused with uneasiness that social planning did not always work as designed. Economic and social instability, a growing change of pace, and the consequent increasing difficulties in predicting and planning for the future gave birth to a new reform or governance strategy where local authorities were ordered to resume a higher degree of responsibility. The new strategy was not limited to education but concerned state governance in general. As the school system had been one of the most centrally regulated and controlled state apparatuses until that time, changes were more dramatic and visible here (Kallós & Nilsson, 1995; Mediås, 1999; Telhaug, 1994).

In Sweden and Norway, the general climate of educational discussions thus shifted to the left during the 1970s. A conflict perspective on education emerged, and the school as a preparatory institution for political participation in a pluralistic democracy was underlined. The content of education, or the subject matter, also entered the political agenda. Competing views of "man," nature, society, and knowledge were focused on, and concepts like "the hidden curriculum," "local, community based curriculum," "learning to learn," and "critical pedagogy" were introduced. Issues concerned with gender relations, the Third World, peace, nuclear weapons, exploitation of natural resources, the global environment, and the potential for change were subjects for more investigative approaches in the schools. Schools were challenged more explicitly by a general sense of cultural liberation and new cultures among youth, who resisted the dominant school paradigm with its demand of obedience and reproduction of texts. In many ways, cultural change and the left turn in policy in general introduced a more conflict-oriented, critical society–centered educational perspective.[1]

The changes in social-democratic educational policy in the 1970s and 1980s were, however, not only reflecting neoradical political movements. They also reflected more general material and cultural changes in the Scandinavian societies. Economic growth, the first wave of immigration from Third World countries, and development toward pluralism and variety in general created a basis for cultural liberation and situated the school in an entirely different context. The new cultural climate created new demands for justification and new visions for education influenced by more individualist or psychological values such as creativity, spontaneity, and realization of the self. Accordingly, schools took on greater responsibilities for improving children's self-confidence, self-acceptance, sense of belonging, and initiative.

Thus the 1970s and eighties marked the end of the utilitarian educational policy of the 1950s and sixties, where schooling was primarily seen as an arena of exercise and qualification for real life through reproduction of a knowledge content and a value system that were taken for granted. Education no longer regarded knowledge either as independent of power relations or as an economic resource or means to be bartered for different benefits such as increased production, increased competitiveness, better grades, promotions, more influence, higher wages, and so on. Education had a value of its own, and schooling was also to relate to the private arena. In the 1960s, the school was relatively free to impart a knowledge that was remote from life itself and everyday experiences. Schooling was seen in light of a utilitarian paradigm aimed more at exploitation and external to aspects of the good life. The utilitarian motivation could reign because the more existential questions and issues of identity still rested on a cultural bedrock (norms, everyday rules, patterns of behavior, habits and pattern of meanings, gender roles, and so on), which had been handed down from one generation to the next and still remained relatively undisputed. As the result of increasing wealth, centralization and urbanization, new technology, commercialization, internalization, demythification, and rationalization, this foundation showed signs of decay in the seventies, and young people filled the void with their own ways of searching for culture, interpretations, and meaning. The private sphere, the world of everyday life, existential question, identity formation, and development of the individual thus appeared on the educational policy agenda.

In this manner, the educational reforms during the 1970s and eighties in many ways established a more radical and critical agenda through school-based development and community-based curricula. But they also implied a social psychological turn and, to a certain degree, a shift away from seeing education as public good and toward individualism and a view of education as a private good.

In many ways, a new educational paradigm arose in the 1970s that defined alternative understandings of and reasons for objectives and strategies for education and school development. Differences in performance were no longer judged on the basis of intellectual capacity but as consequences of cultural differences. Scandinavia entered an era of local-based curriculum and internal school development, emphasizing a more child-centered approach, whole-learning arrangements, thematic curriculum, critical thinking, unit teaching, learning through cooperation, problem- and project-centered methods and process-oriented learning activities, the use of the local environment's learning qualities, and experiential learning. Thus alternative standards for teaching activity were developed. Self-evaluation and internal accountability became central to school development.

After the period of neoradicalism in the 1970s, education became in many ways a nonissue in political and social debates and in the media's eyes in the late seventies and the first half of the eighties. Educational policy was during this period linked only to a small extent to economic and business policy. When educational policy was put on the agenda in Norway in connection with the revisions of the primary school curriculum in the middle of the eighties, economic reasons were not initially particularly prominent. This revision was chiefly initiated by the fact that traces from the dissolution and disintegration of traditions and culture—or viewed more positively, cultural liberation—were becoming more and more clear. Thus rose the demand for the mobilization of values.

The Norwegian national curriculum of 1987, as with the Swedish national curriculum of 1980, also marked, however, changes in state strategy for steering the schools. The curricula gave greater allowances for autonomous and independent action at a local level. The Norwegian national curriculum of 1987 clearly stated that each school within the frameworks of the national curriculum should state its own objectives and carry out systematic development work in order to promote the objectives of the school. The schools were to develop formal local curricula in which each school was recommended to give priority to certain areas of development work, set goals for this work, and follow up on the results of the effort. A national program was also established to promote school development that was widely disseminated through courses and the education of advisers. County directors of schools were also allocated funds for development work on the conditions that schools had established clear goals for development work and for following up important aspects of this work.

In Sweden, the forty-four-year political hegemony of the Social Democratic Party came to an end when a conservative bourgeois coalition government took office in 1976. However, as pointed out by Murray (1995), the conservative coalition governments from 1976 to 1982 actually fulfilled a social-democratic policy rather than introducing a new one. The late 1970s and the 1980s were characterized by a progressive pedagogy as regards the development of school and classroom activities. The implementation of the 1980 National Curriculum represented a change toward a more integrated curriculum, reduction of the role and significance of grading, and emphasis on a unified comprehensive school that limited the role of options and differentiation. In the lower grades, teaching in mixed-age groups became more common and a trend away from textbook-bound teaching and content-specified courses could be discerned.

To summarize, in the course of developing a common comprehensive system of education aiming at national equality, Sweden and Norway instituted a number of controls over the development of institutions of education throughout the countries. In the 1970s, there was a growing realization within the social-democratic movement and among the left more generally, supported by a number of research reports, that schools did not live up to many of the expectations linked to the reforms of the postwar period. Despite the fact that the children went through a nine-year comprehensive education and a large majority received an upper secondary education, class and gender differences, regional differences, and differences between manual and mental work were largely reproduced in schools and society. Based on these premises, a change in governance strategy was initiated. It was believed that resources were better used and creation of quality and equality better solved when decisions were taken at the local level. Thus, in the 1970s and eighties, a loosening of state control was envisaged, described variously as a policy of regionalizing, decentralization, participation, or differentiation. Not only did policy discourse focus on the local, but also, to a growing extent, the arenas of actual policy formulation were also located at the local level. The introduction of new national curricula for compulsory education from 1939 to 1987 in Norway and from 1962 to 1980 in Sweden thus marked a change in strategy for steering schools. The earlier curricula were characterized by a very high degree of central control, manifested in detailed rules laid down by the state, which the schools were obliged to adhere to. In more recent curricula, these detailed rules were to some extent replaced by so called framework rules, which made greater allowance for autonomous and independent action at a local level. The curriculum plans defined a core curriculum but offered considerable leeway for local adaptations.

During the 1970s and 1980s, educational policy introduced decentralization of decision-making power, less earmarking of financial transfers from central to local authorities and to the individual institutions, and a certain building-down of traditional legal regulations. These efforts to decentralize and deregulate the Swedish and Norwegian educational systems were aimed at strengthening local political bodies, increasing the professional autonomy of the individual schools, school leadership, and teachers, and building up strong institutions that were responsive to the social good, as defined through national consensus and client needs. Each school was to become a center for policy and practice, capable of determining its own style and forms of expertise and contributing its own value positions to those of the larger society. Still, however, educational policy was based on the core values within the traditional Scandinavian model. The idea of comprehensive schooling and the need to uphold education of equal opportunities and equal national standards were addressed. A strong state governance at strategic points in order to avoid increased differences between students, schools, and municipalities was defended. In Sweden, a proposal from a parliamentary committee on school governance (SOU 1988:20), served as the basis for a decision in Parliament on school governance in 1989. It combined policies for strong central governance in order to secure equality in education with policies for deregulation and goal governing.

An International Perspective: A New Conservative Accord

In the Western world, continual economic growth, affluence, Western imperial might, and cultural optimism were gradually replaced by years of crisis during the 1970s and eighties. Social-democratic solutions in the form of large-scale intervention in education, welfare, and health to increase opportunities or to provide a minimal level of support were no longer seen as part of the solution. On the contrary, they were gradually regarded more as being part of the problem. With Reagan in the United States and Thatcher in Britain, initiatives taken by the state increasingly came under attack and a new, right-wing activist politics of alteration emerged (Telhaug, 1990). In the United States, Britain, New Zealand, Australia and elsewhere, a new accord was formed combining a market-based, choice-driven, consumerist economy with populist politics connected to the needs, fears, and hopes of groups of people who felt threatened by the range of problems associated with the crises in culture and economy. Michael Apple (1996, 1997) calls this rightward turn the *conservative restoration*. According to Apple, this reorientation in policy was the result of the successful struggle by the right to form a broad-based alliance. Apple identified three major policy positions within this alliance.[2] In analyzing the educational reforms in Scandinavia in the 1990s, I will trace how these three positions or elements—neoliberal, neoconservative, and authoritarian-populist—contested and affected the social-democratic model in Sweden and Norway during the last decade of the twentieth century.

Neoliberal positions are, according to Apple, the most powerful element within the conservative restoration. They are guided by a vision of the weak state leaving the development of society to the dynamics of private initiatives and cost-benefit analysis. Within this economic rationality, efficiency is measured in terms of the possibilities of individuals to maximize their own personal benefits. Within this view, the ideal of the citizen is that of a purchaser. Democracy is transformed into an economic concept where consumer choice within a free-market system is a guarantor of a just, self-regulating society. With reference to education, this perspective implies a shift from the social-democratic view of education as a public or common good toward seeing it as a private good where schooling is to provide opportunities for children to develop the appropriate traits they possess innately and to use them for their own betterment. Students are viewed as human capital and public schools are criticized for not providing adequate results. Through a market-based, choice-driven consumerist policy for schooling, education will more efficiently and effectively respond to individual needs and the financial life of the society.

The second major element within the new alliances is *neoconservatism*. Whereas neoliberalism views public schools more or less as "black holes," neoconservatism is concerned with the content of the schools. Schools are seen as transforming agents for real knowledge, basic skills, morality, Western traditions, high culture, and a national identity. Among the policies proposed under this position were detailed national curricula, national testing, and a "return" to higher standards. Accordingly, unlike the neoliberal emphasis on the weak state, neoconservatives are usually guided by a vision of the strong state. The idea of a strong state is visible in the demand for control over legitimate knowledge and methods and in regulation of teacher autonomy. The neoconservative ideology implies a distrust of teachers, of professionalism in education, and of teachers' unions.

An *authoritarian-populist* position on education is based on particular visions of biblical authority, Christian morality, gender roles, and the family. Perhaps more than in any other major industrialized country, Apple states, educational politics in the United States is influenced by authoritarian populism. In concert with neoconservative elements within the conservative alliance, authoritarian-populist religious fundamentalists have a substantial influence on curriculum policy in this country. By restoring issues of authority, morality, family, church, and "decency," schools can overcome the moral decay of society (Apple, 2001).

In the United States, the power of this new conservative accord of quite contradictory ideas of educational policy leads to: a) programs for "choice," such as voucher plans and tax credits to make schools like the thoroughly idealized free-market economy; b) a movement at national and state levels throughout the country to "raise standards" and mandate both teacher and student "competencies" and basic curricular goals and knowledge, increasingly now through the implementation of statewide and national testing; c) effective attacks on the school curriculum for its anti-family and anti–free enterprise "bias," its secular humanism, its lack of patriotism, and its supposed neglect of the knowledge and values of the "Western tradition" and of "real knowledge"; and d) growing pressure to make the perceived needs of business and industry into the primary goals of the schools (Apple, 1996).

To capture and describe reforms and change in education during the last decade of the twenty-first century, the term *restructuring* was introduced (Ball, 1990, 1994; Carnoy & MacDonell, 1990; Cuban, 1990; Hargreaves, 1994; Murphy, 1991). Marketization, accountability, and the redefinition of the roles of educational stakeholders are central elements in the restructuring of education. Marketization covers attacks on the dysfunctional nature of a bureaucratic, monopolistic state and it appeals to the power of competition as means of improvements in education and the desire to transfer money from the public to the private sector. Demands for greater accountability refer to the need for and use of more outcome-based measures for both student and school performance. Finally, restructuring makes demands on redefining roles for teachers, students, administrators, and parents. In the late eighties, the existing educational system was viewed as too rigid, too bureaucratic, and too inflexible. Restructuring in education was introduced to cope with societal problems of late modernity. Restructuring was of course not a new historical phenomenon. Educational reforms have characterized education throughout the past. While educational reforms introduced within the social-democratic accord after World War II were the point of departure for societal change, restructuring within the new conservative accord in the 1990s can rather be viewed as a response to societal changes (Hargreaves, 1994; Tyack & Cuban, 1995). Restructuring in the form of deregulation, privatization, marketization, consumer choice, and accountability gave, however, new attention to fundamental educational dilemmas or contradictions such as the tensions between utility and culture, between control and autonomy, between homogeneity and plurality, between efficiency and equality, between education as a moral and cultural expressive endeavor and education as an instrumental and technological endeavor, between economic demands and preparation for democratic traditions, and between education as investment and education as a civilizing and cultural activity.

Restructuring of the Scandinavian Model

As in the rest of the Western world during the last part of the 1970s and eighties, in the Scandinavian countries the rationale of the social-democratic order and the belief in continual growth were questioned. The general consensus present in the first decades after the war, with few debates on the principles of educational policy, was followed by a period where powerful interest groups and minority groups voiced their demands. In many ways, social democracy also lost the rhetorical leadership, or the ideological hegemony, it had possessed during the first decades after World War II.

Between 1985 and 1990, a commission initiated by the Swedish government analyzed the distribution of power, resources, and influence in Swedish society (Pettersson, 1991; SOU 1990:44). This study, entitled "The Study of Power and Democracy," gave a detailed picture of a society in transition. What could be observed was a change in the concept of democracy. The society-centered tradition of democracy built on the idea of a sovereign people but where every individual is seen as a member of a collective was gradually replaced by an individual-centered tradition of democracy. Here the point of departure is the sovereign individual taking responsibility for his or her own destiny. In line with this tradition, the individual natural character, ability, and the freedom for everyone to create their own future were increasingly underlined. In broad terms, decentralization, particularization, and polarization had emerged in a context in which the public sector was increasingly regarded as a problem rather than a solution.

The Swedish commission explained this transformation of the Scandinavian model through internal and external causes. Internal causes within the model were tensions between different elements in the model, between

negotiations and the role of experts, and between social equality and efficiency. External causes were changes from an industrialized toward a
postindustrial and international society and cultural diversity due to increased immigration. In other words, the era characterized by strong
public-sector expansion, centralized collective bargaining on a historic
compromise between labor and capital, social engineering, and centrally
planned standard solutions had come to an end. The new period was characterized by individualization and internalization. According to the
Swedish committee, the old institutions linked to industrialization and democratization of Swedish society had become weaker in a process whereby
citizens had become better educated, independent, and autonomous.

In Sweden, such criticisms of the welfare institutions were supported
by a state commission on the economy initiated in 1992 with the tasks of
analyzing emerging economic problems in Sweden and suggesting guidelines for new economic policies. The commission argued that the present
problems were a result of the expansion of public expenditures and the
characteristics of welfare institutions. These institutions were outdated and
were lacking in efficiency. What was needed was a social organization built
on "active citizens" and "distinct and close relationships between efforts
and results" (SOU 1993:16). To get out of the economic crisis, marketization was regarded as an important measure in combination with reduc-
tions in the public sector. Freedom of choice and competition between different alternatives in combination with privatization were regarded as ways
to modernize the malfunctioning institutions of the welfare state, including education.

The Swedish commissions gave a general picture of the transitions of
the Scandinavian countries and the new political rhetoric of the 1990s. In
Scandinavia, as in the rest of the Western world, the ideological climate
changed during the 1980s, and belief in the power of the market increased.
The conflict between "market ideology" and "equality ideology" increased.
The idea of creating a just society by ridding society of inequalities yielded
to the idea of fairness tied to performance and reward. As long as growth
was strong enough to allow private consumption to increase while also sat-
isfying most group demands, the social-democratic distribution policy
worked well. When the crisis arrived in the 1980s, the social-democratic
idea of social solidarity largely digressed into conflicting individual interests without a common idea or purpose. The economic recession turned
the political conflict into a struggle between common and special interests.

Even though mobilization of values was an issue in the revision of the
national curriculum in Norway in 1987, elements from the conservative
restoration did not play a major role in educational policy in the Scandina-

vian countries in the early eighties. The economic crises did not put education on the political agenda. In the late eighties, however, in Scandinavia, as
in many parts of the world, changes in economy, ideology, and mentality
put the focus on the school and education policies. The economic arguments and the ideas of human capital from the 1950s and sixties appeared
again in political discourse on education. We could witness transformations in the public discourse over education concerning what schooling is
for and how education is to be carried out. One way of interpreting the dissolution and decline of the norms of society and the country's lagging behind the competition in the free international marketplace was that neither
schools nor teachers kept sufficiently high standards.

Toward the end of the 1980s and into the nineties, a number of reports
that cast a critical light on the educational system appeared in Norway: the
system was out of national control, standards were too low, and it did not
deliver according to the demands of either the individual or the society.
The public reports were followed by reform measures within the educational system, applying to both its basic structure and substance.

Anxieties that surfaced in the last half of the 1980s about the level of
knowledge children and adolescents had and the focus on the ability of the
educational system to produce future workers with the requisite morals,
knowledge, and skills were in no way a particular Norwegian concern.
These became political issues in all the Scandinavian countries. In this situation, the importance of the socioeconomic role of education was gradually reinstated. The national economy was again linked to the production
of knowledge, and a school system demanding greater effort was called for.
We were facing a new situation with increased international competition
based on production of knowledge, and because of this demands concerning both what schools taught and the level of the subjects intensified.

As an integral part of the shift in political climate, a discourse on educational policy arose in Scandinavia that was no longer based on preparations for participatory democracy, appraisal of social and cultural differences, or the demand for social justice and equality, but on the health of the
national economy. Knowledge and education were again elevated above social conflicts and largely seen as neutral instruments independent of the
social or cultural context. The school was primarily regarded as an instrument to strengthen technical-cognitive know-how and to increase national
efficiency.[3]

When the interest in education as a factor in economic growth and for
national economic competitiveness reemerged toward the end of the
1980s, this was not based on any new research findings. In other words,
contrary to the 1950s and early sixties, it was not due to any push effect.

More important seemed to be the demand from the emerging knowledge industry and the influence of dominant thinking and attitudes in other Western countries. The growing economic crises in the late 1980s and early 1990s also created a general need for symbols demonstrating political authority, efficiency, and ability to act. Educational policy initiatives and education expansion met this demand. In addition, the expansion of upper secondary and higher education had an immediate effect on employment through the removal of individuals from the labor market. Another factor may also have contributed to the restoration of the economic argument. When great reforms are planned and have to be sold to the broad public, general political objectives of concern to everybody are often strongly emphasized. In periods of implementation of politically decided reforms, arguments focusing more on the norms and values of the educational system per se are often predominant.

Internationally, the premises underlying educational policy were changed in the 1980s. Compared to the 1960s, when the economic argument was embedded in the social-democratic accord, authorities no longer tended to place much importance on education as a welfare benefit or a sociopolitical tool. Education was viewed mainly as a production factor. The objective was no longer so much to strengthen the general level of education in society but to develop more specific skills and know-how in the population. High-quality education was needed in order to develop society, business, and economy. The problem was how to wring the most quality out of each dollar invested in the educational system.

As we have seen, restorative school policies in the Western world were characterized by a combination of traditional conservatism with authoritarian attitudes and moralizing demands for more discipline, harder work, and traditional moral virtues on the one hand, and, on the other hand, by neoliberalism with a belief in market powers and competition also in the schools. With this followed an emphasis on knowledge in the form of traditional curriculum and external demands on school from the so-called consumers, that is to say the production sphere and parents. In the 1990s, this policy seemed to burrow itself deeply, even into the social-democratic Scandinavian countries. In Norway, the Labor government started to work on a new educational reform in 1988. The aim was to introduce a more specific national curriculum to enable schools to reproduce common frames of reference and educate more competent students. Structural reforms were introduced in the upper secondary school in 1994, and revisions of the national curricula for compulsory schooling, upper secondary schooling, and teacher education were launched.

In Sweden, the Social Democratic government in 1991 appointed a committee to redraft the national curricula. When the general election in September the same year put a new rightist government in office and two ministers from the Conservative Party in the Ministry of Education, the new government soon announced its intention to introduce substantial changes in the educational system. The members of the National Curriculum Committee were dismissed, new members were appointed, and new directives were written. The shift in government introduced a new rhetoric and a speeding up of the restructuring of the educational system. On the basis of steering by objectives, decentralization, professional responsibilities, and freedom of choice, state intervention was to be subordinated to market mechanisms. The overall aim of the new policy was to develop "the best schools in Europe" by giving school subjects a firmer status in the curriculum and by putting greater emphasis on languages. The committee was directed to both propose syllabi for the different school subjects, permitting a criteria-referenced marking system to be used, as well to recommend quality-raising measures. Both in Sweden and Norway, Christian values, and "Western human values" were pointed to as the foundations for activities in school and knowledge acquisition as the most important task.

In the 1990s, problems of inclusion and exclusion of ethnic groups who had immigrated to Scandinavia during the past decades increasingly became part of the public debate and educational policy. The growing diversity in the Scandinavian countries challenged the previous simplistic conception of a common culture. Globalization and the fear of "the other" undoubtedly gave rise to the more fundamentalist demands of the restoration of a *common cultural heritage* (Apple, 2001).

Following Carnoy and McDonell (1990), restructuring inside the conservative accord was a governance or management reform. In Sweden and Norway, one of the most dramatic changes in the 1990s was the shift from a highly centralized educational system to a decentralized and deregulated system. Radical steps toward local freedom were taken, with the market as a model. The central governing principle was steering by means of goals; the state level is to deliver some general principles for education, and it is up to the local level to interpret and fulfill the goals. The Swedish Parliament decided in 1989 that teachers and other school staff should be employed by the municipalities and not by the state. The nonsocialist government took more far-reaching steps toward local autonomy from 1991 to 1994; decisions promoting the establishment of independent, private schools and the introduction of vouchers were crucial, opening up the possibilities of inviting tenders in certain subjects and the decision to distribute all state subsidies as lump sums and thus leave responsibility and priorities to the municipality level. In Norway, a decentralized budget system had already been introduced in the 1980s.

Since 1986, it has been up to the municipality level to make economic decisions and distribute resources between different sectors like the school system, childcare, and social care. In their Organization for Economic Cooperation and Development (OECD) report on decentralization and centralization in European educational systems, Amelsvoort and Schereens (1996) described the case of Sweden as a tremendous process of deregulation. Decision-making power had been transferred from the central level to the municipalities and schools, while the administrative-authority levels of national and county boards had been abolished. In Sweden, decentralization and deregulation were to a great extent combined with neoliberal enterprises. The consequences of marketization were privatization and the right to choose between schools based on the voucher system. Schools were also given the possibility of developing their own profiles and becoming so-called "free schools," open to more parent and student influence.

Reform Strategy and Educational Research Policy

The introduction of educational reforms in Sweden and Norway in the 1990s marked a break with the traditional model of policy-making. In Sweden, a new national curriculum for compulsory education was introduced in 1994 based on decisions taken by Parliament in 1993. In Norway, a new curriculum for compulsory education was introduced in 1997 based on parliamentary decisions in 1993 and 1994. In both countries, curricula reforms were also introduced in upper secondary schools. In the developing process, the model involving extensive commission work and exploration of possibilities for compromises was abandoned. Reforms were instead decided on and implemented rapidly in order to demonstrate efficiency and ability to act. Follow-up research and evaluation were supposed to serve as a basis for possible corrections of the course of the reforms as they developed. The new visions for central steering reflected a governance philosophy referred to as the rise of the evaluative state (Neave, 1998). Thus in the 1990s the era of lengthy committee preparations was over. The new form of policy-making increased the conflict level in society to a certain degree. The bourgeois government in Sweden (1991–1994) and the Social Democratic government in Norway (until September 1997) started a fast restructuring race with a number of decisions and "turbo" committees.

The curriculum-making process preceding the legislation for the new national curricula in Sweden and Norway was first and foremost a political process steered by political leadership in the ministries of education. In Sweden, the National Curriculum Committee of experts consisted of only four members; two of the members were civil servants at the Ministry of Education. This committee was supported by a secretariat. The composition and small size of the committee were important for the work process. It has been reported that the two members from the ministry had almost daily contact with the minister of education. These members had also been involved in the formulation of the directives for the committee and they were later to be involved in the follow-up work at the ministry (Carlgren, 1995).

In Norway, the minister of education tried to avoid the teacher union, interests groups, and educational expertise in the policy-making process. In the old model for policy-making, it was claimed that too many groups with vested interests became involved in the process, making it almost impossible to implement change. The minister literally wrote the more general and principal parts of the new national curriculum himself.

Restoration or Continuity and Renewal?

On the basis of political documents produced in the beginning of the decade, substantial educational reforms were implemented in Scandinavia during the 1990s. They clearly reflected a shift of views concerning educational politics, how it is initiated and implemented, and the task of the state in relation to schools and education. In what ways does the restructuring of the 1990s reflect neoconservatism, neoliberalism, and authoritarian populism? Has social-democratic progressivism survived in the political decision-making process?

The educational reforms underline the importance of fundamental knowledge. *The knowledge school*—more or less something of an "obscenity" within the rhetoric of the neoradicalism of the 1970s—was reinstated as a positive concept. In a society characterized by rapid change in the demand for competence, the school was to define and convey, communicate, and pass on "real" knowledge and traditional forms. The school was expected to be a unifying, integrative agent in the society and to restore commitment to a common culture. The importance of factual knowledge was emphasized. Due to a rapidly changing society with subsequent changing demands for different types of skills, education had to emphasize basic and *unchanging* knowledge and skills. At the same time, education was given a conservative role through a renewed responsibility for cultural heritage. The reforms also reflected an effort to include the whole population in one cultural framework. Thus in Norway a new subject called "Christianity, religion, and philosophy" was introduced in the compulsory school as part of the compulsory basic curriculum for all students regardless of their religious background. Sweden abolished the option for students not to be taught religion in the compulsory school.

All Scandinavian countries to a greater or lesser extent accepted the principle of management by objectives and results as political rhetoric. Typical for management by objectives is a focus on dual solutions: both national and local control, both political and professional management, both control and freedom, both support and control. In Scandinavia, no country has been so thorough in implementing this principal as Sweden, and no one has abolished this principle step by step in the same way as Norway. The new Norwegian national curriculum for compulsory education spelled out in great detail a syllabus for all school subjects. While earlier, more progressive curricula valued "learning to learn," the new curriculum defined content of school subjects to be perceived as knowledge to be taught and acquired. The curriculum specified and gave detailed instructions for curriculum content, teaching, and learning. The directives for the compulsory school in Sweden stated that there is no need to describe the content of teaching in any detail. A national curriculum was described as participant goal steering, which should enable local interpretations and commitment.

In Norway, the reforms promoted more collective work in schools and marked the end of privacy for individual teachers in their classrooms. New regulations that promoted collaboration between teachers were introduced in all Scandinavian countries. Teacher training also emphasized the fact that education in the future must be based on cooperation between teachers with different qualification as well as on increased social competence. Restructuring in education involved new demands on teachers, such as the making of local curriculum plans, collaborative decision-making, and new ways of communication with parents. Redefinition of teachers' work was argued partly as a way of empowering teachers and schools and partly as a solution to efficiency and accountability problems in the public sector. In a way, this redefinition of teachers' work was about to change the teaching profession from an implicit, tacit, craft-oriented, and oral working culture to an explicit, discursive, theory-informed, and written professional culture.

The effort of social-democratic progressivism to reduce external pressure for achievement on students was in many ways continued in the 1980s and nineties. In Norway, external pressure on students was reduced in 1994 when admission to upper secondary school was made independent of achievements in compulsory schooling. The competitive element in grading in compulsory education was reduced in favor of informal evaluation. Traditional exams in upper secondary schools were partly replaced by "open book" exams. However, at the same time as external pressures on students were relaxed, governments tried to increase pressures on schools as institutions, as well as on teachers. Schools became the targets of various evaluations, reports, incentives, indicators, and efficiency studies. In Sweden, a national system of evaluation was introduced to follow up on the new goal-oriented steering model. National testing became part of this national evaluation system. By the turn of the century, Norway was discussing implementation of similar measures. These measures were introduced as mechanisms for *quality assurance* but they were clearly efforts to gain greater control over teachers and schools. Thus the language of empowering teaching spoke with two tongues. On the one hand, policy documents inscribed an empowered and skillful personality as the ideal teacher, while at the same time they threatened the teacher as a working group that had to be constantly controlled by a continuing report system. This criticism, put forward by the Norwegian sociologist Rune Slagstad (1996b) and others, parallels Stephen Ball's (1994) critique of the restructuring efforts in the United Kingdom during the 1990s. Ball argued that both spaces of professional autonomy and judgment in teaching were weakened and standardization and normalization of classroom practice were strengthened.

At the same time, however, the attempt of social-democratic progressivism to turn receptive and reproductive student activity into productive activity was radically strengthened in Scandinavia in the 1990s. Norway made play, defined as a voluntary activity, a compulsory teaching method for students aged six to ten. In all Scandinavian countries, "responsibility for ones own learning" became a key term in the educational rhetoric. The curriculum directives not only recommended cross-subject teaching and project-work, but also made problem- and project-based teaching mandatory. In Norway, cross-subject teaching and use of the project method secured a prominent place in the compulsory school. The guidelines stated that 60 percent of teaching time in lower primary school had to be used for such activities, 30 percent in grades five to seven, and 20 percent in secondary education. Project-work was also a major issue in upper secondary school reform. In Norway, this activity was made compulsory. Generally in Norway, students were given more freedom while teachers were given less. The sacred principle of a teacher's right to choose her teaching methods was severely challenged when cross-subject teaching, play, and project-work were made compulsory elements. The new Swedish national curriculum, however, was more open and thus, in principle, gave teachers more autonomy and responsibilities. The ability to formulate, discuss, and communicate ideas about the content and organization of teaching and learning was emphasized.

In the policy documents and in the new national curricula, we can clearly identify elements of the conservative restoration: restoration of fundamental common knowledge and tradition; increasingly, weight on quality, standards, excellence, efficiency and accountability, management by objectives, voucher systems, privatization, and decentralization as an opening for diversity; education defined more as a private good as opposed to the traditional Scandinavian comprehensive school; restoration of an instrumentalist view of education which views students as human capital and education in the light of an economic rationality; and increasing national control through evaluation, attainment targets, standardized assessment and management by results. These are all footprints of the conservative restoration that can be seen in the Scandinavian educational reforms of the 1990s.

These elements were, on the other hand, situated within a framework that can also be interpreted as a continuity and renewal of social-democratic progressivism. In Norway curriculum policies in the 1990s, in fact, could imply an opening for a renaissance in progressive education. The restructuring of education in the 1980s and nineties strengthened the participation perspective. Even though there were tendencies to view education more as an individual civil right, education was still also defined as a collective enlightenment project for the public good. The reforms continued the policy of increasing access to education. Education and teaching were viewed as part of a cooperative endeavor or enterprise. The reforms included measures to reduce achievement pressure, and at the same time learning was defined as an active, productive, and democratic process. The reforms included a problem-oriented and integrated curriculum, while advocating a "child-centered education" and a safe and supportive learning environment. Finally, the comprehensive school was defended, and local/community–oriented curricula were promoted.

The restructuring of education in Sweden and Norway showed many similarities. New national curricula, bulk funding, decentralization, deregulation, and goal and result steering illustrate some of these similarities. However, as we have seen, there were also differences between the countries. In Sweden, we could observe a combination of a national curriculum with open goals to pursue, a well-developed national evaluation system, and marketization tendencies in terms of increased consumer choice, a voucher system, and, to a certain degree, increased privatization of schools. In Norway, decentralization was combined with a heavily prescribed curriculum giving detailed instruction to teachers with reference to both subject matter and methods.

Repoliticizing and Empowering Progressive Education?

Within educational reform in Scandinavia, I have identified "artifacts" that undoubtedly point toward a conservative restoration. In his book *The Archaeology of Knowledge* (1972), Michel Foucault stresses the importance of understanding objects for what they are within their particular location, rather than as a symbol of some grand theory. Within the political educational discourse in Scandinavia, neoconservative, neoliberal, and to a certain extent also authoritarian populist positions and measures are definitively present. Following Foucault, however, we might not fully understand Scandinavian discourse over education in the 1990s as a practice if we isolate the different elements and simply interpret them as evidence of a universal conservative restoration. For this very reason I also have identified "artifacts" pointing in a quite different direction, ones which indicate a continuity and renewal of social democratic progressivism.

The social-democratic accord and the progressive Scandinavian educational model of the 1950s and sixties were part of a modernistic project. Knowledge per se was considered as power. Within social-democratic policies in Scandinavia in the 1950s and sixties, education was a main tool for the *Big Leap Forward*. Educational reform was to promote economic growth, not as a goal in itself but as a means to empower the working class and to improve total living conditions for the majority. The enemy was clearly defined as the prewar bourgeois class society. However, social-democratic educational policy also represented a continuance of a Christian and humanitarian tradition and a general rejection of the idea that the value of individuals can be measured in terms of their income-earning capacity or potential. The elderly, the disabled, the unemployed, and the young have the same right to decent living conditions as do the gainfully employed and the affluent. And none should be used solely as an instrument for the interests of others. Everyone should have a say in decisions concerning their life situation, irrespective of their position and their relation to the economy.

Needless to say, in practical policies, the Scandinavian countries have not, by far, been able to realize their ideals. However, the educational model that was developed during the first three decades after World War II represented an attempt to move in such a direction. The model was based on a particular social and cultural commitment, political dreams, and historical experiences. As in all forms of policy-making, it was pierced by compromises with other strong interests in society. The Scandinavian educational model was also a historical phenomenon tied to a certain phase in the development of those countries. Entering the 1980s and nineties, the model was challenged by far-reaching societal changes calling for new and different instruments of policy. As the welfare state reached its goals, some of the most important ideological and material conditions, which comprised its original foundation and generated its popularity, disappeared. The welfare state no longer appeared as a vision of the future in a poor, bourgeois society but as a commonplace with services and equality now regarded as "natural." These changes gradually situated educational policy and schools in a new material, social, and ideological context.

The development of the Scandinavian countries during the 1970s and eighties can be described as a passage from "old deficiencies," referring to the classic shortages and uneven distribution of material goods, to "new deficiencies," referring to needs related not only "to have" but also "to be." This implied a need not only to manage daily subsistence but also to achieve an interesting life and a viable identity. This is not to say that wealth and influence were evenly distributed or that impoverished people did not exist in the Scandinavian countries in the 1970s or 1980s. However, at that time the safety net of the welfare state embraced most of those who were distressed. In other words, economic growth, emancipation from traditions, and an emphasis on cultural liberation continually nourished the sense of the possible. In this way, cultural emancipation included the continuity of a collective progressive potential. But it also opened the door for a society favoring the importance of individual development, private responsibilities, and individual choices. I have identified both these elements in the analysis of educational policy and reforms in Scandinavia in the 1970s and eighties.

Until the late 1970s, the Scandinavian countries were culturally quite monolithic, with a firm knowledge base and normative rules for interpretation and behavior defined as a common good. In the years to come, material and social changes, cultural liberation, and immigration promoted more pluralistic societies. Fundamentally different life patterns, cognitive forms, and norms either clashed or coexisted. Many different life forms appeared, each offering their version of truth. Truth was no longer officially defined once and for all but by repeated hiatuses, which created an apparent need for information. As one of the tabloids put it in an advertising campaign when Sunday papers were introduced on the Norwegian market in the beginning of the nineties: "Reality never takes a break!" General

knowledge and truths were no longer part of an obvious frame of reference. Even people with roots going back generations in Scandinavian societies continually broke with traditions. They oriented themselves globally
and renewed themselves in transient patterns. Their public loyalties often
appeared less than their private desires. Each life form created its own reality. During the last two to three decades of the twentieth century, the Scandinavian countries became multicultural societies. In the 1990s, we could
find inner-city and suburban schools in Stockholm, Gothenburg, and Oslo
with a predominance of children with a non-Scandinavian ethnic background.

More generally, the modernization process in itself promoted new cultural forms. In the pursuit of economic growth, unambiguous rational
truths, and utilitarian applicable knowledge, modern society developed an
unquenchable thirst for posing questions, which in turn led to an erosion
of society from within, not only ecologically but also culturally. Thus in the
1980s and nineties what has been called a risk society (Beck, 1992) appeared with great promises and freedom of choice for the individual but
also with an uncertainty that can never be completely eliminated; all decisions and choices could be questioned. Compared to the modern, rational,
social-democratic model of society, where everybody shared the same
value system and goals for themselves and society, where the mean was solidarity, and where the goal was growth and affluence in town and country,
the society of the 1990s became more shapeless, oblique, ambiguous, and
at times chaotic.

The German sociologist Oscar Negt was one of many who emphasized
the changes within Western societies during the last decades of the twentieth century. He argued that changes in conditions under which children
grew up were greater than those in the previous hundred years (Negt,
1982). It was also Negt's conviction that the Western world faced a new
type of social crisis, one that sent a profound shock wave through the
whole scope of the traditional organization of work and life. He called this
crisis one of erosion, defining it as a process whereby what has been firmly
structured is crumbling. What had been collectively obvious is dissolving.
It was a process comprising all of society and penetrating its very pores.
Nothing could be protected any longer against this basic problem, neither
institutions, subjectivity, intersubjectivity, systems of value, patterns of education, nor existing interest movements like the labor movement. What
sets crises of erosion apart from traditional crises is that they work primarily below the public-institution system as they touch the individuals in
their very rational and mental foundations. According to Negt, this type of

crisis changes individuals in the core of their manifestation of life, in their behavior at work, in their estimation of self, and in their orientation to values and needs.

Late modernity introduced cultural liberation or emancipation, creating both freedom and uncertainty. A parallel was the economic liberation described by Marx. The process of industrialization liberated the feudal village folk from their reins. They received freedom so they could become wage earners having to seek work and a place to live. At the same time, they became homeless and were left to the dynamics of the marketplace. In other words, this created an economic liberation containing both progress and tyranny. We can employ this term in an analogous manner about late modernization and the process of liberation from traditions, from everyday patterns of meaning, from family forms, and so on. Cultural liberation and new forms of communication and knowledge of the information society released virtual explosions of needs, dreams, wishes, and expectations. Subjective possibilities multiplied. Identity was no longer locked to tradition. Others characterized this development as a movement from a society of fate to a society of choice. Previously, the young inherited their future from their parents. By the turn of the century, the young were given more occasions to take part in the planning of their own future. But this development yielded freedom and tyranny simultaneously.

Cultural liberation influenced all age groups, but there is a great difference between growing up in a fixed-identity and norm-based society only to have it break up at the age of forty and growing up entirely without fixed orientation points in a seemingly chaotic terrain of identity totally devoid of charted paths. Hence this liberation hit the young the hardest. They had no solid rituals and strategies of survival to fill the "spaces" of everyday life that adults had. The liberation could be enabling; but not without costs. Late modernity promised wonderful experiences, power, pleasure, personal development, and transformations, but at the same time it threatened the destruction of everything we have, everything we know, everything we are.

With reference to the situation in Sweden in the early 1990s, Lindblad and Wallin (1993) argued that education held a weaker position than it once had. The school's and the teachers' authority was questioned. At the time when the Swedish educational system was constructed, the authority of teachers, the "truth" of content selected, and the obedience of pupils formed a legitimate pattern inside as well as outside schools. In the early 1990s, the situation had changed. The growing independence of citizens was making a system based on external obedience untenable. Thus the school was working under new conditions. Old systems and old patterns did not have the same legitimacy as earlier. William Lafferty (1989), professor in political science at the University of Oslo, gave the same diagnosis of the situation in Norway. He claimed that Norwegian society was facing a profound crisis of values. This appeared through the weakening of two of the most central providers of norms that we have; the Church and the Labor movement. When Marx now also seemed to be dead within the Labor Party, the society faced the real consequences of God being dead.

In many ways, the challenges facing the Scandinavian countries in the 1990s were a repetition of the crises of legitimacy that were raised and responded to by social democracy during the 1970s and 1980s. The cultural emancipation and criticism of education of the 1970s were, however, framed within neoradicalism and concerned mainly with the ideological nature of school knowledge. Thus issues of experience-based knowledge, local and community-based knowledge, the cultural capital of social classes, gendered knowledge, and so on entered the curriculum policy agenda. In the 1990s, postmodern positions entered the discourse. In comprehending and solving problems, postmodern theorists abandoned the enlightenment ambition of unity, certainty, and predictability. Joe Kincheloe argued that students of the late twentieth century faced a different world: *a postmodern hyperreality marked by social vertigo* (1993, p. 84). This loss of balance related to the view expressed by Aronowitz and Giroux (1992) that the former cultural idea of science, with its axiomatic and leading postulates, was in disarray in academic circles. Patti Lather (1991) claimed that postmodernism provided an affective space where individuals felt that they could not continue as they were. This space had been created because the modernist project of control through knowledge had imploded, collapsed inward.

Postmodernist theory questioned concepts of knowledge, truth, objectivity, rationality, neutrality, and logic per se. The position was built on a doctrine that contends that there is no objective reality and no metalanguage against which statements and claims can be tested. Postmodernist theory was, of course, contested. Following Habermas, a postmodern theory is a contradiction and must in itself be incongruent with the very spirit of postmodernism. However, discarding postmodernism as a theoretical position does not necessarily mean rejecting a postmodern reality and a postmodern interpretation of social and cultural changes in the everyday life of people. In the endeavor to scrutinize these changes critically, wider theoretical approaches are indeed needed to situate new challenges and problems within an understanding of the political, economic, and social context to which they surely belong. Exciting grand theories might, however, be insufficient to situate educational problems in the new and often contradictory social reality. In my view, the most important contribution of the postmodern perspective to social science and education was precisely that it rehabilitated the everyday life world. It put everyday life on the agenda. Thus it contributed to a new foundation for revising the pedagogical project.

Everyday life, negotiations of identity, and management of self presented important challenges to schooling when superindividual guidelines were dissolving—that is to say when the reservoir of traditions, patterns of meaning, beliefs, and morals on which one could previously rely for understanding of oneself and the world were disappearing. Traditional identity markers were lost, and self-realization was more an activity of consumption than taking part in production.

As we have seen, the educational policy of the 1990s in Scandinavia showed no signs of postmodernism. However, there definitely were signs of accepting a postmodern cultural diagnosis. Social democracy, schools, and education found themselves in a new cultural situation. The enemy was no longer only the reality of bourgeois class society but also the postmodern reality of relativism, disintegration, and self-centered individualism. The educational policy being formulated by the Labor governments of the early 1990s could be interpreted as an attempt to repoliticize and empower social democratic policy to challenge the relativism embraced by postmodernism. Through postmodernism, the critical potential of relativism easily becomes nihilism, subjectivism, and cynicism. And under the influence of postmodernism, the legacy from the 1970s, with its emphasis on individualism and education as private good, in many ways was turned toward a possessive individualism. Accordingly, social-democratic educational policy in the early 1990s was aiming at social inclusion and solidarity as the cultural and political basis of society.

Within the field of education theory and practice, the influence of relativism had been quite strong because education traditionally had been seen as the development of the rational, autonomous consciousness through the transfer of knowledge. Knowledge had on the one hand been perceived as an objective representation of the world, while on the other hand values had easily been regarded as universal principles of behavior. The relativistic refutation of durable criteria for rationality, objectivity, truth, and morality had challenged this way of thinking. In a situation where common goals, common norms, or visions of what are true benefits no longer existed, it was difficult for educators to create social unity and integration.

In other words, the social-democratic repoliticizing of the educational discourse tried to transcend what was viewed as the destructive consequences of relativism. New questions entered the political agenda: How can educational policy and pedagogy, as a theoretical and practical discipline, play a role in such a process of transcendence so that we could reestablish areas of intellectual and moral unity in society? And if we lack objective criteria to which we may turn when we want to judge the rationality, verity, goodness, or correctness of our notions, statements, and actions, how can education maintain its intellectual integrity in the attempts to establish moral and intellectual unity in society? How can pedagogy engage in such a process where we attempt to rebuild society toward social inclusion, solidarity, and rational conversation? Or in the words of Chantal Mouffe (1992, p. 3): "How can the maximum of pluralism be defended—in order to respect the rights of the widest possible groups—without destroying the framework of political community as constituted by institutions of practices that construe modern democracy and define our identity as citizens?"

Renewal of Social-Democratic Educational Policy

We have seen that the national economic argument reentered educational policy discourse in the 1990s. The economic crises in the 1980s, rising unemployment, and structural changes within the economic system and the mode of production established a base for this argument. In Norway, the Green Paper of 1988 that initiated the reforms of the nineties put it this way:

> The challenge for Norwegian educational policy is that the country does not reap enough know-how out of the talent of the population. . . . Without changes the population will be under-educated and research will be under-powered for the performance required by the cognitive society. The national level will not reach the required international level. This is a comprehensive problem for the whole system from the practice of primary school to the use of time in research. (NOU 1988:28, p. 7)

However, when the economic argument and efficiency of the educational system reappeared in the educational policy discourse in Scandinavia, it was also pointed out that economic growth was not a goal in itself. In both Norway and Sweden it was stated that the aim was for the educational system to be among the world's best. This would constitute an important link in efforts to increase employment and strengthen the national economy. But it was also stated that economic growth and a high level of education for the whole population were important prerequisites for better distribution of wealth and for further development of the welfare society. Put in another way, within the new social-democratic political discourse of the 1990s, the enemy was still poverty, inequality, insecurity, and injustice.

The educational reforms formulated in the beginning of the 1990s represented, in many ways, a continuity of the policy of decentralization from the 1970s. Gunnar Berg and colleagues (1987) have used the terms *legality* and *legitimacy* as analytical instruments in discussions on steering of schools. Legality is focused mainly on those social relations that are formally sanctioned by the state. In concrete terms, this sanction is affected by means of legislation, formal authorization, and other formal controls, directives, regulations, and so on. Legitimacy focuses on such phenomena as morals and systems of values. Legitimacy involves a sanction system that can be expressed in terms of social reliance, acceptance, and confidence in relation to patterns of behavior and norm systems, which do not necessarily have anything to do with the formal legal system. A further method of expressing the difference between legality and legitimacy is to see legality as casting light on a jurisdiction, that is to say a *de facto* juridical rule system. Legitimacy has more to do with a process in which individual actors and pressure groups strive to get their social actions established in some form of internalized norm system, the source of which may be customs, traditions, subcultures, experiences, and so on. Of course, this norm system can be both consistent and inconsistent with the lawful rule system in force at the time.

The policy of decentralization in Scandinavia in the 1980s and 1990s and the reformation of the centralized hierarchical system of steering can be viewed as a conflict between state legality and social legitimacy. Decentralization implied a changed relation between state and society. It represented a shift of power from the state to society. In times when the legitimacy of state interventions and state control are questioned, the shift toward decentralization can be expressed as a process toward a *societification* of the state, in that steering on the basis of legality is reduced in favor of that based on legitimacy (Berg, 1992). However, it is quite possible that the power relinquished by the state via decentralization can be reclaimed and even increased by various control measures. Consequently, on the rhetorical level decentralization can be an expression of a *societification* of the state, but in reality the control mechanisms associated with decentralization may in fact imply an increased *statification* of society. Thus, the state may strengthen its authority rather than weaken it. In other words, decentralization represents only a more legitimate system of control within a strong state.

Niklas Luhmann (1981) has pointed out the appearance of decentered societies divided into autonomous sectors with no unifying core. Modern societies have become more and more functionally differentiated and asymmetric. The asymmetric societies are made up of a number of subsystems such as politics, economy, law, science, education, religion, and family. Each system fulfills a special function in society. And partly due to increasing national wealth, the subsystems are organized around their own unique criteria and their own unique codes. The political system is no longer the central system, which is able to control and regulate the other systems, nor is it possible to reduce it all to economics. Luhmanns's theory is partly confirmed by the contemporary history of education in Scandinavia. During the first decades after World War II, education became increasingly independent of other systems such as the Church, the family, and the political subsystem. The differentiation of education from the political system was reinforced in the 1950s, sixties, and seventies through expansion of central councils, centers, and agencies such as the Norwegian Council for Innovation and Research and the Swedish National Board of Education. This tendency was promoted by the policy of decentralization in the 1970s and eighties. Thus during the 1980s the Scandinavian countries in many ways became decentered.

This was underlined in the OECD examination of the Norwegian educational system published in 1988 (OECD, 1988). With reference to the route chosen by the Norwegian government of moving away from detailed budget control toward general grant and local-based curriculum, the examiners discussed what might be the role of the center within this decentralized scheme. The examiners noted that other countries that had adopted a system of bulk funding and decentralization found that sooner or later some areas must be returned to specificity if national objectives were to be met. The examiners therefore recommended that the center must retain control over the distribution of resources. Granting of general rather than earmarked or specific money should not emancipate the center from the responsibility to state its views on what policies the funding should be used to promote and how resources should be used. The OECD report also stated that the central government had very little information of what in fact was happening in Norwegian schools. The examiners therefore found it appropriate to argue that a move from a centralized system cannot mean that the central ministries simply abandon the national stage. They remain to allocate resources, to create and administer the law, to ensure that curriculum change is legislated and implemented, to consider ways in which good norms of educational practice can be established and better disseminated, and to evaluate goal-attainment and control the results of local activity. In order to perform these functions adequately and to take a central role in continuing development of the system within the frameworks agreed in Parliament, the government was recommended to adopt a more active evaluative and monitoring function.

Educational policy analysis has distinguished between decentralization as delegation and decentralization as devolution (Karlsen, 2000; Lauglo, 1995; Weiler, 1990; Whitty, Power, & Halpin, 1998). Delegation normally implies transmission of tasks and administrative responsibilities related to specific functions, usually defined by the central authorities. Decentralization as delegation does not necessarily mean a shift of power, because local agents are generally given the role only of executing decisions made at the central level. Decentralization as devolution implies the transmission of authority and real responsibility in the decision-making process from central to local bodies. This form of decentralization implies that local authority and independency are clearly increased.

When the decentered society emerged as an enemy in social-democratic educational discourse at the beginning of the 1990s, the political system put pressure on the educational system to regain central political power. The continuity of decentralization policy in the 1990s was therefore balanced with policies of recentralization. In this way, educational reforms in the early 1990s in Scandinavia can be interpreted as *statification* of society. Put in another way, what happened at the beginning of the nineties was that the political system, allied with the economic system to a certain extent, tried to regain a legitimate position as center in society through decentralization as delegation. In this way the Social Democratic government in Sweden (until 1991) and the Labor government in Norway (until 1997) tried to renew social-democratic educational policy.

Entering the Twenty-First Century

The legacy of the Scandinavian educational model is based on a vision of homogeneous societies and a rather simplistic definition of the common good. Within the framework of a global economy, cultural emancipation, growing relativism, and multicultural pluralism, this became more complex. The free flow of information meant that the spatial distinction between *inside* and *outside* collapsed. The rapid advance of technological innovations continually redefined the nature of social relations and altered the conventions of material production in a manner that rendered many aspects of everyday life ephemeral, if not completely unpredictable. In a society of abundance, the social democratic welfare state had lost its ideological and moral base. Those invested in postmodernism strove to understand, but not to reconcile, divisions that existed between ethnic cultures, social classes, linguistic communities, and gender-based identities. Accordingly, distinctions found within and between such groupings should not only be tolerated but also celebrated. Put differently, after World War II the

Scandinavian social democracies asserted human equality, reasoning that everybody is equal. In the 1990s, cultural liberation and emancipation emerged, claiming human equality by reasoning that everybody is different. This became a challenge for schools and educational policy. In a multi-cultural, pluralist society, common goals and the common good are not self-evident. In the 1990s, a great challenge to the renewal of social-democratic policy was to redefine and reconstruct the common good and the modernist quest for certainty, predictability, and the advancement of knowledge and society at large. Educationally, Scandinavia was situated in a new, complex, and contradictory situation. At the same time the neoliberal criticism of the inefficiency, expense, and uniformity of the public sector in general, and of schools in particular, emerged.

Compared with other Western nations, it is nevertheless fair to say that Sweden and Norway in the early 1990s continued to a larger extent the policy of solidarity, a unified school system, equal standards, and social inclusion through measures implemented by governments and Parliament. The educational reforms can be viewed as a renewal of social-democratic progressive education to meet new challenges in late modernity. The educational policy of the early 1990s can be interpreted as an effort to defend the Scandinavian social-democratic political model. However, this effort did not imply enforcing a traditional, coherent, social-democratic philosophy of education. The educational defense took place within a contradictory, dialectical framework that contained residual elements from traditional social-democratic policy but also elements included in the conservative restoration. The social-democratic renewal of education tried to establish legitimacy by seeking balance between essentialism, emancipatory commitment, and contingency. It tended more toward individualism and accepted education as an individual good. But at the same time, it implemented a policy for *statification* of society in defense of education as a public good and as preparation for participatory democracy in a pluralist society. Thus, based on an international comparative perspective, we can conclude that educational policy in Scandinavia carried a metaperspective other than the conservative restoration we observe in the United States, Britain, and elsewhere. To a substantial degree, the society-centered democratic ideal was maintained. It was still within this basic model of state-society relationship that the political leadership viewed education as a prerequisite for greater freedom of action for every individual and for strengthening individual autonomy. The continuity of the welfare state depended on a strong national economy. Education, in terms of both access and knowledge content and standards, was seen as an important incentive in fiscal policy.

Viewed from more of an inside perspective, it was, however, obvious that the more traditional social-democratic policy of education had changed and that it had been contested and challenged in the early 1990s. There was an ongoing struggle over education within each of the Scandinavian countries, and the political solutions that were implemented varied between them. While the principles of equality, social inclusion, and political control were strongest in Norway, Sweden was influenced by deregulation and neoliberalism more than other Scandinavian countries were. Thus measures that were implemented within the different countries were divergent. Accordingly, restructuring of education in the nineties seemed to bring an end to a long period of convergence within educational policy in Scandinavia.

During the bourgeois governance in Sweden from 1991 to 1994, the neoliberal educational policy resulted in further radical changes in education and educational governance. Even after the Social Democrats resumed power in 1994, these changes gained momentum in the latter part of the 1990s as the left failed to provide alternatives (Lundahl, 2000; Mediås & Telhaug, 2000). Typical for Sweden were not only management by objectives, decentralization, national testing, and other measures for quality assessment, but also the right of parents and students to choose their school and faith in a private school system. A positive orientation toward competition, consumer perspectives, and the market was combined with greater responsibility given to principals and teachers.

In Norway, neoliberal rhetoric increasingly entered the political debate and governmental documents at the turn of the century. This became even more apparent when a coalition government came into office in 2001. Within education policy, new actions characterized by result-based funding, performance indicators, quality assessment, competition, and consumerism were taken. In political discourse, matters of equality and social inclusion disappeared. The schools' role in leveling out social differences was no longer a central theme. Accordingly, in the beginning of the century we could observe the contours of a new convergence within educational policy in Scandinavia based on neoliberal ideas and a more elitist educational ideology. However, only future historical analysis will show if the educational reforms being formulated and implemented as we entered the twenty-first century implied a further renewal and empowering of the ideas of social democracy and comprehensive education, or restoration of cultural hegemony, inequality, social exclusion, and stratified Scandinavian societies. However, we can already identify enough evidence to claim that the international movements of neoconservatism and neoliberalism influence the measures that are now being implemented more and more. At the beginning of the twenty-first century, educational reforms both in Norway and Sweden are accordingly less oriented toward delegation of responsibilities and transmission of authority to local political bodies. What seems to be on the agenda is a weakening of the political level for the benefit of individual actors in the local arena, including school leaders, teachers, students, parents, and local enterprises. It is argued that educational change will benefit most from the introduction of quasimarkets and competing alternatives.

What happened, then, is complex and contradictory. It is the result of an array of social movements and a changing balance of forces. While we cannot fully know the future, we do know that without a fuller understanding of such complexities and contradictions, neoliberal and neoconservative influences and transformations cannot be interrupted in serious and long-lasting ways.

Such contradictions and complexities are explored further in the next chapter where we critically examine state policies over knowledge and the economy and the ways in which students and teachers engage in struggles over the identities "on offer" in such policies.

Acknowledgments

For helpful comments on an earlier draft of this chapter, I am grateful to Michael Apple, Alfred Oftedal Telhaug, and Erik Wallin.

CHAPTER 6

Schooling, Work, and Subjectivity

Misook Kim Cho and Michael W. Apple

Creating Manual Laborers

Although there is growing awareness of the importance of subaltern studies (see, e.g., Bhabha, 1994),[1] most analyses of resistance, subjectivity, and identity—especially those that have been most influential and wish to make theoretical as well as empirical contributions—have been developed out of research on predominantly "Western" industrialized nations. While this has led to considerable insight, it has often smuggled in assumptions about the meaning of actions that are grounded in the historical experiences of these nations. This has generated a limited understanding of the importance of historical specificity, of conjunctural relations, and of the ways in which class, gender, and race/ethnic experiences take on specific meanings in different contexts. By focusing on one of these "different contexts"[2]—South Korea and its recent moves to institute career education and to have more students identify as manual workers—we wish to show how such historical and institutional specificities work to produce particular forms of resistance, subjectivity, and identity. In order to do this, we shall have to go inside schools and get much closer to the signifying practices of students and the educators who interact with them.

A good deal of international attention has been paid to the current economic crisis in South Korea. However, it is important to remember that since the late 1980s South Korea, which enjoyed high economic growth for the previous two decades, has continuously faced serious economic stagnation. Even before the current economic upheavals, the dominant faction of the ruling power bloc (Resch, 1992), which consisted of government officials, capitalists, and conservative intellectuals, defined the current Korean situation as a national crisis. The dominant group identified militant labor strikes, the shortage of manual labor, and the Korean people's supposedly "irrational" aspirations for college education and for "mental labor" as the main factors that were weakening national competitiveness. At the same time, labor unions and left-wing groups criticized the government and capitalists for placing the blame on labor or ordinary people and for ignoring the dominant bloc's own contributions to the problem. In particular, they faulted "big capital"-oriented state policies and the capitalists' neglect of technical development and skill training in manufacturing industries for the crisis.

In order to ensure the continued accumulation and legitimation that are necessary to its existence, the state has to regulate such social conflicts. Between 1989 and 1990, then-President Roh announced revisions in the Sixth Five-Year Economic and Social Development Plan. The provision of welfare service was slowed. Economic ministers who were supporters of growth-oriented policies were appointed. In the process, Korean state policymakers reformulated their accumulation strategy in order to strengthen the competitiveness of manufacturing industry and promote high-tech industry (E. M. Kim, 1993).

In relation to these social changes, a number of educational policies were established and revised. With the growing concern about the lack of manual workers, vocational high school policies that had been ignored during the 1980s were newly emphasized. In 1990, the government—which has historically had very strong central control over nearly all aspects of educational policy, funding, and curriculum—announced that it would increase the current ratio of vocational high school students to academic high school students from 3:7 to 5:5. Also, career education at the secondary educational level was emphasized. Mandating more emphasis on career education was seen as the most appropriate way to keep people from continuing their "irrational educational enthusiasm" and would lead more of them to their "proper place" as "unskilled" industrial workers (Y. W. Kim, 1993; RCKCT, 1994).

Despite its ultimate appeal to violence (see Poulantzas, 1978), the Korean state increasingly sought to enhance its political power through an ideological system that was not overtly repressive. Under the rationalization of overcoming national crisis and continuing national growth, the state asserted that all people as responsible citizens should "share the sacrifice" for national economic development and a stable democratic society. The state insisted that the labor shortage could be resolved if people used "good sense." For the hegemonic bloc, "good sense" implied a number of things, but the most important was that "ordinary people" would be both less committed to an academically focused education and more willing to be "industrious" manual workers. In essence, the state discursively separated individuals from social relations, individualized them as "responsible" citizens, and unified them under the "national." In this process, the state selected part of the nation (non-college-bound people) and attempted to transform them into certain subjects (manual laborers) demanded by industries (see Apple, 2000; Jessop, 1990).[3]

Like all hegemonic projects, the success of this project depended on three factors. The first factor is material conditions, which are the contingent outcome of a dialectic of existing structures and the accumulation strategy. This helps shape the production and reception of the hegemonic project. The second factor is the historical power bloc's capacity to articulate its interests as the national popular interest. Finally, this hegemonic project will be successful to the extent to which the dominated people participate in the reconstitution of social subjectivity and ideological integration (Jessop, 1990, pp. 196–219).

This chapter focuses on the third of Jessop's three factors—on the responses of local people to the state's hegemonic project. It is based on an ethnographic study of two commercial high schools. We shall analyze: 1) how the career education stressed by the Korean Ministry of Education was implemented at the individual school level; 2) how commercial high schools and students generated meanings and practices regarding work and workers in their daily school lives; and 3) how their meanings and practices were constrained and enabled by the larger and local contexts.

This chapter has a larger theoretical agenda as well. As one of us has argued at greater length elsewhere (Apple, 1996a, 1996b), rather than the rejectionist impulses that often dominate both sides of the poststructural/neo-Marxist debate, it is crucial that insights from both of these broad and varied traditions inform our critical analyses. Thus, in this chapter, while we cannot fully encompass all of the insights of "post" and "neo" work that might be combined, we shall draw both on traditions which are grounded in analyses of subjectivity, identity, and desire and on those which are more structurally and materially based. Each of these is required to understand the complexities surrounding such programs of career education and how they are played out in real schools inhabited by real people.

Data

Data used in this chapter were collected in a long-term ethnographic study (M. Cho, 1997) of two private commercial high schools in "K City": a mixed-gender commercial high school (hereafter, M School) and an all-female commercial high school (hereafter, G School). Two sophomore classes (one female and one male class) of M School for one semester (the second semester of 1991) and two senior classes at each school for one academic year (1992) are examined. Data were gathered by methods of observation, semi-structured and open interviews, and analysis of relevant documents.[4]

The two schools are located in a small city in the middle-west part of Korea. The great majority of students in both schools came from lower-class families. Their parents were poor farmers (42.1 percent at M School, 46.2 percent at G School), manual workers (20.0 percent and 21.2 percent, respectively), individual service workers (14.7 percent, 10.6 percent), low-status clerical workers (11.6 percent, 6.7 percent), and small shop owners (10.6 percent, 12.5 percent). In both schools, there was no one in the research classes whose parents had professional jobs (e.g., doctor, lawyer, academic) or who were owners of a large business.

Career Education as a State Mandate

In order to produce a new social reality, state power was exercised through its bureaucratic and ideological mechanisms. In 1990, career education, which was implemented in a number of experimental secondary schools during the 1980s, was more widely introduced. Departments of Career Education were established in school boards of cities and provinces all over the country. Principals and vice-principals were advised at workshops that secondary schools should take career education much more seriously to overcome the "national crisis." In addition, official documents and booklets were prepared and widely distributed by educational officials which suggested that—while Korea was moving toward a more democratic society where individual choices and abilities would be recognized and realized—parents and students were still making "irrational career choices." This contributed to the dual problem of the shortage of unskilled labor and the unemployment of college graduates (Chung Nam Provincial School Board, 1991). Thus responsibility for the unskilled labor shortage and the problem of unemployed college graduates was transferred from the larger socioeconomic context to individual parents and students. The government, hence, circulated discourses that were meant to govern and mobilize people's subjectivities in particular ways. Yes, one is increasingly "free" to choose, but only under the guidance of experts (see Rose, 1990).

This, of course, was not the only way in which state power was exercised. It also permeated individual school and classroom sites. However, state power was not exercised over individual schools in a simple way. Rather, power relations between individual schools and the state were characterized by constant tensions and disunity. The particular construction of reality produced and distributed by the government was delocated and relocated into the pedagogical situation (Apple, 2000, pp. 62–66; Bernstein, 1990). Yet as a recontextualizing field (Bernstein, 1990, 1996), the school and the actors within it partly mediated, reinterpreted, transformed, and struggled over these mandated policies. Let us examine how this occurred.

M School ran a career education class twice a month, with the Department of Moral Instruction (what is called counseling and guidance in the United States) within the school being responsible for career education. However, most of the staff were highly critical of the career education policy. This is most vividly expressed by Mr. Kang, the central figure in charge of career education in M School. As soon as he came into the staff room after finishing teaching his career education class, he began to criticize the school administrators and government officers:

> I have a hell of a time in my career education class. I skipped whole difficult concepts. I had to think about how to explain the difficult concepts while I was writing them on the blackboard. Taking account of them makes me sweat. They [government officers] are such bastards. They just command us without considering our circumstance properly. I have lots of troublesome things to do beyond this. They do not know the ordinary teachers' difficult conditions. How could they understand us? . . . All of them [higher status officers] have to be dismissed at this minute. . . .

According to Mr. Kang, he had to teach career education even if he was not especially familiar with the concepts of career education. Furthermore, because of the sudden implementation of this program, he had only five days to create the teaching guidelines for career education that would be given to classroom teachers (see Apple, 2000, for further details).

It was clear to him that career education was suddenly emphasized because of the shortage of manual workers. He predicted that such an educational reform would fail because it was initiated by educational authorities who ignored the reality of the educational conditions and needs of the teachers required to implement such changes. In his words: "Teachers are just pretending to do it in order to avoid the eyes of the bosses."

He was not alone in his skepticism and cynicism. The vice-principal of M School, the individual who was almost entirely responsible for daily school administration because of the principal's predominant interest in "outside [community] activity," also raised serious issues concerning career education. While having some sympathy with the goals of the state, he still questioned its methods:

It [career education] was introduced by the command of the administrators. It was designed so that students can rethink their uncritical desire for higher education and reconsider their careers more seriously and rationally. Every person wants to go to an academic high school and college. Our culture respects mental workers too much. Only college graduates are qualified for this work and they are given high occupational status. College graduates become managers in three years, whereas our students become junior managers in five years. Our students who work in banks cannot even dream about becoming high status managers. No matter how hard they work, they won't be promoted up to the higher status because they are not college graduates. In this situation, how does career education work out properly? . . . Educational policy-makers have to think about their plan more seriously before commanding its implementation. Only the head teacher got the training for career education during the vacation since in order for every teacher to get training from the Ministry of Education a great deal of money is required. It is so problematic to practice on a school level because no concrete program is provided and teachers are not qualified. Our educational policies are too often dragged into politics.

According to this vice-principal, education policies were too often politically motivated. Career education was just such a case. Because of the wide social gap between college graduates and non–college graduates in wage and promotion, he too believed that this type of career education would not work out very well.

All of this influenced how career education was implemented at the classroom level. In M School, career education was taught by classroom teachers based on handouts provided by the Department of Moral Instruction. During a representative career education class of second-year students, the classroom teacher, Mr. Song, came in and said: "Pass this around and read it." The title was "Who Should Survive?" The content was as follows:

The whole world is facing death because of nuclear war. Scientists have made a special space ship which can survive. Only eight people can ride in that special space ship. Write who should survive and explain the reason. Also explain who has to be sacrificed if I were to be a survivor? There are college students, a habitual criminal, a pregnant woman, an old clergyman, an armed policeman, a male traveler, a very bright man, a girl friend of a student, and an enthusiastic Christian.

The classroom teacher gave students time to answer. Students followed the teachers' direction. When the bell rang, the teacher collected the handouts and went out of the classroom.

These handouts were designed to develop students' "general sensibility or judgment" about their possible social conditions. Since the late 1980s, the general direction of vocational high school education had been changed from training for specific job skills to developing basic and common knowledge and "flexibility." This change was a response to criticisms by employers and managers that vocational high school graduates were unable to understand and adapt to rapidly changing work structures. In 1990, career education was introduced throughout the country in order to resolve this problem as well as to secure a sufficient manual labor force. However, in the specific lesson described above—and in many others that were observed—there was no discussion between teachers and students or among students, and the students did not receive feedback about their writings from their teacher later. Thus the growth of "general sensibility and judgement" in the search for flexibility went unguided and was dealt with in a *pro forma* way.

Another career education class that was observed involved the relation between occupation and aptitude. Here is a segment taken from the field notes:

> Mr. Lee gave handouts to the students and read the section about clerical work. A student asked: "What is the difference between a planning and management job and an ordinary office job? It states that both need similar abilities." The teacher answered, "The high achievers get clerical and managerial jobs and the low achievers become salesmen or doorkeepers." The students laughed for a while. The teacher said: "Read the rest of them by yourselves." According to the handouts, salesmen needed social ability in addition to memory, language, and cognition which were required by planning and managerial jobs. The teacher glanced at the students and looked out the window. He sometimes asked his students to be quiet. Students secretly chatted with their partners. When the bell rang, the teacher said: "Don't miss class." The students answered in a loud voice: "Yes, sir." The career education class was over.

From these examples, it is obvious that although career education was strongly stressed by the Ministry of Education, it was performed very superficially at M School. The great majority of M School teachers and students perceived it as an "easy" and unimportant subject and did not invest much time or intellectual/emotional energy to it.

However, the situation at M School was actually better than at G School. G School had no separate formal career education classes. The head teacher of the Department of Moral Instruction of G School (Ms. Lim), who was supposedly in charge of career education, said: "We don't care about career education that much. Rather, it is the job of the employment department and of classroom teachers."

The principal of G School had a somewhat less dismissive view of the situation:

> When I came to the study meeting of the principals last year, an officer of the Economic Planning Board presented something on the Korean economy. According to him, our country desperately needs factory workers. Before going there, I wanted our students to be employed as office workers for better companies as much as possible. However, I have changed my mind a little bit. I am worried about our country's future. So I am thinking that it is not so bad for young students to go to key industries and contribute to our economy before being contaminated with the 3D phenomenon.[5]

Yet despite saying this, while the principal said that he changed his mind "a little bit" about manual labor after participating in the training meeting of principals, this did not mean that he would actively encourage students to get factory jobs. This was largely due to the fact that he was very concerned about his school's reputation, a key element for all commercial high schools. The two commercial high schools competed with each other and with other types of high schools such as industrial and academic high schools. They were constantly worried about the ratio and quality of jobs publicly signified by the employment of their graduates. In this situation, having many students entering factories could jeopardize the legitimacy of the school, since a "good" commercial high school supposedly helps students obtain "attractive" clerical jobs, not factory jobs. Not to do this puts the reputation of the school at grave risk, in a manner reminiscent of the dilemma of many schools in, say, England that must attempt to manage their images in marketized contexts (see, e.g., Ball, Bowe, & Gewirtz, 1994; Whitty, 1997; Whitty, Edwards, and Gewirtz, 1993).

Thus, as we have seen, in both schools career education was not stressed as much as the Ministry of Education expected. Even though M School ran a career education class twice a month, it was only superficially implemented. And the fact that G School had no separate class at all for career education demonstrates that this school also did not have a commitment to obeying the order of the Ministry of Education, even superficially.

Although the new regime of capital accumulation and legitimization was accompanied by a new rationale of vocational education, its implementation at both the school and individual classroom levels did not closely correspond to the rationale. Why did the two schools resist this educational policy, one that was so clearly stressed by the Ministry of Education? First of all, as in many other countries, there is a strong classification (Bernstein, 1977) between academic and vocational high schools and within vocational high schools (commercial and industrial arts high schools) in Korean society. In addition to the strong boundary between different types of high schools, the competition between schools compelled these two schools to be predominantly concerned with preparing students for careers as clerical workers, not for manual labor or other jobs—and for demonstrating through employment results that this was, in fact, the case. In a paradoxical way, the relatively autonomous needs of local markets act in partly contradictory ways against larger state-driven plans for capitalist expansion, even in situations of strong states.

Yet another reason that career education was only superficially carried out was precisely because of the long-lasting hierarchical relationship between the Ministry of Education and individual schools. In Korea, the Ministry of Education has played a commanding rather than cooperating role for quite a long time. Thus, for individual schools, the Ministry of Education has been seen as a threatening force, given the powers of supervision and evaluation powers it has not been hesitant to use repeatedly. Because its authority has historically been highly dependent upon coercive or authoritarian methods, the policies of the Ministry of Education are often largely ignored, or, at best, responses to them are frequently highly ritualized, especially when they are seen as compulsive, as having a direct effect on teachers' and administrators' interests or security, or where power is slightly weaker than before. Although M School showed more cooperation with the policy directives of both the Ministry of Education and the Board of Education of K city, it, too, was also largely a matter of form. The "hidden transcript" embodied in actors' actions was relative noncompliance through doing the bare minimum. (It is worth noting as well that, since there were no concrete guidelines and since it was not included in the more high-status formal curriculum, career education was often perceived as simply an extra burden for teachers who already were burdened with heavy workloads, intensified conditions, and small salaries [see Apple, 1986].)

Differentiating Work

We have seen how historical relations between strong states and local schools, and between existing demands and newer ones, strongly influence "reforms" and acceptance of and resistance to them. Yet focusing on to what extent and how the career education mandates were implemented does not tell us everything we need to know about why local actors such as teachers responded in the ways that they did. It does not enable us to see how the students who were to develop this new work subjectivity themselves "read" and responded to the situation as well. Nor is it sufficient to help us understand the differentiated gender and class readings that structure these experiences. This can be done only if we think across the entire school experience, since it is not only in career education where students learn to differentiate among work and workers. Studying the subtle and at times contradictory ways in which students appropriate, rework, or reject these "truths" is crucial. It enables us to understand better different levels and meanings of contestation, and the ways in which "absent presences" work throughout school programs and daily lives. Most important, it opens up generative ways of thinking about the relationship between identities and cultural politics (Epstein & Johnson, 1998). In so doing, we shall have to unpack how work is differentiated and how it is differentially valued. Work subjectivities are relational. They are not seen in isolated ways by teachers or students, but are consistently placed in comparison to each other. These relational constructions offer a key to uncover how actors attempt to carve out spaces for movement in contexts riven with contradictory ideological meanings and material consequences. As we shall see, the values attached to office work, factory work, and ultimately working for oneself all have very different meanings and are mobilized in different ways. They all offer different subject positions and are connected in complex ways to each other and to gender, class, and the construction of identity.

Office Work

The fact that, for a variety of reasons, creating factory workers was not seen as their primary task does not mean that creating efficient workers was rejected by the schools. It is taken for granted in Korea that commercial high school students will become office workers. As Butler reminds us, established meanings often become the inferential bases that lead people to identify with a preconstituted relation (Butler, 1993). The "dominant imaginary relation" between commercial high school students and being an office worker, however, is not automatically materialized by the transmission of signification. Through the active social practice of selecting, excluding, and organizing elements of meaning in a particular way, the taken-for-granted meaning is sustained (Hall, 1985) and, as we shall see, is sometimes changed in significant ways.

This will be made clearer if we examine students' ideas about their future work position. When interviewed, the vast majority of commercial high school students answered that their future jobs would be in offices:

Interviewer: What are you going to do after graduation?

Joo-Yeun (F): I am going to be an office worker, because I am a commercial high school student.

Soo-Kyung (F): I want to be an ordinary office worker in a medium-sized company.

Interviewer: Have you thought about other kinds of jobs?

Soo-Kyung: All my neighbors and friends know that I am attending a commercial high school. They would laugh at me if I worked in a factory.

Byung-Kil (M): I am going to have a humdrum life.

Interviewer: What do you mean by a humdrum life?

Byung-Gil: Being an ordinary office worker.

While some male students came to a commercial high school because of their lower grades and actually wanted to go to industrial arts high schools, the great majority of young women and men in the two schools came to a commercial high school to be office workers. Even before attending these schools, they had already identified themselves within the dominant imaginary relation designated for commercial high schools and being a clerical worker.

Even with this overt aim, however, as is evident in the above interviews, there is something which needs to be examined in more detail. When asked about their futures, many students responded with phrases like "just an office worker" or "an ordinary office worker" or "a humdrum life." For them, an ordinary life meant having an office job for which "the social position is neither high nor low." Students had already assumed that their future jobs would not have high social status when they decided to go to a commercial, not an academic, high school and college.

The social category of "commercial high school student" did not work as a simple expression of a certain image. It was more active than that. Rather, it embodied a set of regulatory practices, a regulatory discourse (Bernstein, 1996), whose materialization was partly compelled from the outside and certainly lived out in the daily existence of students in these schools. While the dominant definition of a commercial high school student had significant effects on constructing the identity of commercial high school students in a particular way even before attendance, the schools themselves acted strongly to materialize and thus sustain the category of commercial high school student. They did this through a number of internal mechanisms, such as the organization of curriculum, rewards and punishments, and the regulation of meaning and the body in the students' everyday school lives.

For instance, students had a formal curriculum that required that they spend twice as much of their time on commercial subjects as on general subjects. Commercial subjects were also given more weight in evaluation. Students were often told that as commercial high school students, they should deal with numbers and letters more quickly and accurately. In the morning and evening meeting times that were standard at these schools, homeroom teachers quite often advised students to attain the technical qualifications (typing, bookkeeping, abacus, and so on) demanded by companies as soon as possible by working hard on commercial subjects throughout their high school years. Teachers in both schools frequently checked on how much their students' technical qualifications had improved. There were reasons for this. These subjects served as proxies for other valued characteristics. Based on this knowledge, in an almost Foucauldian way, teachers judged students normatively—that is, as an "industrious" or "lazy" student and as a "high-quality" or "low-quality" student (see also Apple, 1990; Foucault, 1977; Tavares, 1996).[6]

In addition, students often heard that: "You will only be simple office workers. Don't expect too much from your future work. It'll be just simple work." According to teachers, they had to discourage their students because many students dreamed longingly about their future jobs and romanticized white-collar work. Teachers were certain that students would be deeply disappointed with what would prove to be simple, boring, and repetitious jobs. The result would be unhappy working lives and frequent changes of occupation. To protect students from quitting, frequently transferring jobs, or having an "unsatisfactory work attitude," teachers felt that they needed to be honest. They had to let the students know about "reality" before their students entered it. Such teaching practices seemed to have a clear impact on the way their students thought about who they would be or what they wanted to be. As we have already addressed, many students assumed that they would be "ordinary clerical workers."

Of course, the meaning of what it means to be a commercial high school student and an "ordinary" clerical worker was not gender-neutral.

For instance, here is a typical example involving Mr. Choi, a G School employment teacher. Mr. Choi begins this interaction in the following way:

> "You are going to be the lowest worker when you enter a company. You should arrive earlier than others and clean up the table of bosses and the office." Some students shouted, "We are not cleaners but [clerical] workers. We go there to work, not to clean." The others supported this by saying: "Yes" or "Woo-." He responded: "Don't you clean up your father's room? Don't you do errands for your brother?" The students intervened before he ended, saying "No way." The young women did not give up their view: "It is different. The company is not the house." He smiled and continued: "Be quiet. I am telling this for your well-being. Follow me and you will be loved by everyone in the company. Think of your bosses as your father or brothers. I really mean it. Keep it in your mind."

Gendered specificities are also present in M School. Here is Mr. Shim, an M School employment department teacher.

> This company has a bright future, even if its present condition is not so good. I suggest that students apply. However, they are not interested in the company because it does not pay a lot of money now. . . . I often advise them to choose the company which deserves to earn their lifetime loyalty after they think about its prospects seriously. . . . For men, it is necessary to accept challenges. By having the difficulty, one's feeling of achievement gets bigger and his life becomes satisfying.

In both schools, the general practices for preparing students for clerical jobs were largely associated with the traditional sexual division of labor. Teachers constantly emphasized that young women should be concerned with making people feel comfortable at the workplace, whereas young men were encouraged to think about long-term career planning and accept challenges.

However, as one might well expect, the teachers' transmission of this message about low-status work and gender was not internalized by the students without conflict or ambivalence. Some students were clearly angry with the ways teachers treated them. A student described her feelings in no uncertain terms:

> **Jae-Soon** (F): A teacher overtly and frequently said to us: "You will be just ordinary workers. After all, you are destined to be drivers of rice cookers no matter how highly you think of yourselves." We

knew that very well without their saying it. It made us very mad and frustrated. We had been previously discouraged because we had to give up going to college. Now I have almost overcome that complex. But whenever teachers ignore us, I feel terrible.

Furthermore, a number of students questioned why they had to take for granted that their future jobs would be just office jobs. They believed that the commercial high school itself was forcing them to narrow their goals. According to these students, the commercial high school drove them to focus exclusively on being an office worker while marginalizing other possibilities:

> **In-Sun** (F): I wanted to be a lawyer when I was a child. Now [smiles] I want to be an office worker in a medium-sized company. . . .
> **Interviewer:** Do you think that attending commercial high school has an impact on your future plans?
> **In-Sun:** Yes. This school is. . . . You know, I had lots of dreams even before I went to high school. But this school makes us think about only being an office worker. Every student won't be an office worker and every student is not employed, though.
> **Young-Joo** (F): The teachers are trying to kill our dreams. They say: "Your job is to have a good marriage and meet a good husband. If you are employed in a big company, you will have more chance to meet a good husband." [Young-Joo had a plan to get a job for a couple of years and go to college because her mother was sick.]

However, the fact that female students were very critical about what they recognized were unreasonable and unfair practices of school and society did not necessarily mean that they totally rejected the dominant ideal image that was presented by them. There was something considerably more complex going on. Some of them wanted social success as a means of resistance, and at the very same moment they combined this with a partial sense of resignation. This is a crucial theoretical and political point. It directs our attention to the centrality of the tensions between what Gramsci would call "good" and "bad" sense in people's common sense (see Apple, 1995, 2000). The following interview segment documents these tensions in powerful ways:

> **Moon-Hee** (F): Some teachers even overtly say to us: "You are just goods. You have to do your best in order to be sold well. To be sold out quickly, you have to get good qualifications and wrap yourself up very well." They say so, right in front of us. How dare they speak to us that way? Why are we goods? We are human.

Interviewer: How do you respond to the teachers' comments, then?
Moon-Hee: We scream. And then, I say to myself: "OK, I want to be somebody so that I will knock the breath out of you guys. Look, I am going to have college graduates as my employees and make them do what I command. I will come to this school and donate lots of money, while looking down arrogantly at the teachers." [She stopped giggling.] However, [sighing] I am sometimes afraid that I might end up being just an ordinary clerical worker, serving tea and typing. I am so funny, aren't I?

Thus, under the unfavorable conditions where students felt that they were socially mistreated and where the subject positions offered by the schools were not consistent with the students' personal desires, students contested the meaning that was given to them in a suggestive yet paradoxical way—by dreaming about how they would succeed in life. At the same time, they feared that they would end up as "just an ordinary clerical worker." This tension between fantasy and insecurity and partial resignation was very clear ("I am so funny, aren't I?"). Yet it should not be understood as merely an individual's way of coping with one's probable social destination.

The power of ruling ideological practices lies in continuously setting limits on the horizon of intelligence and feelings of security—what the world is, how it works, what is reasonable and safe (Hall, 1985). While we do not want to overstate this argument, as some postmodern theorists of "desire" have done, it is still the case that dominant ideological systems are unstable to the extent that there are residual feelings and desires (I, as a woman, will be in "command" and will "donate lots of money") within subordinate people that are excluded but not easily extinguished by these dominant ideological practices. Often such residual feelings and desires become elements of fantasy, elements that speak to the potential of opposition. In this sense, individual and collective dreaming, while perhaps seeming narcissistic on first examination, also need to be understood as partly a positive moment of contestation, not as merely a failure to "adjust" or as an escape from reality. Indeed, the very moment when desires are negotiated and repressed is one of the scenes where creative and autonomous agency is performed. It requires the process of transformation of meaning and intervention (Donald, 1992, pp. 89–98; Walkerdine, 1990, p. 199). Once again, we want to be cautious about placing too much weight on these arguments. They are suggestive, however, and need to be thoroughly considered, not simply rejected out of hand because they are not "materialist" enough. Yes, it should be clear that desires cannot be easily fulfilled without changes in material circumstances. However, there is a world of difference between claiming that everything is reduced to the body, desire, and culture (few "post" theorists actually ever make this claim in such a totalizing manner, of course) and claiming, as we are, that, say, fantasy and desire represent one of the many spaces where ideological contestation occurs, where it is worked through in all its contradictions, and where what Williams (1989) would call "resources of hope" may be found. This is not automatic, however. We are speaking about potentiality here.

Having said this, we should be cautious of overgeneralizing. These schools also had differential effects. Despite the fact that the majority of male students took for granted that they would be office workers after graduation, they did not think that commercial high schools affected their lives as much as female students did. Thus there were different views according to gender as to how commercial high schools had an impact on the way that they thought about the future. Female students tended to feel more sensitive and more negative about their school lives, in the sense that the commercial high school limited their dreams. In contrast, many male students replied that the school did not make much of an impact on their future.

Some of the gender differences seemed to stem from the following facts. Given the particular construction and history of patriarchal relations in Korea, by and large commercial high school boys had much more support from their families for going to college. More male students attended commercial high schools because of their lower academic achievement or their decided lack of interest in studying. However, for them, attending a commercial high school did not mean that they had abandoned the hope of attaining higher levels of education. These young men were still expected to go to college. In contrast, female students who tended to have higher school grades came to commercial high schools both because of their poor economic situations and because of unequal support from their parents. Generally, for these young women, attending a commercial high school meant giving up going on to a higher level of education, unless they earned money for college fees themselves. Thus these often markedly different material and ideological circumstances generated different interpretations of the meaning of commercial high schools among many females and males.

However, even with these differences, there also were very real similarities. In general, nearly all of these students perceived office work more positively than factory work because it featured higher job security and better working conditions. In addition to the above advantages, working in offices was seen as more advantageous for young women who wanted to get married. Its image was clean and "gentle." Perhaps even more than similar young women in studies of other "more advanced" countries (Griffin, 1985; Valli, 1985), they too wanted to avoid presenting themselves as "wild" and "masculine." In fact, these Korean female students were even more deeply concerned about the ways they would be treated socially on the job. Whatever differences exist undoubtedly stem from Korea's strongly patriarchal structuring of paid and unpaid labor and from its specific sociohistorical background, where there has typically been an exceptionally wide gap, one that is even deeper than in many Western nations—between blue-collar labor and white-collar labor in terms of wage, promotion, working conditions, and social status. How this works its way out in these students' possible identification with manual factory work is of major import. This is discussed further in the next section.

Factory Work

By and large, being a factory worker was regarded as a less desirable alternative by most teachers, parents, and students. It was a job for those who were less qualified or who were "troublemakers." Commercial high schools overtly and covertly played a significant role in "disqualifying" factory work. In the context of reaching their objective of preparing students to be clerical workers, commercial high schools created and mobilized a deauthorized subject—the factory worker. Teachers quite often told students that lower achievers or troublemakers would end up as factory workers. They actively referred to factory workers as what Butler (1993) would call the "constitutive outside" to office workers. That is, the image of the factory worker was required to define the "proper" domain of the subjects (in both senses of that term—the curriculum and the people) of commercial high schools.

The schools did not consciously teach any skills related to factory jobs, although in actuality, because of the employment situation in this region, significant numbers of their students ultimately went on to factories. In fact, about 30 percent of the female and male students found employment there. It is important, then, to ask more about what the students thought about this "constitutive outside," about factory work. The students also identified factory work as lower status and as difficult, dangerous, and dirty—the 3Ds.

Young-Suk (M): I've never seen higher-achieving guys go to factories. I won't go there although I am not good at studying.

> **In-Sook** (F): It is said that there is neither noble nor humble work. However, it's not true. In reality, people don't think of it [factory work] as good.

However, there were some students who wanted to be factory workers, despite the 3Ds. These students constructed the meaning of factory work in various ways that showed both the importance of contestations over bodily control (Mellor & Shilling, 1997; Shilling, 1993; Tavares, 2002) and students' own strategic decisions of short- and long-term goals.

> **Do-Il** (M): I want to work in a factory. It is because I am so active that I will not put up with just sitting all day.
>
> **In-Soo** (M): I wanted to go to an industrial high school. I don't fit in at the commercial high school. I am acquiring qualifications for auto repair and will accumulate those skills by working in an auto shop or a factory. In the future, I will have my own auto shop.

It was not just male students who had such different images of factory work. Some female students intentionally failed to identify with the ideal image of a woman clerical worker emphasized by the schools. They consciously chose to get a manual job. This was beyond the schools' understanding, as indicated by the remarks of Ms. Park, one of the teachers at a commercial high school.

> There was one very good student last year. She was the second best achiever in our class. She had a good appearance and her personality was very good. So I recommended her for a large company and she was accepted by the company. But she quit the job because it was too oppressive and boring. After all that she got a job in a construction company. That place was known to be so wild. We usually send boys. . . . With such good qualities, why should they go to a factory? I can't understand them. They were too good to be factory workers.

It is not too difficult to understand why some students did indeed want to go to factories rather than to engage in clerical work. For a few, like the young woman who is described in the teacher's comments above, factory work seemingly offered an alternative to "oppressive and boring" office work. However, in general, there were two groups of female and male students who wanted to go to factories. One group went to factories for a simple reason—to earn money quickly.[7] Another group wanted to be manual workers because they thought that factory jobs fit better with their interests. The first group of students strategically and temporarily decided to get manual jobs. They wanted to quit their manual jobs after making some money or before marriage. The majority of students who entered factories belonged to the former group.

However, even with their strategic rejections of the dominant imaginary and their appropriation of the constitutive outside, their plans to get factory jobs were often blocked, especially by strong opposition from their parents. In the words of a teacher who said what was commonly thought: "Eight or nine out of ten Korean parents would not allow their kids to go to factories. They say that was why they educate their daughters and sons at the high school level."

As the statistics show, some students, of course, were strong enough to resist such pressures. However, all did not always turn out well for those students who did find themselves working in factories after overcoming such opposition. Many of them wanted to quit their factory jobs after experiencing them. Other, more hidden reasons that involved the schools themselves also became evident. For example, the schools asked these students neither to return to the school for visits nor to continue to be in contact with their teachers or counselors once they got such a job. This was partly for the sake of the school's reputation. It is clear, then, that the school's regulatory power over one's habitus and hexus (Bourdieu, 1984, 1996) does not always end once the student enters the paid labor market. The power of the school may be heightened in the Korean context because of its specific cultural history (of which we shall say more shortly), but this is worth further research in other nations as well.

Yet the more proximate labor-process reasons for students to want to leave these jobs are very powerful. A number of students were interviewed about this. A former student who worked in a mid-sized factory which dealt with polyethylene states the following:

Song-Hyun (M): If I stayed longer there, I would get an occupational disease. There was so much dust in there. I don't want to work at such a place. I don't want to hurt my health.

Another male student also had a plan to quit his factory job at an electric company in the near future. He said that it was too boring to put the same part in at an electric machine. He went there because his close friend had suggested it as a way to earn some money and his family also thought that it was better to earn money than to be idle. Of course, there were many students who stayed with such work. But one thing was clear: for the vast majority of teachers, parents, and students, factory work was anything but desirable.

The reasons for this are complex and cannot be reduced to something that is only discursively based. As poststructuralists imply, the negative representation of factory work was made through overt or covert contrasts whereby the positive meaning of office work depended on the negation of factory work. However, does the hierarchical relation between office work and factory work come largely from the exclusionary logic of signification we noted earlier? We do not think that this is always or necessarily the case. Rather, we think that the hierarchical relation between office work and factory work in Korea for the most part comes from their different social and material contexts.

Since the Yi Dynasty, Confucianism, which valued a "scholarly deposition," has significantly shaped the Korean people's views on how they value, and devalue, manual work. This cultural tradition continued under Japanese colonization. In fact, colonization policies largely excluded Koreans from doing "mental work." Only selected intellectuals who received postsecondary education were allowed to engage in such work, and they received far better salaries and treatment than manual workers.

The valuing of mental work was solidified by the state's industrialization policies. The government aggressively carried out export-oriented policies, focusing on large firms. These large firms had employed a high-volume, price-competitive business strategy for the past three decades. In order to continue high economic growth, the state repressed labor unions and controlled the wages of factory workers by using its coercive power. As a result, large firms expanded enormously and required a considerable number of clerical and managerial workers. Over the past two decades, these firms have maintained lower wages for production workers in order to reduce production costs and have maintained relatively higher wages for clerical and managerial workers. In addition, labor markets have developed around male, white-collar workers who have college credentials (see Dore, 1976). Blue-collar workers with high school diplomas are discriminated against in recruitment, job allocation, compensation systems, and skill training. Inferior material rewards remain, although the wage gap was significantly lessened by the intense labor struggles during the 1980s. The different material and social rewards shaped by various historical processes became a crucial factor in creating a strong hierarchical relationship between office work and factory work, although poststructural theories are clearly correct in recognizing that these hierarchical relations were and are discursively mediated.

In addition to different material rewards, direct and indirect bodily experiences (intensification, constant movement among factory shifts, unsafe conditions, injuries, etc.) became another solid foundation for supporting a view of factory work as negative and subordinate. The students at the schools examined in this research clearly knew this from their own local experiences and from interacting with their neighbors or families. Thus their indirect and direct experience was certainly another important factor shaping the differentiation of work and students' work subjectivities (see also Ezzy, 1997).[8]

"Having My Own Business"

So far we have examined the relation between and the construction of two kinds of work subjectivities. However, as we shall now see, the subject positions authorized and deauthorized by the schools did not cover the entire universe of such positions and of the ways in which students gave meaning to work. The official ideology of the school and the state's hegemonic project are effective to the extent that they have the cultural leadership to be able to articulate their particular definitions of the social imaginary as general and that they have the regulatory power to realize these ideas. In mediating the state's hegemonic project, the commercial high schools provided students with two job possibilities: clerical work and factory work. The official ideology of the schools suggests that clerical jobs are obtainable when the students work hard in school. Factory jobs are appropriate for those who do not work hard enough. By and large, the official ideology of the schools parallels students' perceptions.

However, there were unanticipated contestations by students. Significant numbers of students rejected both of these forms of work and the "subject positions" associated with them (see Apple, 1996a). Rather, they wanted to have their own businesses, to become what some might call "petite bourgeoisie." In the case of M School, about 30 percent of the students hoped to open their own businesses. This long-term vision, not the one officially sponsored by the schools, represented "ideal" work for them. In the case of G School, about 20 percent of students wanted to have their own businesses or own small shops. Only this, they believed, would allow for more autonomy, freedom, and opportunities for personal development:

> **Hyun-Ae** (F): I will be a clerical worker for a while. And I would like to own a small shop like a gift shop or a clothing shop.
> **Interviewer:** Why do you want to have your own shop instead of keeping your office job?
> **Hyun-Ae:** Even if it will be a small shop, it gives me freedom and autonomy. I don't need to stick to bosses and please them.

A sense of resentment that is partly class-related is visible here in some ways as well. Owning one's own shop also enables a reduction in status differentials between academically prepared and commercially prepared students. This description from the summary of field notes makes this clear:

> Gi-Soon felt very bad when she met her friends who were attending an academic high school. Her friends often asked curiously but cynically: "What are you learning?" This kind of question made her mad because she felt like a second-class citizen. She decided "not to be mad about it but to show them by making a difference." She said: "It is so naíve for us to limit our job goals to only clerical work. I would like to be a factory worker and make a lot of money. After earning enough money, I will have my own business."

Small business ownership, then, provides an "imaginary" solution to other forms of social hierarchy. It enables one to be "better" than someone who works for a boss and "merely" earns a salary. This cuts across gender relations as well:

> **Eun-Joong** (M): I will earn a lot of money and live decently. I will engage in a sort of distribution industry.
> **Interviewer:** Why do you want to work there?
> **Eun-Joong:** My parents are farmers. They have a really hard time, working on the farm. No matter how hard they work, they are always poor. The distribution businessmen collect all the money. So I made up my mind to run my own distribution business. Even by working hard to death for an entire lifetime, a salaried man could not be rich. At first, I am going to enter a company. And then I will have my own business after saving enough money and learning the business.

In addition, other things were at work here. For some young women, having their own small shop embodied elements of a very different construction of good sense than that implied by the state's or the schools' definition. It showed how they mediated the pressure of the sexual division of domestic labor. For them, owning a small shop would enable them to deal with the many problems associated with responsibilities such as housework or child rearing by giving them flexibility to adapt to unexpected occurrences.

Yet it was not only these students who dreamed of being owners of small shops. For some "troublemakers," students who were often called into the Department of Student Affairs because of long absences or fighting, having their own business provided a mechanism for rejecting external control and perhaps for supporting particular definitions of masculinity (Connell, 1995; Mac an Ghaill, 1994). For instance:

Dong-Jin (M): I want to run a business.

Interviewer: How come you want to run a business?

Dong-Jin: Well. It is good to make lots of money. And I don't work under other people. I won't obey a boss's orders. If they make me feel bad, I will beat them up again [He implied that he did not want to get in trouble like going to prison for assault as he had done before.]

All of this went on in the face of the fact that the schools did not actively encourage students to have their own businesses. A few teachers talked on occasion about a number of graduates who owned a small business or a profitable shop. Some teachers used such stories of successful graduates to encourage those students whom they perceived to be discouraged or frustrated with the fact that they could not go to an academic high school and college. But aside from this, dominant school practices focused on producing clerical workers.

In the dominant culture of G and M Schools, the main differentiation revolved around dichotomies such as clerical work/factory work, a good workplace/a bad workplace, an employer/an employee, and a good worker/a bad worker. The schools' main practices were to prepare students for jobs that were offered and needed by others. Yes, a significant number of students, regardless of school grades, sex, and general attitudes about schooling, wanted to be employed by themselves rather than by others; but in the matrix of the dominant ideology of the commercial high school, self-employment is rarely thinkable and hardly possible.

Self-Employment and the Politics of Desire

What are the conditions that underpinned the reasons so many Korean commercial students—regardless of school grades, gender, and general attitudes about schooling—dreamed of self-employment? A number of studies of Korea report that self-employment is gradually decreasing overall due to the rapid shrinkage of the agricultural population as a result of industrialization (D. M. Cho, 1994a; Hong, 1983; Suh, 1984). However, interestingly enough, the ratio of petite bourgeoisie in nonagricultural sectors has increased, whereas the ratio of agricultural petite bourgeoisie has rapidly decreased (D. M. Cho, 1994b; B. J. Kim, 1986; Suh, 1984).

There are a number of sociological accounts for the increase of self-employment in nonagricultural sectors. For instance, people may become self-employed because good jobs usually demand higher educational credentials, which require more economic and cultural capital than they have (Steinmetz & Wright, 1989). The expansion of the petite bourgeoisie or self-employed in the service sector in Korea may be a result of the fact that self-employment would allow higher income. The higher income of the petite bourgeoisie might be possible because increases in productivity in the service sector grew far more slowly than in other sectors, and capitalists are moving from a higher marginal utility to a lower marginal utility (Cho, 1994a; B. J. Kim, 1986).

The ethnographic data reported here do not allow us to provide a direct explanation for the mechanism behind the expansion of self-employment in the nonagricultural sector. However, this chapter does have at least some important implications for better understanding the growth of self-employment in Korea, something which is considerably marginalized by established, overly economistic theories. It is social actors' identities, feelings, desires, and fantasies about themselves and social relations that compel them to act in a particular way. When students were asked to answer the questions of why and how they came to think about having their own businesses, they often referred to their neighbors', friends', *sunbays*' (former graduates), and families' negative experiences while working under other people. It was clear to the students through these accounts from families, neighbors, and former graduates that all too many workers in any kind of paid employment were arrogantly supervised, mistreated, and humiliated by (mostly male) bosses who largely had college degrees. Both male and female students were also depressed by and resented their schooling as well as the surrounding society, which largely encouraged them to be second-class citizens and submissive workers.

These young women and men sought alternative ways of making sense of themselves and their social conditions in order to have decent lives. In the process of finding alternatives, they were actively drawing from and rearticulating their classed and gendered cultures, or experiences of trauma, which were neither adequately signified by nor included in the dominant culture. The sanctioned fantasies and sanctioned imaginary in the lower-class school systems that had legitimated the ruling definitions of social order, as a constitutive outside, became a force to subvert it (Butler, 1993). This says something important about the continuing power and emancipatory potential of past cultural forms when they are reappropriated in new contexts.

Following Williams (1977), we might say that the Korean commercial high school students' subculture in which self-employment is valued is not a newly "emergent" culture but is at least partly a "residual" cultural form. Self-employment had historically been "normal" in preindustrial Korea and still contains compelling themes. While it originated in the preindustrial past, it is still active in the current sociohistorical process. What seems newly developed in this subculture, then, is partly the effect of older forms being taken up and mobilized in powerful new ways in a new setting. Thus the meaning of self-employment and petit bourgeois forms may not be totally the same as that of earlier periods. This is actually in keeping with Williams's own intuitions about the changing meanings of social processes over time (Williams, 1977).

With rapid industrialization and growing managerial/employer control, ordinary workers came to be closely supervised and thus grew even more alienated from their labor. Thus the excluded and prohibited meanings, experiences, and fantasies that were not verified by the dominant culture were "lived and practiced on the basis of the residue, cultural as well as social, of some previous social and cultural institution or formation" (Williams, 1977, p. 122). Students did not want to be subordinate to others. To do so meant less autonomy and more alienation. In this sense, these commercial high school students' desires for self-employment could be interpreted not as a simple reflection of the ideological formation of the petite bourgeoisie—a category of considerable and often negative commentary within some traditional Marxist appraisals (see Wright, 1985)—but as something more complex. It functions partly as an oppositional practice that, while based on past "stories" and sentiments, rejects the growing encroachment of managerial control, the exploitative nature of the employment relationship, and their feelings of alienation from work and school (Scase & Goffee, 1981). In the words of Bernstein (1996), retrospective and prospective identities are complexly intertwined.

Their desire for self-employment and work autonomy is not radical in the sense that it denies fundamentally capitalist values and practices. However, students do resist subordination to others by using the tools and the social imaginaries that are at hand. Many of these students wanted to run their own businesses and to be employed by themselves because they perceived that it would allow them more autonomy and self-respect. Of even greater importance, particularly for female students, was that running their own shops or businesses was a way to creatively cope with their assigned gendered responsibilities. But it also went further; it also enabled them to avoid oppressive or boring homes and workplaces where males dominated.[9] Having their own businesses meant that they had a real space in which they could refuse to take orders from or be mistreated by their future husbands or male bosses. But the desire of these young lower-class women to run their own business was not only a simple reaction to avoid classed and gendered oppression. Rather, it was an active pursuit—to express and realize their sense of capacity and autonomy and to have the pleasure of participating in a larger social world.

Such personal desires and fantasies, which were deeply class- and gender-embedded, did not occur purely in their minds, separated from other material practices. Rather, they became a significant force for actual materialization through conscious and unconscious interconnections with specific material conditions.

Conclusion

The Korean state attempted to resolve the problems of insufficient manual labor and unemployment of college graduates. Its solution was an expansion of career education at the secondary-school level. As part of a hegemonic project, the state tried to reconstitute social subjectivity though the use of its educational system so that people would be willing to become manual laborers. Non-college-bound high school students were targeted especially.

But there is little evidence in this study that the current hegemonic project is effective. In M and G Schools, career education was not carried out as seriously as the Ministry of Education expected. The actual practices that dominated these two commercial high schools still focused on preparing students for clerical work rather than encouraging them to think again about manual labor or other careers. Teachers, administrators, and others working within the schools engaged in ritualized or weak compliance. The strongly institutionalized definition of commercial high school education (what commercial high schools are and what social positions commercial high school students are entitled to or expected to have) strongly affected school practices. The sustaining representation of commercial high school education forced the young people to identify themselves with the preconstituted category of the subject, being clerical workers, which was highly class- and gender-coded.

Some writers have correctly argued that education is, at least partly, a process of producing certain forms of subjectivity (Donald, 1992). However, the transformation from concrete individuals to concrete subjects (being commercial high school students or being clerical or factory workers) is achieved in complex, unstable, and often contradictory ways. As we have demonstrated in this chapter, in the identification process with the dominant imaginary, many of these students actively created other possibilities, possibilities that were marginalized by the official discourse of the state and the commercial high schools. Thus some female students re-

garded becoming a clerical worker as gender-oppressive or boring and became factory workers in spite of the opposition of teachers or parents. A
significant number of students, regardless of gender, school grades, and
general attitudes toward school, wanted to run their own businesses after
working at an office or factory and saving money. They wanted to be employed by themselves, not others. Even within "an effective dominant culture" (Williams, 1977), the excluded and repressed dimensions of students'
lives within that culture—dimensions that were class- and gender-embedded—undermined the regulatory power of the ruling signification in a variety of ways in relation to schools and work. Subordinate people's desires
were expressed and materialized through a creative process of interweaving
resources, desires, and "oppositional" subject positions like being "petite
bourgeoisie" available in that specific material and cultural conjuncture.[10]

Let us not romanticize this, but let us also be open to its complex meanings and use in a particular conjuncture. Students sometimes creatively use
resources our accepted theories may easily ignore or frown upon (Willis,
Jones, Canaan, & Hurd, 1990). They do it in order to live in, transform, or
even gain control over the unfavorable social conditions of their existence.
The political and educational potential of these creative actions is worth
further thought. Only by combining the insights of both "neo" and "post"
together, as we have done here, can critical researchers go even further in
dealing with these issues.

In the next chapter, we will see both how teachers as well can create and
take on oppositional subject positions and how this is situated within
changes in state policies. Once again, contradictory processes will be visible.

Acknowledgments

We would like to thank Parlo Singh and Geoff Whitty for their comments
on earlier drafts of this chapter.

Democracy, Technology, and Curriculum: Lessons from the Critical Practices of Korean Teachers

Youl-Kwan Sung and Michael W. Apple

Introduction

All curricula have complex connections to differential relations of power. As one of us has argued at considerable length elsewhere, the politics of curriculum involves a selective tradition in which only certain groups' knowledge becomes "official knowledge" (Apple, 1990, 2000). The politics of the social studies curriculum provides a clear-cut example. In nations that have a history of strong state control over the content and organization of the curriculum and of repressive governments, such politics are even clearer. This is certainly the case in the instance we again discuss here—South Korea.

Korean society is in the midst of a great transition. For decades, there have been periods of intense resistance against the excessive central control of the curriculum and over textbook production and adoption policies. This resistance has been connected as well to the ongoing struggles by teachers—and a large portion of the Korean people—for political freedom and for the right to teach democratic values in schools. Indeed, the struggle over the social studies curriculum constituted one of the most distinguished movements of opposition to military dictatorship. While there have been some significant social, political, and economic transformations because of such resistance, much remains to be done. For example, the process of curriculum selection is still heavily regulated by the national government and the standards it has often imposed. This centralized process is

178 THE STATE AND THE POLITICS OF KNOWLEDGE

still in place even though the long-standing military dictatorship has collapsed due to the constant pressure for a more democratic government by progressive movements.

Political conditions in the Republic of Korea have indeed changed. It is the case that a more democratic and civilian government has been installed. Civil society, including various social interest groups and nongovernmental organizations, is gaining power in terms of participatory democracy. However, in order to secure and deepen these transformations, it is even more crucial at this time that we ask how the area of the curriculum that became so politically vital during the years of struggle against the military dictatorship—social studies and its accompanying classroom practices—should itself be transformed so that it is organically connected to the continuing efforts to build an even more vibrant civil society in the reformed political environment that has evolved after military rule.

In order to take this issue seriously, it is first necessary to examine critically important parts of the context in which teachers operate in Korea. What discourages educators from creating a more fully democratic social studies curriculum, a curriculum in which students might call dominant interpretations into question? Despite the hard work of many teachers and the rhetorical claims about the importance of building more democratic classrooms by government officials, many obstacles still block the path of teachers whose pedagogical agendas include transforming the school context and content. Just as important is the question of what teachers are actually doing to overcome the barriers to what they believe is a "true education" based on democratic dialogue.[1]

This chapter analyses the tensions between the complex situations in which teachers find themselves and their attempts to transform these situations in politically and educationally progressive directions. In the process, we will examine the ways teachers have attempted to employ technology to teach each other about what is possible in spite of the very real obstacles they face. This will involve focusing on the discourses expressed in an on-line communication group for social studies teachers and the accompanying off-line movement that links teachers to progressive lesson plans, counterhegemonic discourses, political issues for use in classroom, and a wide range of views and voices. In Korea, as in many other nations, on-line discussion is being used increasingly in education, often as a means to provide discussion forums for, say, university classes. But this particular group's use is different from other approaches. It is overtly meant to facilitate the development of a language of critical discourse, political engagement, and an alliance with progressive-minded social studies teachers. It is meant to counter critically not only the central control that we noted earlier, but also the ideological vision that such control embodies.

In the following section, we explore the politics of the national curriculum and situate social studies education in its larger historical politics. We then examine how progressive-minded teachers conceive of democratic discussion for praxis, how they think about their pedagogical agendas so that they can build a "true education," and how they constantly have to adjust their practices to deal with the realities of Korean education. As we shall see, their students' obsession with college entrance exams, for instance, places a major limit on what is possible for critical teachers to accomplish.

Web Sites and Political Pedagogy

The socioedu.njoyschool.net Web site is an on-line discussion group for social studies educators that connects teachers together. It is meant to be a tool for the conscious building of coalitions with other teachers. On-line collaboration and dialogue between teachers at this site have provoked a set of enthusiastic responses in terms of, on the one hand, resistance against the national curriculum and, on the other hand, the creation of new resources to be shared with other teachers. The educators in this group are committed to the idea that successful on-line communication among professionals can be a crucial factor in contributing to the creation of new spaces for democratic voices to evolve (see Bromley & Apple, 1998). The site is also designed as a virtual meeting place for critically oriented social studies educators to share parts of their day-to-day practice in classrooms with each other. The participating group consists of like-minded individuals who are engaged in democratic practices in their classrooms, who want to provide mutual support and advice, and who see the exchange of electronic resources as an opportunity to build a larger movement in education. Thus these teachers are not simply devotees of the new technology in education. They are all committed to grassroots movements that support socially critical and democratic activities in classrooms in the name of "true education."

Even a brief examination of teachers' discourses illuminates the complexities of the situations they face as they attempt to build and defend more socially critical and democratic practices in their classrooms. The majority of discourses we examine here are taken from the on-line group discussions, e-mails, or bulletin boards, teaching materials and resources, supplementary resources, lesson plans, and related off-line documents. At

the Web site, participants can post messages or opinions to all other sub-
scribers of the group. The site is designed so that others can respond to
posted messages and views over a period of time. This usually leads to the
emergence of debate, or discussion topics, where a number of contributors
provide responses and counterresponses to original postings, thus forming
a dialogue. Given the fact that for these teachers a classroom that stimu-
lated serious discussion, rather than what Paulo Freire (1970) would call
"banking" education, was a crucial sign of educational transformation, we
will focus on this and on the possibilities and limits of such action within
the existing material and ideological realities of Korean society.

"True Education" in Social Studies Classrooms

As we mentioned, the teachers who participate in the socioedu.njoyschool.
net Web site are strongly oriented toward the ideal of true education and
are equally committed to the recently legalized independent Korean Teachers Union (KTU). In 1989, a number of Korean teachers initiated their first
trade union with the slogan "educational democratization." Nearly fifteen
hundred teachers were dismissed for joining and supporting the union and
one hundred were arrested. Nonetheless, on July 1, 1999, after a long legal
struggle and multiple demonstrations, the KTU became a legal union with
62,000 members. The existence of the teachers' union, a union that had
been banned by the government for the past decade, was finally given official legitimacy. This was an historic event, since for the first time it guaranteed basic labor rights for teachers. As the first president of the KTU said
in the inaugural declaration of the Korean Teachers Union: "The pseudo-
education, which was forced on us by a dictatorial regime, seriously de-
meaned the prestige of teachers and drove them to become knowledge
salesmen or examination technicians." In recognition of the KTU's efforts,
the introduction of the socioedu.njoyschool.net site starts with a distinct
link to the homepage of the KTU and a statement that shows the participants' political and educational affiliation with the KTU. It declares that
"we refuse to become knowledge brokers or transmitters based on pseudo-
education." This is a very different view of teachers' roles and of who
should control the selection of knowledge.

In line with these political and educational commitments, the on-line
discussion at the Web site has become an important linkage among teachers. First, it has enabled the development of a more collaborative culture.
Second, and of considerable import, it seems as well to have helped teachers construct alternative identities and perceive new roles for themselves
within the teaching profession. These identities are strikingly different

from the prevailing bureaucratic and conservative expectations for teachers historically found within Korean policies. For example, one of the official statements at the site asserts:

> Basic direction of our organization: We are committed to support for democratic social studies education in which both teachers and students participate. For this reason we are different from the established official academic association for social studies education. . . . Our primary concerns are to put the aims of participation into practice and to carry the belief of true education into action.[2]

This declaration of support for true education against the traditional conservative solutions that had been imposed during military rule involves two major tasks: democratizing school governance and creating alternative curriculum. The true education movement argued for a democratization of education, one that not only allows but also actively sponsors critical engagement in issues of governance and educational policy-making at both the macrolevel of the state and at the school district level. It also maintained that a socially just and democratic education must enhance the initiative of teachers in creating their own curricular knowledge at the microlevel of the school and classroom. It stood in opposition to the national curriculum, seeing this as the main barrier to democratic practice in classrooms. Here their arguments about the dangers of a national curriculum were similar to those raised by one of us elsewhere (Apple, 1996). For these progressive educators, even though some gains have indeed been made in Korean education through organized action, the overall structure and content of the curriculum is still much too uniform, rigid, and controlled. They recognized that such features are still rooted in a political environment in which curriculum design and the agenda for its implementation had been monopolized by the strong state. One of the curriculum's major historical roles had been that of legitimating the successive military regimes' genesis, dictatorship, and immoral actions. For more than thirty years, the military government had taken advantage of curriculum control as an ideological instrument. The lineage of this is still very visible even in a new political environment.

This history of centralized control has meant that curriculum organization and administration have become key tasks of the national Ministry of Education (MOE). Thus the state, for example, is exclusively responsible for the publication and authorization of school textbooks for the primary and secondary levels. The MOE is also responsible for supervising textbook compilations and for monitoring whether or not the national curriculum has implemented lessons that are within the range of standard and "legitimate" knowledge. The annual schedule of subject matter that can be taught and the time allotment for each subject are both specified in great detail in the teacher's guidelines. Both are to be regulated and are under the control of the principal, *not* the teachers (Nam, 1994, p. 32). The fact that this centralized process of curriculum determination provides little allowance to be made for the specificities of gender, class, and disability has made it even more resented by many teachers.

Yet the endorsement of the ideal of "true education" was by no means the sole feature on the socioedu.njoyschool.net site. The site participants' next step was to articulate the specificities of what would be a new definition of "official knowledge," to elaborate new forms both of desirable knowledge and of effective teaching methods that would bring the ideal of true education in social studies to life. In the process of doing this, the initial group of teachers caught the attention of other social studies educators by both creating and then publicizing democratic curricula and teaching practices. For them, these methods and content embodied the primary ways in which the school could be used to create a new—and much more democratic—Korean citizen. They connected with many teachers who wanted fresh and workable models to replace the rote learning and classroom recitation that had dominated schools. For all of these teachers, there was a clear preference for pedagogy that involved having students discuss topics by incorporating them into a style based on problem-posing questions. And for all of them, these discussions were to be based on the students' encounters with a variety of social issues and community predicaments that require democratic participation to resolve.

In a number ways, this technique has much in common with what Dillon (1994, p. 40) defined as a method of teaching grounded in the "discussion question." For him, the questions that students are to discuss concern what to think and how to act about the subject matter under discussion. The method then moves on to a second step, that of "joint inquiry," which invites students to develop possible resolutions of the problem. The parallels between Dillon and the Korean teachers can be seen in the fact that the lesson plans that they post on the site also are intended to foster democratic dialogues using discussion questions and joint inquiry as a means of breaking out of the traditionally rigid disciplinary structures that organize the curriculum in Korean schools.

However, while there are some similarities with Dillon and similar discussion-based teaching methods, there are significant differences that are deeply connected to a much more critical political and educational vision. For the teachers influenced by the true education movement, this process can neglect content, especially politically charged content and questions.

Under orientations such as Dillon's, there is no guarantee that the questions and content that are raised are indeed socially critical. This is not where the true education model stands. Thus the discussion topics based on true education are closer to, say, Ira Shor's (1992) work on critical pedagogy or to the models that are found in the book *Democratic Schools* (Apple & Beane, 1995) than they are to Dillon. Unlike Dillon (1994, p. 32), who holds that a topic for discussion would be anything that perplexes us, that we wonder about, that we are unsure of, or that we need to work out, the discussion topics suggested for true education are oriented much more toward political issues. Certain *specific* kinds of "puzzlements" take priority here.[3] This is more than a little understandable given the history of repressive regimes in South Korea.

Let us give a concrete example of what this might mean. Some of the posted lesson plans for democratic discussion are organized around critical dialogues on the political aspects of social movements, exploring topics closely linked to pressing social problems such as the exploitation and dehumanization of South Asian laborers and the malnutrition of children within low-income families. Teachers are encouraged to help students think critically, to recognize the social function of particular forms of knowledge, and to realize that dominant relations of power produce unequal and unjust policies. Through discussion, students are asked to find alternative ways to cope with the lack of infrastructure for democracy and, at the same time, to fight for their rights as citizens. According to a posted message:

> I believe we share some assumptions about the role of social studies teachers. Social studies teachers should educate [students as] conscious agents in order [for students] to be capable of making alliances with others who have provided the grounds for social movements.

This aim, to stimulate the critical capacities of students and to enable them to become active agents of social transformation, is common among all advocates of true education. For these teachers, only through creating democratic dialogue around the most serious social problems facing society today can real transformations in the school curriculum come about. Yet they also recognize that currently students are exposed to history or social and cultural studies through textbooks that barely address politicized topics. For this very reason, recommendations are made that students learn Korean modern politics both from the historical experience of their families and from thematic reflections on historical and political events of the democratization movement. Even though some teachers were not completely free from the textbook they should cover, nearly all of the lesson plans that are posted are intended to promote critical thinking through which students examine social and cultural studies with a variety of lenses, not simply the ones imposed by the MOE. All of the plans expect that critical discussion, rather than a linear step-by-step teaching model that is concerned only with the mastery of atomized "facts," will help youth construct alternatives. Democratized conditions in schools, and they hope in the larger society, will arise only when students learn to construct alternatives. And this can be accomplished only if students are given time and space actually to do this in schools. In essence, it is a politicized version of John Dewey (1916)—with the politics kept intact and extended. Democratic values and dispositions can be learned only through concrete practice in one's daily life.

This is clear in another posting to the site:

> As you see, the substance of education in Korea has not been free of the reins of government and has not been suited to the qualities needed for democratic citizens, either. Learning social studies should be more than the acquisition of social knowledge in fragments. Students have been no more than the objects of education, and teachers have been mere instructors of fragmentary facts given by the government. Instead, we need to put open-ended discussion to students so that they are conscious of problems in thinking them through. I might say we should avoid teaching a simple technique of picking one out of multiple-choice short-answer questions, which degrades students, making them like machines calling out the one right answer.

The position taken by this teacher and many others who are represented on the Web site is once again very similar to the arguments advanced by Ira Shor. According to Shor, a democratic learning process is one in which teachers and students negotiate and share mutual authority, but without a romantic giving up of all leadership by the teacher. For him, one of the ultimate aims of all serious educational projects should be to help in the formation of a democratic civil society. Such projects are supposed to end in actions that are established through genuine participation among all involved, thereby creating active *agents,* not passive recipients of prechosen knowledge. Thus full participation is to be the main door to empowerment within civil society. In elaborating a series of empowering pedagogies, Shor recognizes that "it is not the fault of students if their learning habits wither inside the passive syllabus dominant in education" (1992, p. 17). For this very reason, in order to guarantee an actively participatory attitude on the part of students, attention must be consciously and consistently directed toward sharing the teacher's authority with students in educational environments. This will require time and the taking of risks. But only in this way can students unlearn passivity.[4]

So far we have talked about the ideals that are the driving force behind these teachers' activities and of some of the kinds of material that they have posted on the Web site. However, neither Shor's nor others' critical and participatory pedagogies are always successful in practice. For example, as Hemmings (2000) shows in her study of academically oriented secondary schools in the United States, democratic dialogues sometimes not only yield contradictory results but also can invert the teachers' desired ends. One teacher in Hemmings' interesting study—someone whose overt pedagogical agenda was to transform the school context through a very critical reconstruction and use of democratic dialogue—constantly faced serious resistance from students. The students had constructed their own identities that ran counter to those advanced by the teacher. They were university-oriented and wanted only what would supposedly be guaranteed to help them reach that goal. They exhibited a truly tenacious determination to push their own educational ends, ones that were directly counter to the teacher's seemingly more emancipatory ends.

This is exactly the situation within academic high schools in Korea. As we shall see, it is one of the main causes of what discourages educators there from using democratic discussion in classrooms. The electronic mailing list documents repeatedly that teachers are often frustrated; they experience a good deal of difficulty in convincing all of their students to take on roles that embody active participation. As we shall also see, given the oppressive realities of the system of educational mobility that these students face, there are elements of "good sense" as well as "bad sense" in their rejection of alternative forms of curricula and teaching methods.

Resisting Participation

It has long been known that students may resist pedagogy and curricula, even ones with liberatory ends (see, e.g., Apple, 1995; Luke & Gore, 1992; McNeil, 1986; Willis, 1977). Shor himself recognizes part of this problem when he notes how difficult these ends may be to accomplish. According to him, teachers themselves need to initiate some form of critical resistance to dominant perspectives, since students cannot do it on their own and it may feel quite "un-natural" to them (Shor, 1986).

The development of a variety of new approaches to critical pedagogy over the past decades has been underpinned by a robust critical research tradition on the role of schooling in reproducing and interrupting dominance. These joint efforts at the level of research and practice have helped to stimulate a number of critically oriented reforms in educational policy and practice. One of this literature's key insights has been that students should be understood as far more than a mere captive audience in the educational process. Even though students often mediate, transform, are cynical about, and may even reject the dominant ideology that orients so much of schooling, this does not mean that more critical approaches will be easily accepted.

Teachers who actively seek to empower students may ironically find themselves forced back into traditional roles by students' resistance or opposition (Shor, 1986, p. 186). In Korean social studies classrooms, student resistance can function to discourage progressive teachers from creatively acting on their democratic intentions. It is clear, for instance, that the teachers who are actively using socioedu.njoyschool.net do seek to promote a form of critical thinking and discussion instead of perpetuating a curriculum based on a predetermined package of knowledge and a passive model of instruction. But, it is also clear that they often confront a situation strikingly similar to that found by Hemmings. Students want the instructor to teach only what they perceive is "legitimate" content, only that knowledge which will enable them to achieve higher marks on the all-important college entrance examination. Participating in a discussion seems almost a "waste of time."

Let us examine this situation more closely. The most important examination for upwardly mobile parents and students in Korea (this means the majority of Korean parents and students, given the utter importance they give to educational achievement) is the Scholastic Ability Test. (Students are supposedly tested on "ability" rather than "aptitude" on this examination, so immense preparation is actually required.) Most parents possess what Koreans call "educational zeal" and see themselves and their children as involved in a contest to get into the most highly reputed universities. Succeeding in such a contest is absolutely crucial for a very large proportion of Korean parents. In essence, they have learned Bourdieu well. They are attempting to accumulate particular kinds of cultural capital that can ultimately be converted into economic and social capital by their children later on (Bourdieu, 1984).

With the significance of "educational zeal" in Korean society, this means that the majority of Korean parents are willing to give up their own economic hopes and dreams to such an extent that they spend large amounts of money on the additional (private) education that is seen to be necessary for their children to get into a distinguished school. Given the pressure from these parents—and it is often quite intense—teachers are often frustrated. They realize that they cannot have the same high expectations for all students. They feel as if they are forced to focus on creating a classroom environment aimed increasingly at students who might be accepted at highly esteemed colleges. Teachers on socioedu.njoyschool.net hence feel conflicting demands between democratic instruction and students' resistance and oppositional behavior. An e-mail response to a question that one of us asked of a participant in the electronic mailing list shows this well:

> To be honest with you, a dominant teaching method for me is not discussion but lecture. I talk and students listen. I know well that discussion is one of the best ways to help young people seek out a range of ideas and to have their own voices. Unfortunately, the students do not ask teachers to pose a critical discussion but to give them a lecture. I am always trying to stress the importance of a just and caring society in their lives—within the limitations of a lecture, though. That's the way I compromise with my impasse.

The sentiment behind this e-mail could be multiplied many times. Teachers feel frustrated by the fact that the primary concern of so many students (and their parents) is simply their test scores. Progressive pedagogical intentions are interpreted as involving content and teaching processes that would diminish their examination results. The existence of this kind of reaction from students and parents can serve as a corrective to some of the relatively naïve literature in education that discusses impediments to creating a more democratic curriculum and to using in-depth discussion of subject matter as a dominant teaching technique. Dillon (1994), whom we drew upon earlier in this chapter, for example, has pointed to a number of elements that discourage discussion. He highlighted teachers' and students' inexperience with discussion along with a possible lack of "know-how" in leading discussions. However, like many others, he did not take into consideration how students themselves (to say nothing of their parents) respond to such pedagogic moves, how in specific contexts student resistance becomes a major pedagogic force.

Because of this lack in the literature, there are important lessons to be learned from South Korea. Even though politically and educationally progressive teachers there desire a more democratic education, the existence of both a powerful national standardized test and fierce competition discourages democratic practices and distorts the instructional process—and paradoxically supports content and methods that are exactly the opposite of those the teachers we have been discussing are working so hard to build, defend, and share. As the electronic mailing list documents, these progressive-minded teachers on socioedu.njoyschool.net do explore and advocate various methods such as having students—not just teachers—speak to the class and critically discuss issues with peers or asking students questions to encourage open-ended and socially critical thinking. But teachers who have tried these methods have often faced two disappointing responses from the students. The first response of the students is boredom in being made to think for themselves. For them, this is *not* what teaching and learning is about; therefore, it can't be "serious." This is then quickly linked to discontentment with and disassociation from a method that they perceive will not be effective in improving their college entrance examination scores.

These responses are confirmed in Lee's ethnographic research in a Korean academic high school. Lee's respondents had much in common with much of what is found on socioedu.njoyschool.net. Teachers experienced high levels of stress, largely due to their students' obsession with "overheated competition." As the students in Lee's study said about what they considered "real" teaching: "We want to listen to the teachers' explanation" and "Discussion is hassling us" (1994, p. 16). These were typical responses given to high school social studies teachers by significant numbers of students.[5]

Lee also documented that there was yet another response to discussion-centered classroom interaction: it was a "waste of time." When the teacher asked a question that was meant to encourage students to investigate a topic for themselves, the students responded by saying: "We need to count on the textbook, to cut down on the time of working with other students, and to be taking the mock-exam of the SAT to be a good test taker" (p. 16). We need to remember that this response by the students is not simply a product of some misguided false consciousness. It is a realistic response to the pressures they are under. And in the intensified and highly pressured world of teaching (Apple, 1995, 2000), when day in and day out teachers are confronted with such reactions, they usually decide to meet the students' immediate needs and not to draw as much upon or attempt too rigorously to enhance their students' critical thinking capacities. The political urge to create new forms of civic participation through actions in schools runs afoul of the material and ideological circumstances and the discursive conditions that create student identities and their dreams and nightmares about their futures.

All of this tells us something very significant about what discourages discussion in classrooms in nations such as South Korea, and perhaps in many similar nations. This is due not so much from a lack of teachers' abilities as it is from the fierce competition for college entrance. This leaves the specific teachers we have been discussing and Korean educators in general in a truly difficult position. In order for classroom transformations to occur, there must be concomitant changes in the methods of assessment that have been so dominant there. In recognition of this, after intense discussion and considerable pressure from teachers and others, some changes in assessment have been made that do provide (limited) space for teachers to act in a more progressive manner.

For example, in 1999, the Korean Ministry of Education ordered all high schools to employ modes of student evaluation based on "performance assessment" for college entrance courses. Behind this was something similar to portfolio forms of assessment, where more "authentic" assessments are used rather than the usual traditional evaluations such as multiple-choice examinations grounded in rote learning. While part of this reform can also be seen as the state's response to its legitimation needs within a new and rapidly changing political situation (Apple, 1995), for the teachers involved in the Web site, this partly opened up new ways of justifying their more socially critical and democratic methods and content.

This is worth saying something more about. The teachers' responses to performance assessment at socioedu.njoyschool.net centered around two claims, one positive and one negative. First, for some teachers, performance assessment is ideally suited for a progressive social studies curriculum. The teachers believe that by its very nature it tends to foster democratic practice and participation. For them, performance assessment allows for much more than behavioral assessment, mastery learning, and textbook-based management. Students construct, rather than simply select, knowledge and ways of demonstrating their understanding. Furthermore, the teachers argue that these kinds of assessment formats allow them to observe student activity through a more varied set of tasks, ones that reflect democratic requirements from real life. Thus the new lesson plans based on performance assessment that are posted on socioedu.njoyschool.net are focused on purposeful, collaborative, and self-reflective collections of student work that can be generated during the process of participatory activities.

A teacher who posted his teaching plans about participating in nongovernmental organization (NGO) programs summarized this by stating that portfolio assessment has the possibility of functioning as both a teaching tool and an assessment medium. It empowers students and teachers to encourage teacher-student collaboration, foster critical thinking, and promote democratic discussion.

Yet not all teachers agree with this position. There is a second, more critical claim made. For these other teachers, who are much more critical of performance assessment, their experiences indicate that the majority of students have not acquired critical thinking skills. Students did not perform as well in large classes. Their responses indicated that students used surface approaches to discussion more than deep approaches. While most of the critics agree about the procedure's *potential* success, they have quite serious worries about the "fuzziness" of the criteria used for performance assessment and especially about class size. Since class sizes tend to be large in Korean schools, without major changes in the numbers of students in each class, merely altering assessment procedures will have minimal effects.

While these conflicts reflect the lack of unanimity among the teachers involved in the electronic mailing list, these examples do point to something very positive. Given the history of military dictatorships and strong state control, the fact that there is open and honest discussion among teachers about what might lead to a more critically oriented classroom itself points toward the growth of more public debate about how curriculum and teaching might be organized to contribute to the processes of political, economic, and educational democratization. The very existence of the Web site and electronic mailing list points to the seriousness of the teachers' endeavors.

Conclusion

In this chapter, we have employed a key example, the socioedu.njoyschool.net Web site, to demonstrate how technology is being used to create partly counterhegemonic spaces for teachers to resist dominant forms of curriculum and teaching and the centralized modes of control that accompany them. As we have seen, the teaching practices in academic high schools in Korea are characterized by rote recitation and lecture. This has become the major strategy to prepare students for the college entrance examination, a strategy that has been kept in place not only because of mandates from above but because of intense pressures from parents and students. In the face of these obstacles and pressures, teachers have strategically taken a new government mandate—the use of performance assessment—and have attempted to use it in partly progressive ways.[6] Yet, as the teachers themselves note, this can be accomplished in lasting ways only when conditions exist that enable the generation of serious and critical discussion around socially important themes in classrooms, where there are clear (and democratically arrived at) criteria, and where there is a reduced teacher/student ratio. Thus changes in assessment may help but do not necessarily guarantee democratic practice when this continues to be hindered by the dominant politics of official knowledge in Korea.

In responding to this predicament, teachers are constantly faced with the question of how they can make a real difference in terms of democratic curriculum and instruction in the new political environment that has arisen after decades of military dictatorship. This is made even more complicated by the fact that, with the progress toward political democratization in the 1990s, many radical and/or progressive groups lost their initiative. Because so many social movements and organizations had concentrated all of their activities against the dictatorship, once the military was no longer in power, the press for more radical transformations weakened. A number of progressive-minded groups are more than a little pessimistic about what is currently happening. Democratization did accomplish a weakening of the repressive social environment; but as a result, the point of convergence for continued political struggle, for even further democratization in the economy, in education, and in so many other institutions, has been lost. This has presented considerable hardships for the many teachers and social activists who rightly saw the successful struggle against military rule as the beginning, *not* the end, of the movement toward a society that was more equal in both means and ends.

In spite of these difficulties, the Web site we have focused upon and the voices represented on it embody several important tenets of "true education" and point to the possibility of continued action. Both a rejection of the teacher's status as merely a knowledge broker and an emphasis on a critically engaged education are very visible. And both are increasingly important in the politically changed situation of South Korea today. Based on their numerous discussions of actual practice and their development and sharing of detailed lesson plans for social studies classrooms, teachers on the site clearly still believe that they can overcome a number of the obstacles they and their society so obviously face. They are committed to providing resources for building a more empowering education and to teaching each other possible ways in which students and teachers can change their traditional approaches and identities into more critically democratic ones.

Given the new and still-changing political environment in Korea, it is hard to be certain about what the future of curricula and teaching there will actually be. Will there be continued movement toward "thick" democracy, rather than the "thin" democracy that currently exists? Can social studies teachers successfully contribute to this movement? It would be arrogant to see the choice that teachers must face as only one of all or nothing: either transmission or transformation. The teachers we have described here are learning to be strategic. They have begun to find the spaces where openings within a system still dominated by traditional educational values and centralized control can be found and widened. In the process, the teachers from socioedu.njoyschool.net have begun what we hope is a continuation of part of a process that Raymond Williams called "the long revolution" (Williams, 1961), the transformation of official knowledge and values in the name of "true education."

What a new politics of official knowledge and a thick democracy would actually look like when they are put into practice is the topic of the next chapter's examination of the reality of large scale counter-hegemonic education in Porto Alegre, Brazil.

Acknowledgments

We would like to thank Diana Hess of the University of Wisconsin-Madison for her help on this chapter. Many of the ideas expressed here have emerged from discussions with her.

Educating the State, Democratizing Knowledge: The Citizen School Project in Porto Alegre, Brazil

Luís Armando Gandin and Michael W. Apple

Introduction

We are living in a period of crisis that has affected all of our economic, political, and cultural institutions. But one of the institutions that has been at the center of the crisis and struggles to overcome it is the school. We are told by neoliberals that only by turning our schools, teachers, and children over to the competitive market will we find a solution. We are told by neoconservatives that the only way out is to return to "real knowledge." Popular knowledge, knowledge that is connected to and organized around the lives of the most disadvantaged members of our communities, is not legitimate. But are the neoliberal and neoconservative positions the only alternatives? We do not think so.

The great Brazilian educator Paulo Freire constantly stressed that education must begin in critical dialogue. Both of these last two words were crucial to him. Education must hold our dominant institutions in education and the larger society up to rigorous questioning, and at the same time, this questioning must deeply involve those who benefit least from the ways these institutions now function. Both conditions are necessary, since the first without the second is simply insufficient to the task of creating a critically democratic education.

Of course, many committed educators already know that the transformation of educational policies and practices—or the defense of democratic gains in our schools and communities—is inherently political. In-

deed, this is constantly made visible by the fact that neoliberal and neoconservative movements have made teaching and curricula the targets of concerted attacks for years. One of the claims of these rightist forces is that
schools are "out of touch" with parents and communities. While these criticisms are not totally wrong, we need to find ways of connecting our educational efforts to local communities, especially to those members of these
communities with less power, that are more truly democratic than the
ideas of "thin" democracy envisioned by the right. If we do not do this,
neoliberal definitions of democracy—based on possessive individualism
and where citizenship is reduced to simply consumption practices—will
prevail (Apple, 1999, 2000, 2001).

While it is crucial to recognize and analyze the strength and the real
consequences of neoliberal and neoconservative policies (something we
both have been doing for a long time—Apple, 1996, 2001; Gandin, 1994,
1998, 1999), it is also essential to understand the renegotiations that are
made at regional and municipal levels. As Ball emphasizes: "policy is . . . a
set of technologies and practices which are realized and struggled over in
local settings" (1994, p. 10). Thus, rather than assuming that neoliberal and
neoconservative policies dictate exactly what occurs at the local level, we
have to study the rearticulations that occur on this level to be able to map
out the creation of alternatives.

Educators in a number of nations have had to cope with these transformations of ideology, policy, and practice. For us, it is important to learn
two things from the experiences of other educators who are struggling
against the forces of inequality. First, we can learn about the actual effects
of neoliberal and neoconservative policies and practices in education. Second, and even more important, we can learn how to interrupt neoliberal
and neoconservative policies and practices and how to build more fully
democratic educational alternatives (Apple, 2001).

One of the best examples of this can currently be found in Porto Alegre, Brazil. The policies being put in place by the Workers' Party, such as
"participatory budgeting" and the "Citizen School," are helping to build
support for more progressive and democratic policies there in the face of
the growing power of neoliberal movements at a national level. The Workers' Party has been able to increase its majority even among people who
had previously voted in favor of parties with much more conservative educational and social programs *because* it has been committed to enabling
even the poorest of its citizens to participate in deliberations over the policies themselves and over where and how money should be spent. By paying
attention to more substantive forms of collective participation and, just as
important, by devoting resources to encourage such participation, Porto

Alegre has demonstrated that it is possible to have a "thicker" democracy, even in times of both economic crisis and ideological attacks from neoliberal parties and from the conservative press. Programs such as the Citizen School and the sharing of real power with those who live in *favelas* (shantytowns), as well as with the working and middle classes, professionals, and others, provide ample evidence that thick democracy offers realistic alternatives to the eviscerated version of thin democracy found under neoliberalism (SMED, 1999b). In many ways, the policies and practices now being built there extend in powerful and systemic ways a number of similar reforms that are being built in other countries (Apple & Beane, 1998). Yet just as important is the pedagogic function of these programs in Porto Alegre. They develop the collective capacities among people to enable them to continue to engage in the democratic administration and control of their lives. This is time-consuming; but time spent in such things now has proven to pay off dramatically later on.

In this chapter, we describe and analyze the policies of the "Popular Administration" in Porto Alegre. The proposals for the formation of a Citizen School are explicitly designed to change radically both the municipal schools and the relationship between communities, the state, and education. This set of polices and the accompanying processes of implementation are constitutive parts of a clear and explicit project aimed at constructing not only a better school for the excluded but also a larger project of radical democracy. While the reforms being built in Porto Alegre are still in formation, what is being built there may be crucial not only for Brazil but for all of us in so many nations who are struggling in classrooms and schools to create an education that serves *all* of our children and communities.

In order to understand the limits and possibilities of such attempts during a time of what has been called "conservative modernization" (Apple, 2001), we will need to examine closely a number of things: how the proposal for the Citizen School connects to the larger project of the Popular Administration, the major normative goals and institutional design created by this ongoing project, and the possibilities and problems in generating the new realities the Workers' Party committed itself to create. The first part of the chapter briefly situates the experience of Porto Alegre in the larger political and educational context of Brazil. The second part presents the normative goals of the Citizen School and examines the mechanisms that helped to forge these goals. In the third part, we discuss the consistency between the normative goals and the institutional design constructed to implement those goals, and in the fourth part we discuss some of the potential problems of the project. Finally, we offer some considerations about

the future of the project and its potential contribution for the enhance-
ment of democratic relationships inside and outside education.

Porto Alegre and the Popular Administration

Porto Alegre is a city of 1.3 million people, situated in the southern region
of Brazil. It is the capital of the state of Rio Grande do Sul and the largest
city of the region. Since 1989, it has been governed by a coalition of leftist
parties under the general leadership of the Workers' Party (Partido dos Tra-
balhadores or PT, formed in 1979 by a coalition of unions, social movements, and other leftist organizations). PT has been reelected three consec-
utive times, thus giving it and its policies even greater legitimacy.

According to one of the former mayors of Porto Alegre (a nationally re-
spected member of the Workers' Party), the purpose of the government is
to "recuperate the utopian energies," to "create a movement which contains, as a real social process, the origins of a new way of life, constructing a
'new moral life' (Gramsci) and a new articulation between state and society . . . that could lead social activity and citizenship consciousness to a
new order" (Genro, 1999, p. 9).[1]

The municipal administration, the "Popular Administration," has
brought significant material improvements to the most impoverished citizens of the city. To give just one example, as Santos (1998) points out: "as
regards basic sanitation (water and sewage), in 1989, only 49 percent of the
population was covered. By the end of 1996, 98 percent of the households
had water and 85% were served by the sewage system" (p. 485). In terms of
education, the number of schools has more than doubled since the Popular
Administration took office.

One particular measure adopted by the Popular Administration—*participatory budgeting* (Orçamento Participativo or OP)—is credited with the
reallocation of resources to the impoverished neighborhoods. The OP is a
mechanism that guarantees active popular participation and deliberation
in the decision-making process for the allocation of resources for investment in the city. Santos offers a compact description of how the OP works:

> In a brief summary, the OP centers on the regional and thematic
> plenary assemblies, the Fora of Delegates, and the Council of the
> OP (COP). There are two rounds of plenary assemblies in each of
> the sixteen regions and on each of the five thematic areas. Between
> the two rounds there are preparatory meetings in the microregions
> and on the thematic areas. The assemblies and the meetings have a
> triple goal: to define and rank regional or thematic demands and

priorities, to elect the delegates to the Fora of Delegates and the councilors of the COP, and to evaluate the executive's performance. The delegates function as intermediaries between the COP and the citizens, individually, or as participants in community or thematic organizations. They also supervise the implementation of the budget. The councilors define the general criteria that preside over the ranking of demands and the allocation of funds and vote on the Investment Plan proposal presented by the executive. (Santos, 1998, p. 469)

The OP is at the core of the project of transforming the city of Porto Alegre and incorporating the historically excluded impoverished population into the processes of decision-making. Just as importantly, as a number of researchers have shown (Avritzer, 1999; Azevedo, 1998; Baiocchi, 1999; Santos, 1998), not only have the material conditions of the impoverished population changed, but also the OP has generated an educative process that has forged new organizations and associations in the neighborhoods. The citizenry of the city has been engaged in an extensive pedagogic project involving their own empowerment. There has been a process of political learning through the construction of organizations that enable full participation in the OP. In essence, the OP can be considered a "school of democracy." The learning acquired within the OP is transferred to other spheres of social life (for more on this see Baiocchi, 1999; see also Bowles & Gintis, 1986). Yet there may be an even more significant educational aspect in the OP. The government agencies themselves are engaged in being "re-educated." Popular participation "teaches" the state to serve the population better.

Working in tandem with the OP, there is another more specifically educational project for the city, the Citizen School, implemented by the Municipal Secretariat of Education (Secretaria Municipal de Educação or "SMED"). The Citizen School is pushing in the same direction and aims to initiate a "thick" version of education for citizenship very early in the formal education process through the creation of democratic institutional mechanisms.

Before we describe some of the mechanisms created by the Citizen School project, we want to situate this initiative within the global context of predominantly neoliberal reforms. If we are to understand the case of the Citizen School, we have to investigate the particular rearticulations being forged at this locale.

The concept of articulation is central here, because it helps us to understand the ideological "work" that has do be done to disconnect and reconnect ideas and practices. To disarticulate a concept historically associated with counterhegemonic movements and rearticulate it to a hegemonic discourse actually requires a good deal of creative ideological work. To disarticulate this concept from the hegemonic discourse and then rearticulate it back to progressive and counterhegemonic initiatives is even more difficult. This is a dynamic, not static, process. As Hall states: "an articulation is . . . the form of the connection that *can* make a unity of two different elements, under certain conditions. It is a linkage which is not necessary, determined, absolute, and essential for all time" (Hall, 1996, p. 141).

The concept of articulation provides us with a tool to understand that the apparent homogeneity and solidness of a given discourse is' actually a historical construction, one that has to be constantly renovated if it is to be maintained. Connections that are established between groups and specific ideologies are not given. They are better understood as "nonnecessary," as more or less contingent relations made possible in a specific context and in a specific historical moment.

This conceptual framework can help us to better understand the case of Porto Alegre. As we already noted, there is a process of conservative modernization going on in education around the world. One of the key claims such a movement has put forth is that education is not only a crucial cause of the economic and cultural crises many nations are experiencing but is also a major part of the solution. If "we" prepare students for a world that is increasingly governed by the relations of an ever more competitive new capitalism, "we" will be better prepared to excel in the globalized market. Education hence is stressed as a privileged site in this hegemonic discourse.

However, when this discourse reaches Brazil, and more specifically the city of Porto Alegre, some interesting rearticulations are forged. In the dominant discourse, an emphasis on education is related to a consistent attempt to colonize the space of "legitimate" discussions of educational policy and practice and, hence, to produce an educational environment more in tune with the economic needs of the market. But when this global process enters Brazil, contradictions are created and a hybrid product is formed. This is the case because even though the hegemonic discourse tries to colonize the educational sphere, once it meets the realities of the Brazilian context it creates unintended spaces for alternative experiences.

The idea that education will solve the problems of the country paradoxically allows for a discursive space that can be reoccupied by arguments for more investment in education. The Popular Administration uses this space to prioritize education for *everyone*, in a country where education for the poor has been decidedly neglected. Once the space is rhetorically reoccupied by a discourse of more investment in education, the Citizen School can deploy its alternative agenda. It can work on a very real transformation of priorities and can invest in a project aimed at building a "thick democracy" that focuses on an emancipatory education for the excluded. In the process, the Popular Administration can also recuperate and reinvent concepts such as "autonomy," "decentralization," and "collaboration." Even though these concepts were taken up and rearticulated by neoliberals, they have historically had a completely different meaning in the popular movements in Brazil. The Popular Administration has itself begun successfully to disarticulate these key concepts from neoliberal discourse and to rearticulate them to the Citizen School project.

However, we need to be conscious of the complexities of the politics of historical movements. The fact that these disarticulations and rearticulations are happening does not mean that the Popular Administration has permanently won the battle. Hegemonic groups themselves are constantly attempting to win back the meaning of key concepts and to reoccupy the terrain of educational policies and their meaning. Thus education remains a site of struggle. But it is still crucial to realize that a dominant hegemonic bloc cannot control all spaces simultaneously. As the Citizen School project shows, even dominant groups' own discourses can be rearticulated to favor counterhegemonic purposes.

This is visible in the use of the concept of citizenship, a "sliding signifier" that can be used by both neoliberal and more progressive agendas. This concept, central to the project in Porto Alegre, has a very specific meaning in contemporary Brazil. It is not a random category; it symbolizes the struggles against the ongoing attempts to introduce market logics inside public sites such as education. Thus an emphasis on the formation of citizens within public schools has to be read within this context of discursive struggle. The category of "citizenship" serves as a discursive weapon against the rival notions of "client" or "customer" that have played such an important part in the language of neoliberalism.

It provides very different subject positions for agency from those offered by the idea of the consumer in a set of market relations. The political meaning of citizenship has been rearticulated to a set of more socially critical ideas and practices, one that intends to construct a new common sense that is truly focused on collective as well as individual empowerment.

This is not a simple task, though. Certain discourses more easily gain truth effects; others do not have access to the channels of distribution or, when they do have access, have to struggle to rearticulate concepts that have already been framed in dominant ways. The fact that the municipal government has access to a large number of schools and that the schools themselves are sanctioned by the municipal level of the state does not mean that the rearticulation will go smoothly. The Popular Administration must constantly struggle against dominant groups' ability to sustain hegemonic control by their power to restrain the spaces of visibility of alternatives, to use the media to circulate negative readings of the educational and social transformations in which the Popular Administration is engaged, and to win back the discursive spaces that have been successfully reoccupied by progressive groups and governments.

Because of this, it is important to realize that the discursive struggles about both education and its major goals that are taking place in Porto Alegre are significant. They are not epiphenomenal but have real and material effects. As we mentioned above, the language of citizenship is used in a way that tries to "accent" it in the struggles over meaning. Again, talking about "citizenship" in opposition to "client" or "consumer" is a conscious move to bring "political" words into the arena of public discussion. Part of the project is to bring to the very center of the debate alternatives that have been marginalized. Thus, as we shall see in the next section, there is an attempt to bring to the very core of political practice the idea—contrary to what many "experts" would say—that impoverished communities, for example, can participate in the definition of their social destiny through the channels created by the Citizen School. Not only are concepts that were relegated to the margins brought back to the center of public discussion, but even more important, an entire group of people who were marginalized and excluded from the economic, social, and political goods of the society are affirmed as having the right to space, to voice, to social existence. In order to accomplish all this, there is a constant struggle to legitimize the experience of the Citizen School, to make it socially visible, to pose the discussion over education in terms other than those of neoliberalism, to pull education from the technical economistic realm favored by neoliberal assumptions and to push it to a more politicized one that has as its basic concern the role of education in social emancipation.

These creative transformations have affected common sense. The Popular Administration has been reelected three times. Certain issues are already established as being at the center of electoral discussions in the city of Porto Alegre. No political party can win the election in Porto Alegre if it does not guarantee that certain elements created by the Popular Administration—such as direct participation of the communities in the decisions of the municipal schools—will be maintained. There is a new set of expectations about the relationship between communities and the municipal government, and this has been incorporated as a new common sense of the city.

This has occurred in large part as well because there has been a recognition that counterhegemonic struggles must be able to connect with popular memory, with the residual idea that there is a more than just one way to structure social life, where social exclusion is not a daily reality. In the case of Porto Alegre, where a strong history of popular organization and politicization of daily life is part of this popular memory, latent in the local common sense, the project of the Citizen School and its repoliticization of the educational arena, along with the activation of community participation, does exactly that. The project was able to connect with this residual element already present in common sense and not totally expunged from popular consciousness by the experiences of neoliberal economic and social policies. By constructing social relations that actually recuperate this popular participation in reality, it has created a new common sense. High levels of participation by the people are now considered as a new minimum for the relationship between the state and communities.

Now that we have laid out the terrain of discursive struggle, we examine some of the institutional mechanisms created to implement the Citizen School project in the reality of the school system and in the daily lives of the schools themselves.

Creating the Citizen School

Public education in Brazil is governed in a complex manner.[2] It is simultaneously a responsibility of federal, state, and municipal governments. The federal government is responsible basically for postsecondary education (universities). Recently a national education law was passed giving the larger responsibility for elementary education to the municipalities and for secondary education to the states.[3] Nonetheless, because a considerable number of state schools were attended by elementary school students, the law actually established a coresponsibility of state and municipal governments. In the city of Porto Alegre, therefore, elementary education is under the responsibility of both state and municipal administrations. In reality, however, the municipal administration of Porto Alegre is responsible for early childhood and elementary education, and because of that, the Citizen School project involves only these levels of education.[4]

Historically, as a rule, schools in Brazil have had little autonomy. In the majority of states and cities, there are no elections for the city or state council of education (traditionally a bureaucratic structure, with members appointed by the executive), let alone for principals in schools. The curriculum is usually defined by the secretariats of education of the cities and states. The resources are administered by the centralized state agencies; schools usually have very little or no financial autonomy.

Although recently Brazil has achieved a very high level of initial access to schools (close to 95 percent), the indices of failures and dropouts are frightening. This reality is where the Citizen School, and the entire educational project of the Popular Administration, begins. It represents a sharp contrast with the policies that produced such indices. The field of education has become central to the Popular Administration's project of constructing new relations between state, schools, and communities. The Citizen School is organically linked to and considered a major part of the larger process of transforming the whole city.

The municipal schools of Porto Alegre are all situated in the most impoverished neighborhoods of the city—the *favelas*. This is because the expansion of the system occurred recently (since the Popular Administration took office in 1989), and the schools were built in the zones where there was a clear deficit of educational institutions and programs. In fact, some of the schools were constructed as a concrete result of the OP. A number of the regions of the city prioritized education and, specifically, a school in their assemblies.

Dealing with the excluded of Brazilian society, the Citizen School has a clear and explicit project of transformation. It: "institutes the possibility for citizens to recognize themselves as bearers of dignity, to rebel against the 'commodification' of life. . . . In the Citizen School, the conformist and alienated pedagogy that sustains the idea that history is a movement rigorously pre-organized as a realization of capitalist needs is denied" (Genro, 1999, pp. 10–11).

The grounding of the SMED proposals can be seen in the words of one of the most recent secretaries of education in Porto Alegre:

> The Citizen School is not a product of a group of enlightened administrators that had formulated and executed a "new proposal." It is not, as well, a spontaneous construction, without intentionality. . . . The Citizen School nourished itself from and was inspired by theoretic-practical contributions of academic progressive educators, by contributors in the public schools, and by the experiences of democratic and transformative struggle of social movements. Many of the builders of the Citizen School were actors of the movements in unions, communities, and in the popular trenches of the struggle for redemocratization of the country. (Azevedo, 1999, pp. 12–13)

This political origin of the coordinators of the Citizen School is an important factor in the democratic component of the proposal. It constitutes one of the reasons that there is a clear political commitment to constructing participatory and democratic alternatives. In fact, although the SMED plays an essential role in coordinating the actions of the schools and pushing a democratic agenda, the principles that officially guide the SMED's actions were created collectively, with active participation of teachers, school administrators and staff, students, and parents in institutionalized forums of democratic decision-making.

In order to construct the principles that would guide the actions of the Citizen School, a democratic, deliberative and participatory forum was created—the Constituent Congress of Education (see Freitas, 1999). Through a long process of mobilization of the school communities (using the invaluable lessons learned in the mobilization for the OP), a congress was constructed whose objective was to constitute the organizing principles that would guide the policy for schools in the city. From the Constituent Congress, the main normative goal for education was defined as a radical democratization in the municipal schools along three dimensions: democratization of management, democratization of access to schooling, and democratization of access to knowledge.

It is important to clarify that, for the Popular Administration, democratization of management is not simply a "technical" but a political and ethical issue. It involves the democratization of the relationships inside the schools, between the school and the community, and between the school and the central administration (SMED). It requires the creation both of mechanisms that enable the full participation of teachers, staff, parents, and administrators in the construction of democratic decisions about education in Porto Alegre and of a system of monitoring that guarantees that the collectively constructed decisions are being implemented. It is also grounded in the recognition of the centrality of the culture of the community as part of the educational and administrative spheres of the school and school system. In this sense, the democratization of management involves a clear educational process, because both the state agencies and the communities learn together to construct new mechanisms that represent the will of the communities.

The decision-making and monitoring processes in education occur at various levels: the establishment of a larger policy for education in the city and a constant evaluation of it, deliberations about how to invest the money allocated by the central administration to the school, and decisions about creating mechanisms of inclusion that are overtly linked to the ongoing struggle against a society that marginalizes impoverished students and denies knowledge to them.

The task that the SMED had to engage in was hence complex, but the basic question was simple: "How [do we] develop a transformative and democratic project inside a state apparatus that has a logic that goes in the opposite direction of democracy and transformation?" (Azevedo, 1998, p. 309).

In order to implement these principles of democratization in the educational system of Porto Alegre, the SMED and the Popular Administration created several mechanisms designed to achieve this goal. The following sections examine some of these mechanisms.

The New School Configuration

The first transformation involved one of the most pressing issues facing schooling throughout Brazil—the terrible exclusion of students. In order to democratize access both to the school and to important knowledge, the SMED implemented a new organization for the municipal schools. Instead of keeping the traditional structure of grades with the duration of one year (first to eighth in what is called "fundamental" education), the idea was to adopt a new structure called "cycles of formation."

The administrators at the secretariat were convinced that the issue of access to schools could be dealt with in a much better way using cycles. According to the SMED: "the cycle structure offers a better way of dealing seriously with student failure, because its educational perspective respects, understands, and investigates the sociocognitive processes that the students go through" (SMED, 1999b, p. 11). The idea is that by using a different conception of learning/time, the Citizen School would not punish students for being "slow" in their process of learning. In this new configuration, the traditional deadline—the end of each academic year—by which the students had to "prove" that they had "learned" is eliminated in favor of a different time organization.

The democratization of knowledge is also addressed by the adoption of the cycles: "the cycles of formation contribute to the respect of the rhythm, the timing, and the experiences of each student, enhancing the collective organization and interdisciplinarity in the schools" (SMED, 1999b, p. 10). The establishment of the cycles is a conscious attempt to eliminate the mechanisms in schools that perpetuate exclusion, failure, and dropouts and the blaming of the victim that accompanies these.

How do the cycles of formation actually work in the Citizen School? The schools now have three cycles of three years each, something that adds one year to fundamental education (one year of early childhood education inside the schools). This makes the municipal schools responsible for the education of students from six to fourteen years old. The three cycles are organized based on the cycles of life: each one corresponds to one phase of development, that is, childhood, preadolescence, and adolescence. The idea is to group together students of the same age in each of the years of the three cycles. This aims at changing the reality in the majority of public schools that cater to popular classes in Brazil, the reality with which the SMED was faced when the Popular Administration started to govern the city: students with multiple failures inside classrooms intended for much younger ones. By organizing education by age, having students of the same age in the same year of the cycle, the SMED claims to remotivate the children with multiple failures and fight against the commonsense idea that there are prerequisites to be learned without which it is impossible to comprehend the next knowledge in line. As the secretary says, the institution using the cycles of formation is:

> the redesigned school, with space and time that are geared towards the development of the students. Children and adolescents are beings in permanent development that should not be ruled by the school calendar or the school year. . . . The school using the cycles of formation sees learning as a process in which preparatory periods or steps do not exist; instead, there is a permanent process of development. Instead of punishing the student because he/she did not learn, the Citizen School aims at valorizing the already acquired knowledge. . . . (Azevedo, 2000, p. 129)

In the schools that are using cycles, students progress from one year to another within one cycle; the notion of "failure" is eliminated. Yet the SMED understood that the elimination of mechanisms of exclusion was not enough and it alone could not achieve the goal of democratization of knowledge. Because of this, the Citizen School created several mechanisms that aim at guaranteeing the inclusion of students. It established "progression groups" for the students who have discrepancies between their ages and what they have learned. The idea is to provide those students with multiple failures in their past with a stimulating and challenging environment where they can learn in their own rhythm and fill the gaps in their formation that exist because of the multiple failures they have experienced. Furthermore, the progression groups also provide a space so that the students who come from other school systems (from other cities or from the state schools, for example) and have experienced multiple failures are given close attention so that they are ultimately integrated in the cycles according to their respective ages. The idea here is that the school has to change its structure to adapt to the students and not the opposite, which has been historically the case (Souza, et al., 1999, pp. 24–25).

This idea of constructing a new structure to respond better to students' needs is connected to the creation of another entity: the learning laboratory. This is a space where students with special needs get individual attention but also a place where teachers conduct research in order to improve the quality of the regular classes.

Transforming "Official" Knowledge

The cycles do not stand alone, however. Curriculum transformation is also a crucial part of Porto Alegre's project to build "thick democracy." It is important to say that this dimension is not limited to access to traditional knowledge. What is being constructed is a new epistemological understanding about what counts as knowledge. It is not based on a mere incorporation of new knowledge within the margins of an intact "core of humankind's wisdom" but on a radical transformation. In the Citizen School, the notion of "core" and "periphery" in knowledge is made problematic. The starting point for the construction of curricular knowledge is the culture(s) of the communities themselves, not only in terms of content but in perspective as well. The whole educational process is aimed at inverting previous priorities and instead serving the historically oppressed and excluded groups.

The starting point for this new process of knowledge construction is the idea of "thematic complexes." Through action research (one that the teachers do in the communities where they work, involving students, parents, and the whole community), the main themes, ones that come from the interests or concerns of the community, are listed. Then the most significant interests and concerns are constructed into a thematic complex that will guide the action of the classroom in an interdisciplinary manner during a period of time. In this way, the traditional, rigid, disciplinary structure is broken and general interdisciplinary areas are created.

Let us give a concrete example of how this works. One of the schools organized its thematic complex in the "sociohistoric" area in order to examine questions directly linked to a particular set of interests and problems of the community. At the center of the complex was the issue of the community's standard of living. Three subthemes were listed: rural exodus, social organization, and property. In the rural exodus subtheme, the issues reflected the origin of the community—living now in a *favela* but originally from rural parts of Brazil. This is a common story in the *favelas,* where people who had nothing in the rural areas come to the cities only to find more exclusion. In this subtheme, the issues discussed were migration movements, overpopulation of the cities, an "unqualified" workforce, and marginalization.

In the subtheme of social organization, the issues were ordered in terms of temporal, political, spatial, and sociocultural relations. The issues, again, represent important questions in the organization of the community: the excessive and uncritical pragmatism of some in the local groups and associations, the connections between neighborhood associations and the OP, and cultural issues such as religiosity, bodily expression, African origins, dance groups, and "samba schools." In the third subtheme—property—the issues were expressly linked to the realities of the living conditions of families in the *favela:* living in illegal lots with no title, having to cope with the lack of an infrastructure, and the constant need to fight for their rights as citizens.

This example shows the real transformation that is occurring in the curriculum of the schools in Porto Alegre. The students are not studying history or social and cultural studies through books that never address the real problems and interests they have. Through the thematic complexes, the students learn history by beginning with the historical experiences of their families. They study important social and cultural content by focusing on and valorizing their own cultural manifestations. Yet it is important to note that these students will ultimately still learn the history of Brazil and the world, "high" culture, and so on, but this will be seen through different lenses. Their culture will not be forgotten in order for them to learn "high-status" culture. Rather, by understanding their situation and their culture and valuing them, students will be able to simultaneously learn *and* have the opportunity to transform their situation of exclusion. By studying the problems (rural exodus, living in illegal lots, and so on) and not stopping there but also studying the strengths of self-organization (in the OP, in neighborhood associations, in cultural activities and groups), the Citizen School helps to construct alternatives for these communities who live in what are clearly terrible conditions.

We also can see in this example that the historic silence about race in Brazil is being challenged. Bringing the African origins of the music (samba) and the religion (*candomble*) and openly discussing racist practices in Brazil in the process of constructing critical knowledge, teachers and students are learning that the silences about oppression only help in the reproduction of exclusion and racism. Thus the Citizen School has embarked on a dual path. It has recognized the necessity of creating empowered channels where people can speak openly, but it also knows that at the same time one must unveil the meanings behind these voices, question their hidden presuppositions, and construct new knowledge. Beginning from the insights of the community, it is necessary not to stop there but rather to construct knowledge that fights discrimination, racism, and exclusion. This experience overcomes the limited forms of multiculturalism that usually are put in place in the curriculum offered to the excluded (Giroux, 1995; McLaren, 1995). Not only does this new model of where knowledge comes from incorporate elements of "ethnic information" but it also aims at constructing a new form of "official knowledge" (Apple, 2000) by shifting the center of discussion to the lived experiences of the dispossessed.

School Councils

These transformations are made legitimate by a different politics of participation in educational governance as well. School councils are the most central part of the democratization of the decision-making process in education in Porto Alegre and are the product of concerted political efforts both by the Popular Administration and by a number of social movements involved with education in the city. These councils are composed of teachers, school staff, parents, students, and one member of the administration.

Each school council has half of the seats for teachers and staff and half for parents and students. One seat is guaranteed to the administration of the school, usually the principal (elected by all members of the school), something to which we shall return shortly.

The task of the school councils is to deliberate about the overall projects and aims of the school, the basic principles of administration, and the allocation of economic resources. Their responsibilities also extend to monitoring the implementation of these decisions. The principal and her or his team are responsible for the implementation of the policies defined by the school council.

In terms of resources, it is important to say that before the Popular Administration took office, there was a practice (common throughout Brazil) of centralized budgeting. Every expense (even small daily ones) had to be sent to the central administration before it was approved. Only then would the money be sent to the school, or a central agency would purchase the necessary product or service. With such a structure, school councils had their hands tied and possessed no autonomy at all. The SMED changed this structure and established a new policy of making the resources allocated to each school available every three months. This measure institutes financial autonomy for the schools, and allows schools to manage their expenditures according to the goals and priorities established by the school council. At the same time, such autonomy gives parents, students, teachers, and staff present on the council a notion of social responsibility in administering public money. It also teaches them to determine their spending priorities with solidarity in mind (SMED, 1999c):

> Along with the financial tasks, the School Council has these responsibilities:
>
> III—Create and guarantee mechanisms to effective and democratic participation of the school community in the definition of the political-administrative-pedagogical project of the school;
>
> . . .
>
> VII—Propose and coordinate the discussion in the school community and vote alterations in the school curriculum, in the scope of the attributions of the school unity, respecting the current legislation;
>
> VIII—Propose and coordinate the discussion in the school community and vote methodological, didactic and administrative alterations in the schools, respecting the current legislation; (SMED, 1993, p. 3)

Furthermore, the school council also has the power to monitor the implementation of its decisions by the principal and her or his team (SMED, 1993, p. 3). In fact, the school council is an empowered structure in the schools. It is the main governance mechanism inside the schools, and its limitations are only the legislation and the policy for education collectively constructed in democratic form. Decisions about the curriculum are part of the deliberation, and the inclusion of parents, students, and staff (or even teachers, in the majority of cases) in this process is a great innovation of the model. Because the school has a relative large amount of autonomy (decisions of the Congress of Education must be implemented in the schools, but these are general boundaries, not content-specific), this is an empowered instance.

It is important to realize that participation in the school council demands a certain level of technical knowledge. Because of this, in order to enhance the participation of parents, the SMED has been promoting municipal meetings of the school councils (six up until the year 2000). This is a space where parents, students, teachers, and staff acquire the tools and construct the necessary knowledge to administer the schools. It also generates an arena where the individual councils meet and share their knowledge and their doubts, allowing for a larger perspective beyond a corporatist or a "localist" view that tends to dominate in situations such as these. Furthermore, the SMED has a permanent program of "formation" (continuing education of all the participants) inside the schools. This provides an additional space for the education of the councilors. Finally, in order to make participation truly substantive, the SMED has been stimulating the building of connections between councils and local associations or unions. This gives the councilors more representativeness. In short, the process of education is not only happening inside the classrooms of the schools but in every instance of the school that involves democratic participation.

Although the school council is a remarkably democratic institution, there is another structure that guarantees representativeness as well. In the schools of Porto Alegre, the whole school community elects the principal by direct vote. Thus the one responsible for the implementation of the decisions of the school council is her- or himself elected, based on the program that she or he articulates. This enhances administrative legitimacy in the community. The principal is hence not someone who represents the interests of the central administration inside the school councils but someone with a majority of supporters inside that particular educational community. But the responsibility of the community does not stop with the election; through the school council the school community also monitors the activities of the principal and holds her or him accountable.

The process of direct election of principals by the whole educational community produces considerable levels of mobilization. In the 1998 elections for principals, data from the Popular Administration indicate that almost thirty thousand people voted. Once again, this provides an important part of the democratic learning of the communities, especially because the very process provokes a good deal of debate about the varying proposals for managing the school. The direct election of the one responsible to implement the directives created by the school council and a school council that is elected directly by the school community together represent a pedagogic mechanism that aims at both generating and teaching the principles of democratic management at the local level of the school.

Judging Success

Up to this point, our focus has been on the processes and mechanisms that have been put in place in Porto Alegre. Yet a final question remains: Are the mechanisms created capable of realizing the goals? Here we can only offer some tentative conclusions, since the reforms in Porto Alegre are ongoing and still "in formation."

Obviously, we have already offered some elements of an evaluation throughout this chapter. The Citizen School, through the collective creation

of goals and mechanisms that generate active involvement of the communities, so far seems to be a genuinely transformative experience. The Citizen
School has broken with the separation between the ones who "know" and
will "educate" (the administration) and the ones who "don't know" and
need to be "educated." A new form of thinking not only about education but
also about the whole society seems to be in gestation. Here the project re-
flects Paulo Freire's (himself a member of the Workers' Party) dictum that
"the Workers' Party cannot be the educator that already knows everything,
that already has an unquestionable truth, in relation with an incompetent
popular mass needing to be rescued and saved" (Freire, 1988, p. 17).

The epistemological rupture that plays such a major role in the experiment also allows for optimism. The challenge to what counts as knowledge,
to what counts as core and periphery, represents the essence of the educational proposal. Instead of creating isolated multicultural programs or
content that have little efficacy in the context of a largely dominant whole
structure, the Popular Administration has been creating a structure, with
popular participation, where the question of diversity of cultures has space
to flourish. The Citizen School created spaces where multicultural practices are organically integrated, not added artificially to a bureaucratically
determined structure that is averse to "difference." To construct a powerful
and democratic set of multicultural experiences, the whole institutional
structure had to be changed. An important example is the fact that the
SMED has been acting to create a context where the problems of racism
not only can surface but can be treated seriously. At the same time, the
SMED is acting proactively by establishing advisory boards that can
quickly discuss with the community and incorporate new agendas in the
curriculum and in the relationship of the school with the community. This
is enhanced by the establishment of and participation by popular organizations that are organized around the powerful issues of race, gender, and
sexuality. Local knowledge is valorized and considered essential to the educational and democratic quality of the project.

This vision of "thick" democracy is crucial. As we argued earlier, the
project of the Citizen School has also radically challenged the roles of the
traditional school. In these transformed schools, all the segments of the educational community collectively construct the principles that guide their
daily actions. But the project not only constructs this as a goal; it also consciously takes up the task of *creating* concrete participatory mechanisms to
implement these goals. In the process, a new conception of respect for the
diversity of cultures is generated. Challenging the elitist belief that impoverished people from poor neighborhoods or slums cannot participate because they are "ignorant," the Citizen School inverts this logic, placing the

212 THE STATE AND THE POLITICS OF KNOWLEDGE

ones who live the problems at the center as the people in a privileged position to construct alternatives.

In this sense, the Citizen School advances in relation to the "mainstream" notion of multiculturalism. In fact "multiculturalism is too easily depoliticized" (Pagenhart, 1994, p. 178). It is exactly this depoliticization that the Popular Administration wants to avoid. The project seems to perfectly fit what Giroux calls an "insurgent multiculturalism," one where: "all participants play a formative role in crucial decisions about what is taught, who is hired, and how the school can become a laboratory for learning that nurtures critical citizenship and civic courage" (Giroux, 1995, pp. 340–341).

A major difference here is the fact that the objectives are not simply the formulations of a team of experts in the SMED but are a democratic and collective construction with the participation of all the segments involved in education (including especially those people historically excluded from nearly all of the processes involved in education). As we showed, taken in their entirety, the participatory mechanisms created as part of the whole design for reform by the Popular Administration are powerful ways of implementing the goal of democratization of decision-making and of implementing and monitoring processes in the schools and in the educational life of the city.

The SMED clearly wants the decentralized local school councils to achieve the larger goals for the education of the city; but these larger goals were themselves forged through a democratic process. In this sense, what the Popular Administration is avoiding is a common practice in Brazil and in many other countries, where power is devolved to local units but these units themselves are held accountable by criteria not based on democratic decisions.

The SMED understood that participation is a process that had to be *constructed*. Therefore it consciously launched a program of providing advice and education so that people could participate knowledgeably in the OP, in the school councils, and elsewhere. Thus the transfer of technical knowledge has been an important part of the process. The SMED seems to have recognized Claus Offe's observation that the functional superiority of a new model of participation does not by itself solve all the problems involved in major democratic reforms (Offe, 1995, pp. 125–126). The mechanisms of the Citizen School reconstitute the participants as subjects, as historical actors. Participants are not only implementing rules but are part of an historical experiment of reconstructing the structure of the municipal state.

This can be seen in the fact that the school community gets to decide the allocation of economic resources. The schools are granted autonomy in the management of their share. This has had a significant impact on the reality of the schools themselves. Of just as much import, unlike many other parts of Brazil, where decentralization has actually meant a decline in real resources, the decentralization that has occurred in Porto Alegre has not been accompanied by an allocation of fewer resources. This process has produced a real empowerment of the school councils and not—as in the majority of the cases in the rest of the country—a mere formal transfer of responsibility from the centralized agencies to the local units, a transfer whose ultimate effect has all too often simply meant that local units have been forced to cut needed programs. Such decentralization is usually merely part of the legitimation strategies of the regional or national state as the state exports fiscal crisis downward (Apple, 1995, 2000).

We still need to ask, however, whether such participatory processes and the changed curricula have had real and substantial effects on issues such as exclusion in schools. While data are limited, they do seem to show significant improvement in terms of quality. Since it took office in 1989, the Popular Administration has increased the number of schools by more than 220 percent. The number of students enrolled has risen from 24,332 in 1989 to more than fifty thousand in 1999. But without any doubt, the success of the Citizen School can be measured by the sharp decrease in the number of student dropouts. In 1989, when it took office, the percentage of dropouts (and remember that we are talking about elementary and middle schools) was a frightening figure of nearly 10 percent. The consequences of this for already disadvantaged and excluded children were truly horrible. Through the Citizen School's emphasis on parental and student involvement, curriculum transformation, teacher education, and other similar mechanisms, the SMED reduced this dropout rate to 0.97 percent in 1998. This is clearly one of the most important educational achievements of the project. If the children stay in school, then clearly the new curricular proposals can actually affect them (SMED, 1999a).

Another telling fact is the virtual nonexistence of vandalism against the majority of the municipal schools. School vandalism used to be a serious problem in public schools (and still is in the state schools). The fact that the community actively participates in the governance of the schools, and actively uses them as a space for the community (for sports, cultural activities, etc), creates a sense of responsibility and enhances the notion that public goods are the property of all. That many of the new schools are fruits of the OP makes the school "theirs" as well.

Potential Problems

While we have been very positive in our evaluation of the project here, we do not want to be romantic. Although the mechanisms and the curriculum constructed by the Citizen School have a good deal of potential to create an education that helps to include the historically excluded, there are a number of potential problems that need to be carefully examined.

One potential issue is the possibility of the re-creation of hierarchies within the cycles. The cycles represent a very thoughtful innovation. They allow students to stay in school, thereby combating the serious problem of dropouts. The overall structure also allows a more integrated construction of knowledge, which valorizes the knowledge that the students bring from their community. Yet we need to step back and ask whether parts of this structure could ultimately lead to the production of new hierarchies of students within the cycle. Even though they are seen as temporary, the progression groups have the risk of creating a "second-class" group of students.

Another potential problem of the Citizen School project is related to the issue of social class. The Workers' Party has historically had its roots in a Marxist understanding of the primacy of class. Parts of the Marxist tradition have been accused (correctly, we think, in many cases) of choosing class as not just the central but often the only category of analysis, thus subordinating other forms of oppression to class (see Apple, 1986; Apple & Weis, 1983). Thus in the material produced by the Popular Administration, there are several explicit references to class oppression—and rightly so— but there are fewer references, for example, to racial oppression, a major element within Brazilian society. Because of the documents' relative silence on race, this could signal that even progressive-oriented state agencies can still be dominated by those who believe that successfully struggling around class issues alone will solve all the problems of oppression. This ignores the specificities of racial oppression, ones that are not totally reducible to class (see Dyer, 1997; Fine, Weis, Powell, & Wong, 1997; Omi & Winant, 1994).

This is made more important due to the racial specificities of the city and the region. In this "whitest" of Brazil's regions, the "whiteness" of school practices has to be discussed and challenged if transformation is to happen. Although the documents analyzed seem to show that this process is one that is being slowly constructed in the schools of Porto Alegre, further research, preferably ethnographic, about the politics of whiteness (Apple, 2001; Dyer, 1997) would be necessary to evaluate this construction.

Furthermore, in terms of gender and sexuality, in a region of Brazil where male virility and specific forms of masculinity are stressed because of their association with the traditional *gaucho* (the Brazilian "cowboy"), the consequences to issues for "traditional" male/female roles and sexual orientation should be obvious (see Connell, 1995). Again, there is not enough evidence in the material examined to evaluate the project in this area.

It is to the SMED's credit that these potential problems are not unrecognized. As we demonstrated, there is some evidence that the practical experiments of the Citizen School are incorporating race issues into their thematic complexes. In addition, the various mechanisms of continuous education of teachers in the Citizen Schools do provide sites where explicit discussions of race, gender, and sexuality are brought up, thereby creating theoretical spaces for the construction of new practices that challenge the silences about these themes. These movements represent positive signs, in the sense that the members of the school communities are using the open channels to problematize the issues of daily life, issues that certainly include moments of prejudice and racism. It is also true that the Popular Administration has several advisory boards (with both budget and structure, and the power to act) that have the explicit task of bringing up the themes of gender, race, sexuality, and religiosity.

Hence, although these potential problems should not be ruled out, there are reasons to believe that there are open spaces for popular organizations such as the growing activist movement among Afro-Brazilians, women's social movements, and gay and lesbian organizations to operate and demand from the state agencies the inclusion of issues that we believe should be part of the agenda of every citizen who fights oppression.

Of equal significance, however, is another possible problem for the project. This is the possibility that participants who have historically had more power will dominate the school councils and the other mechanisms of popular participation. This is a serious issue that should not be pushed into the background, given the experiences of such experiments elsewhere. However, we think that the case of Porto Alegre has some specific attributes that can lessen the probability that this will occur. First, the municipal schools are all situated in the most impoverished areas of Porto Alegre. Therefore, the classical cases of middle-class people dominating the discussions (see McGrath & Kuriloff, 1999) are avoided because, as a rule, there are no middle-class people in the regions where the schools are situated. Two recent studies of the OP in Porto Alegre offer some indirect evidence (Abers, 1998; Santos, 1998) and one study offers direct empirical evidence (Baiocchi, 1999) to show that there is no domination by powerful groups in the deliberative processes. In the OP, there is gender parity among the participants at the meetings and the proportion of "less-educated" people corresponds to the city average (Baiocchi, 1999, p. 7). While it is true that there are more men and educated people speaking at the meetings, the research has also shown that the main factor is the number of years of participation. There is a learning curve that encourages people with more years of participation to speak. In fact "participation over time seems to increase participation parity" (Baiocchi, 1999, p. 10). This is a very encouraging conclusion that leads us to be optimistic about the process, especially given its conscious pedagogic aims.

This said, no data about the composition of the various mechanisms of the Citizen School itself are yet available, and therefore we cannot evaluate whether this potential problem has surfaced in the specifically school-related parts of the experiment of Porto Alegre. There are no data about the race of the participants or about whether teachers—because of their more technical "insiders' knowledge"—play more dominant roles in the various forums and councils. This is clearly worth further research.

Another potential issue needs to be mentioned. The very fact that the entire project is based on an active engagement of the citizenry could have serious consequences in terms of sustainability. Because the city adminis-tration is using citizen participation in all sites where a process of policy decision-making is necessary, the requirement for active engagement of the members of the communities is multiplying. There are dozens of sites where an active and involved citizen or activist is asked to contribute with her or his perspective. This could generate an "overload" for those who are already integrated into other sites of deliberation. How many hours can a working-class person, with two or three jobs necessary to feed her or his family, allocate to deliberative instances? Can the levels of active engage-ment with the participatory institutions be maintained over time? Our own involvement in political and educational work of this type, with the intense time commitments this requires, leads us to worry about whether such involvement can be sustained.

Yet once again, our worries are lessened by the fact that the SMED seems to be trying to deal with these potential problems proactively. We are witnessing an *increase*, not a decrease, in participation in the democratic mechanisms that have been put in place by the Popular Administration. The community agents of the city administration are constantly stimulat-ing the involvement of individuals and neighborhood associations. Be-cause the idea of participation is not isolated in the action of one secre-tariat but is something incorporated in the daily practices of the city administration as a whole, we can see an integrated effort to generate active involvement of the communities in the definitions of the directions that the city will chose to go. If it is true that this could demand too much from communities accustomed to being only the recipients of policies, and espe-cially could overload activists already involved in the existing sites of decision-making, it is also true that the city administration has an aggressive policy of actively involving and educating new participants. This policy has been more than a little successful so far. The visible results of participation—translated in the much lower dropout rate and better education for the community's children, as in the case of school councils—are the best guarantees both of maintainability and of the creation of new generations of participants.

All this should not make us overly sanguine. It is important to point out that because of the electoral success of the Popular Administration—currently in its fourth term—the previously hegemonic conservative forces have responded with renewed vigor. There has been a major reorganization of the center-right forces in the city to challenge the policies of the Workers' Party. So far these attempts have been unsuccessful. Nevertheless, one should not minimize the strength of the possible center-right coalitions that are being formed to defeat the Popular Administration and its comprehensive program of reforms. As we have seen repeatedly in other contexts, rightist movements have been able to mobilize successfully around issues of racial backlash, economic worries, and antigovernment sentiment (Apple, 1996, 2000, 2001). It remains to be seen whether such mobilizations will have any marked effect in Porto Alegre.

As a final problem, one could ask how a municipal administration has been able to implement an educational policy that clearly stands in opposition to Brazilian national policy, a policy that has been highly influenced by neoliberal impulses. Here it is important again to point to the rearticulations that have been created by the Popular Administration. Following the recipe prescribed by those who defend neoliberal practices, the structure of education in Brazil has been greatly decentralized to municipalities. As with other areas, here too the Popular Administration explored and expanded these impulses to the maximum in order to create an educational system that challenges traditional models of education that have consistently failed. In this case, there is little that the federal government can do to interfere with the project of education that is going on in Porto Alegre. However, having said this, we also recognize that currently there is an increasingly strong tendency to introduce national testing in Brazil. The combination of neoliberal and neoconservative polices that such testing entails at a national level could potentially influence the degree of autonomy of the municipalities and states in implementing dominant educational policies. This is something we shall need to follow closely in the near future.

Conclusion

In this chapter, we have sought to situate the processes of educational policy and reform into their larger sociopolitical context. We have described
the ways in which a set of policies has had what seem to be extensive and
long-lasting effects *because* they are coherently linked to larger dynamics of
social transformation and to a coherent set of polices and practices that
aim to change the mechanisms of the state and the rules of participation in
the formation of state policies. All of this has crucial implications for how
we might think about the politics of education policy and its dialectical
role in social transformation (see also Wong & Apple, this volume).

The Citizen School has been important not only as a way of giving an
impoverished population a quality education that will enable them to have
better chances in the paid labor market and at the same time operate as
empowered citizens, but also because it has generated structured forms of
"educating" the communities both for organizing around and discussing
their problems *and* for acting on their own behalf through the channels of
participation and deliberation. In the process, it has "educated" the state
agencies as well. The OP, the Municipal Congress of Education, the New
Educational Configuration of the Schools, and the school councils have—
together—helped to create the beginnings of a new reality for the excluded.
They have forged new leadership, brought about the active engagement of
the communities with the communities' own situations, and led to much
more active participation in the construction of solutions to these problems.

In spite of the potential problems we have discussed above, we are optimistic about the lasting impact of the Citizen School's democratizing initiatives and its construction of a more diverse and inclusive education. By
itself, the Citizen School has been very successful in including an entire
population that, if it were not for this project, would be out of the schools
and even further excluded in an already actively excluding society. But the
larger educative aspect of the Citizen School—empowering impoverished
communities where they are situated and transforming both the schools
and what counts as "official knowledge" there—is also of significant moment. Together with the OP (with its own cumulative effects), they represent new alternatives in the creation of an active citizenry—one that learns
from its own experiences and culture—not just for now but also for future
generations. For these very reasons, we believe that the experiences of
Porto Alegre have considerable importance not only for Brazil but also for
all of us who are deeply concerned about the effects of the neoliberal and

neoconservative restructuring of education and of the public sphere in general. There is much to learn from the successful struggles there.

Some of the other lessons we might learn from the analyses and political/cultural theories employed throughout this book are pointed to in our final chapter.

Acknowledgments

This study was made possible, in part, with funding provided by the Brazilian National Council of Scientific and Technological Development (CNPq). A different version of this chapter appeared in the *Journal of Education Policy*.

CHAPTER 9

Afterword

Michael W. Apple

The State and the Politics of Knowledge has had an ambitious agenda. One of the things it has aimed at is extending the conceptual, empirical, and historical tools I first employed in the series of volumes that preceded this one. But while an important goal, this is insufficient in itself. The book also has provided concrete examples of how such tools might be used in understanding the complexities of real situations so that we might use such understandings to further an agenda of interrupting dominance.

Taken together, these chapters carry a number of messages. The first is to "think contextually." Understanding—and acting on—the very real relations of power in any situation requires us not to apply simple formulas. This does not prevent us at all from examining major axes of differential power, such as class, gender, race, or colonial forms of domination. But it does ask us not to assume that we automatically know what these relations are beforehand. Second, think about multiple levels. That is, examine the mechanisms that link the global to the local; yet at the same time, also think about the specific relations of power at each level, ones that may not always be reducible to the automatic working out of global power onto the local. Third, while we must *never* forget the massive structuring force of the economy and class dynamics, think about multiple relations of power. More than one dynamic may be acting at a specific site: colonialism, race, and gender; class and gender; not only forms of economic domination but cultural relations of power as well. And these may not all act in the same direction. Thus things may be simultaneously progressive and retrogressive depending on their use, and they may have different effects on, say, class and on race or gender or religion. Hence, the concept of *contradiction* is crucial. Fourth, think historically. In order to understand what the limits and possibilities of social transformation are and the role that education can play in these processes, it is crucial to situate each site into the historical movements and tendencies that have been such powerful forces in bringing the present into being. Fifth, following on my last point, don't assume that education is simply a passive actor, a mirror of relations outside itself. It can and does have relative autonomy and is a critical site in the formation of both positive and negative movements and identities. Sixth, pay attention to social movements, and *not* only progressive ones but the range of progressive and retrogressive movements that provide much of the impetus behind the politics of education. Seventh, and finally, don't be satisfied with slogans—"get your hands dirty" by detailing histories, presences and absences, social movements, and real peoples' lives. Thus rhetorical skills are crucial, but we also need skills in qualitative, quantitative, historical, and textual analysis, and we decidedly need to generate evidence that cannot be easily refuted.

There is another message that stands behind a number of these chapters, one that is spoken about directly in Chapter 6, for example. This relates to the unfortunate stereotype among some scholars in education that "critical" work arising out of, say, political economy or the neo-Marxist, neo-Gramscian, or cultural studies traditions is totally incommensurate with postmodern and poststructural traditions. This is an unsustainable claim, one that is more than a little overstated. Such a position may be due to the lack of familiarity with the very interesting attempts to draw upon these two seemingly distinct kinds of traditions, or may simply be due to sloppy scholarship. But whatever the reason, work associated with issues of identity and constitutive outsides, with hybridity and multiplicity, with discourse and power, and with the state and governmentality has been and can be integrated with interests in the economy and ideology, social movements, and a more structural sense of the state—and the combination can be extremely useful in enabling us to focus on real schools, curricula, teaching, and the relations of all this to real movements and communities. Indeed, this very set of mutually self-correcting tendencies lies behind some of the work in this book. Even though there are differences between and among these traditions of critical analysis, it is where they meet and "sparks fly" that progress can be made.

As I argue at considerably greater length elsewhere (Apple, 1996, 1999), I fear that for too many people within the critical educational studies communities, having to find their way among the various tendencies and tensions among what might be called "neo" and "post" may have taken up all too much of their political/educational energies, thus causing such anguish that political or educational action may get pushed aside until the moment when there is supposed certainty about what the "correct" theoretical position is determined to be. Such a situation can be dangerous. It can sap the emotional and intellectual energies that are so very needed at a time of neoliberal and neoconservative restructuring of many of the things we hold dear.

Yet there is another, perhaps more insidious danger. This one is a bit reminiscent of Bakhtin's discussion of the function of balconies during carnival in Europe hundreds of years ago. The affluent were both attracted to and repelled by the cultural, political, and bodily transgressions that accompanied carnival. The smells, the noise, the possibility of loss of control, the undercurrent of danger, all of this was fascinating. But the bourgeoisie could not let go of their safe havens. The balcony was the creative solution. The carnival of the streets could be experienced—vicariously. The sights and smells and sounds could be safely lived—and commented upon, which also had its own politics of pleasure—from the balcony overhanging the street. One could be in and out, almost participant but mostly observer, at the same time (Stallybrass & White, 1986).

The universalism of the intellectual who stands above it all, observes, and deconstructs the positions of others has of course a long tradition in education and elsewhere. Adorno's vigorous attack on such "innocuous skepticism" is telling here. As he put it, such a standpoint "calls everything into question and criticizes nothing" (Osborne, 1996, p. xii). While there *is* much to question, my own position and that of the authors of this book has little in common with such "innocuous skepticism." Unlike, say, Karl Mannheim's view of the unattached intelligentsia where the relative classlessness of free-floating intellectuals enables them to stand aside from the political and ideological struggles of the larger society and to look at the "interest of the whole" (Osborne, 1996), I believe that we are *already* deeply positioned.[1] We must attach our criticisms to identifiable social movements that expressly aim to challenge the relations of exploitation and domination of the larger society.

This of course is easy to say but harder to do, given the multiplicity of "emancipatory" political projects and movements today. It is clear that there have been significant transformations in the political imaginary. At times, claims for the recognition of group differences have eclipsed claims for social equality. As Nancy Fraser clearly puts it in her description of the growth of identity politics and the decentering of class politics:

We are witnessing an apparent shift in the political imaginary, especially in the terms in which justice is imagined. Many actors appear
to be moving away from a socialist political imaginary, in which the
central problem of justice is redistribution, to a "postsocialist" political imaginary, in which the central problem of justice is recognition. With this shift, the most salient social movements are no
longer economically defined "classes" who are struggling to defend
their "interests," end "exploitation," and win "redistribution." Instead, they are culturally defined "groups" or "communities of
value" who are struggling to defend their "identities," end "cultural
domination," and win "recognition." The result is a decoupling of
cultural politics from social politics, and the relative eclipse of the
latter by the former. (1997, p. 2)

Fraser may be overstating the split in some ways, since many of us are
familiar with and/or participate in groups demanding (correctly) recognition who also are deeply committed to a politics of economic justice. However, there is enough truth to what she is pointing to for us to take her worries seriously.

I believe that we are increasingly faced with a false antithesis between
what might be called the "social left" and the "cultural left." One of its most
telling iterations can be seen in the *Social Text* hoax of a few years ago,
where a social left writer parodied the language and concepts employed by
many "post" authors in their analyses of the relationship between science
and power. He got it published as a serious contribution to the debates in
the journal, and only after its publication did he admit that it was a hoax.

The fact that it made national and international news says something of
great import about the eagerness of the dominant media to look for any ex-
cuse to pillory the left. But no matter what the merits of the case (as a former board member of one of *Social Text*'s editorial collectives, I have mixed
emotions here), the entire incident points to a divide that I believe is not
very useful. "While one side insists in retrograde accents that 'it's all the
economy, stupid,' the other retorts in hypersophisticated tones 'it's the culture, stupid'" (Fraser, 1997, p. 3). Both seem to evade what I and others take
to be crucial tasks: interrogating the distinction between economy and culture; understanding how both work together in complex and sometimes
contradictory ways to produce injustices; and, finally, figuring out how, "as
a prerequisite for remedying injustices, claims for recognition can be integrated with claims for redistribution in a comprehensive political project"
(Fraser, 1997, p. 3). The task before us is to combine the two, in essence to

think "about" and "across" at the same time. It is when sparks *don't* fly that there are problems. The creative tensions between and among these traditions are productive of some of the best scholarship available. Political and conceptual paralysis in the face of the question of "what's the best approach" is not very useful. A disciplined (and I don't mean this in a Foucauldian way) intersection of multiple traditions is more than a little important.

One of the tasks we have set in this book is to let the sparks fly in multiple ways: letting different traditions of critical social and cultural analysis rub against each other; pointing to the limits and possibilities of sparking social movements that can create lasting changes; illuminating the ways that education is itself a crucial actor in such social transformations. The phrase *social transformation* is a key here. In Chapter 1, I stated that all of the material included in this book is "engaged." As authors and activists, we hope that our efforts assist all of us in the process of supporting what Williams (1961) called the long revolution. And, as a number of the chapters here so eloquently document, let us remember that "long" does not equal impossible.

Notes

Chapter 1

1. A comparison is useful here. In sixteen of the Organization for Economic Development and Cooperation countries, the average rate of incarceration in 1992 to 1993 was 78 per 1,000,000 people. In the United States, it was 519 to 1,947 for African Americans and 306 for European Americans. This extraordinary disparity bears *no* relation to differences in the rate of violent crimes in these nations. See Katz (2001, pp. 16–17). Interestingly, many of the people who are in prisons in the United States are indeed working within the walls of the prisons for private companies that pay extremely low wages. This both saves the companies the cost of paying liveable wages and certainly reduces the possibility that unions would form.
2. Nancy Fraser's discussion of the gendered nature of the split between public and private spheres is very useful here. See Fraser (1989).
3. While the phrase "on offer" has become an accepted way of referring to the state's role in creating subject positions, there is a danger that accompanies such usage. It can tacitly lead to an assumption that the state—or hegemonic forces and institutions in general— "gives" such positions to passive actors, instead of individuals and groups participating in creating and taking them. My own position entails more of the latter than the former. See, for example, Apple (2000). My thanks to Marcus Weaver-Hightower for this point.
4. Indeed, in my most cynical moments, I tend to think that the only true Gramscians left are on the right. Interestingly, Gramsci's writings on the formation of hegemonic blocs and on how to disarticulate people from their previous identities and political positions and rearticulate them to new positions and identities actually has influenced rightist strategists. See Brock (2002).

Chapter 2

1. For further discussion of identity politics, see Bromley (1989). One of us has raised issues concerning the relatively uncritical appropriation of poststructural and postmodern theory but has also argued that it is crucial to let both neo-Gramscian and postmodern/poststructural positions interact with each other creatively. See, for example, Apple (1995, 1996).
2. The formation of social movements and how they are connected to ideological tensions and beliefs has received a good deal of attention historically. See, for example, Melucci, Keane, and Mier (1989), and Tarrow (1994), Tilly (1995).
3. These assumptions may not be totally the same in other nations, especially in the relative power of religious fundamentalism. Further, not all segments of the cultural and reli-

gious right agree. For ease of presentation here, however, we will gloss over some of the differences within this movement.

4. It is important not to see such positions as "irrational." For many right-wing women, for example, such a belief is wholly sensible given the conditions in which they live. DeHart (1991, p. 261) gets it exactly right when she states that: "we must recognize the screams of antifeminist women as the rational responses of people who live in a deeply gendered and profoundly precarious world—a world in which identity, social legitimacy, economic viability and moral order are deeply rooted in conventional gender categories."

5. Curtis adds domination and exploitation to this list. There is, of course, a vast literature on the state both as an arena of class, gender, and race conflict and as a contradictory assemblage of publicly financed institutions. While this is more fully discussed in Apple (1994, 1995), representative examples can be found in Evans, Rueschemeyer, and Skocpol (1985) and Jessop (1990).

6. The material in this section is drawn from Oliver (1993). This study took place over a two-year period of research on site. It included long-term and repeated observations of public and private meetings of the school board, parents, community, and protest groups, and detailed and longitudinal interviews with administrators, teachers, parents, and activists on all sides of the controversy. It also involved attending such events as press conferences, court hearings, and church services and the collection of relevant written documents, both official and unofficial.

7. We want to be cautious not to overstate our reading of the class dynamics of this situation. The new middle class is itself divided. Not all fractions of it support "invisible pedagogies" such as whole-language approaches. Bernstein (1990) hypothesizes that those members of the new middle class who work for the state are much more likely to support such loosely classified and loosely framed pedagogies than are those who work in the private sector. This, and particular professional ideologies, may partly account for the fact that most teachers (though not all) in Citrus Valley supported the whole-language emphasis found in the state guidelines and in *Impressions*.

8. This is one of the volumes in the *Impressions* series.

9. About the same time as parents first complained about the books, some teachers also brought complaints, but of a very different nature. Teachers reported that some of the stories in the books did not match the table of contents in the student anthologies. Obviously, there was a distinct possibility that the wrong books had been shipped or that there were misprints. However, as the conflict intensified, the local teachers' union became increasingly vocal in its support for the *Impressions* series and for the school district administration. Of all the groups involved in this study, teachers were the most reluctant to be interviewed. This is understandable given the tensions and fear in this situation.

10. Some aspects of how the belief in the power of the "ordinary individual" works its way out in our daily lives are discussed in greater detail in Gans (1988) and Reinarman (1987).

11. See, for example, the widely discussed and hopelessly flawed volume by Richard Herrnstein and Charles Murray, *The Bell Curve* (1994). The sponsorship of this volume and its authors by conservative foundations and these groups' ability to place the authors on highly visible media outlets are worth noting. It would be important to investigate the role of such conservative groups in sponsoring and circulating and thus helping to make publicly legitimate positions that have been discredited scientifically many times before.

12. Examples of more democratic responses can be found in Apple and Beane (1995).

Chapter 3

1. On the image and term of the "hula girl" as distinct from "hula dancer," see Desmond (1999), especially Part I.

2. My discussion of semiotics draws on the work of Roland Barthes (1972; 1977a) and Kaja Silverman (1983).

3. The *linguistic sign* for Ferdinand de Saussure (1959) has two parts: the "signifier" and the "signified." The signifier refers to a meaningful form, while the signified designates the concept which that form evokes. Within the linguistic system, the signifier would be what Saussure calls a "sound-image," that is, the image of one of those sounds that we shape within our minds when we think, whereas the signified would be the meaning that this sound-image generates. To put it differently, the signified is not "a thing" but a mental representation of the "thing" (Barthes, 1967, p. 42). The *semiological sign* is also compounded of a signifier and a signified.

4. Barthes attempted to resolve this problem in *S/Z* (1974), a publication appearing more than fifteen years after *Mythologies*.

5. The question of the determinacy or indeterminacy of meaning has become an important rallying point in American philosophical and critical debates. Jonathan Culler (1981) examines this debate in the context of American literary criticism and points out how partisans of determinate meaning, in fact, rely on an arbitrary consensus:

> If a work [or text] has in principle a determinate meaning, it is because there is something that determines it, something that is responsible for the true meaning. Unfortunately, the partisans of determinate meaning have not made much progress in determining what determines meaning. Is it the author's intention, the norms of language and genre, the comprehension of competent readers of the day? (1981, p. 14)

6. See Michael Kimmelman (1996). In terms of deflecting criticism about Barbie dolls, Erica Rand says that in the 1980s, when feminism and calls for diversity posed a threat to the status of Barbie dolls, Mattel in a clever move turned Barbie into a role model for girls by inventing "career options" and by introducing "black and Hispanic Barbies" (1995, pp. 64–68). But perhaps the most effective way to maintain control over unauthorized uses and versions of Barbie is the threat of litigation, because "Barbie" is a registered trademark of Mattel. As Mattel's vice-president for corporate communications, Sean Fitzgerald, remarked: "We're a very diverse society—Barbie respects that. But if somebody's marketing repackaged Barbies, selling them as a 'Barbie' that's trademark infringement" (Fitzgerald 1996).

7. For a discussion of primitivism, see Lovejoy and Boas (1935).

8. This is a point made by Johannes Fabian's (1983) discussion of the temporal concepts and devices used in the construction of anthropology's object.

9. Kamehameha Schools is a nonprofit, private, charitable trust created by the 1884 will of Hawaiian Princess Bernice Pauahi Bishop (Bishop Estate), great-granddaughter of King Kamehameha I, to educate children of Hawaiian ancestry.

10. The Hawaiian Promotion Committee was renamed the Hawaii Tourist Bureau in 1919, the Hawaiian Travel Bureau in 1944, and the Hawaiian Visitors Bureau in 1945. See Robert Schmitt (1977).

Chapter 4

1. Of course, some scholars studying the state and education have pointed out that schools are sites of contestation and that education systems are by no means mechanically determined by external powers such as the state and the dominant class (see, e.g., Apple, 1995, 2001). However, people working on state formation and education (Boli, 1989; Curtis, 1988; Green, 1990, 1997; Harp, 1998; Melton, 1988) have often failed to incorporate insights from these areas of literature to create more sophisticated theoretical formulations.

2. The discussion in this chapter does not go beyond 1965. This is not because we regard state formation as having been completed in that year. Instead, we believe that state formation is always an ongoing process and that the ruling regime of Singapore continued to struggle to consolidate its dominance after 1965. The post-1965 educational politics of Singapore, once it became a sovereign state and entered a new phase of state formation after "withdrawing" from Malaysia, are clearly worth further study and should be the topic of another article.

3. Because of space limitations, we have omitted many crucial struggles over the state and Chinese schools in postwar Singapore and have provided a relatively abbreviated theoretical framework of state-building and education in this chapter. Readers interested in a fuller theoretical and historical account may read T.-H. Wong (2002).

4. The constitution of the Malayan Union granted local citizenship to those born in either Singapore or the union and those who had resided in either territories for ten of the preceding fifteen years. This policy in effect gave local citizenship to almost all Chinese and Indian residents. This scheme was advanced because the British wished to give the Chinese residents a definite status and curb possible interference from the Chinese government in the affairs of those Chinese. This pro-Chinese opinion gained support in Whitehall because during the war the Chinese people were the most dedicated group resisting the Japanese while the Malays collaborated with the enemy. Singapore was excluded from the Malay Union because the British wanted to preserve it as a free port and naval base. Also, by leaving out Singapore, the British hoped that the Malays, who would still be the numerical majority in the union, would consider the scheme palatable. On the controversy over the Malayan Union, see Allen (1967), Cheah (1978); Lau (1989; 1991); and Sopiee (1974).

5. For instance, Adkins had judged that the only way to resolve the problem of Chinese schools was to replace them with English institutions (CO 825/90/7; CO 1022/285). The British colonial bureaucrats in Singapore and the peninsula had this anti-Chinese disposition chiefly because, considering the Malays as the only indigenous group, they had put very minimum effort into learning Chinese language and culture. For the formation of this anti-Chinese attitude, see Allen (1970).

6. Before automatic registration, the number of registered voters was very small and the majority of the electorate were Indians. After that, the electorate increased from 76,000 to 300,299 and the Chinese became predominant (Yeo, 1973b, pp. 256 and 259).

7. On the responses of some mainstream Chinese education bodies, such as the Singapore Chinese Middle School Teacher Association and the Chinese School Management/Staff Association, see related reports from *Sin Chew Jit Poh,* March 1 and 6, and April 4, 1956.

8. In 1958 the government needed to reschedule the Senior III examination so that the timings of these two tests would not be too close and candidates from English schools sitting for both the COSCE and the Senior III would have enough time for preparation (SCJP, April 21, 1958). This decision of the government implied that the two exams had different requirements.

9. Monthly Reports by Chief Inspector of Chinese Schools, April 1955, SCA (declassified files, Secretary for Chinese Affairs, Singapore) 15/5.

10. For more on the admission policy of the Nanyang University, see *Sin Chew Jit Poh* (January 26, 1956), Nanyang University (1956, pp. 195–199), and Ting-Hong Wong (2000). For the China-oriented inclination of this university, one can check the backgrounds of its professors from pages 189–191 of Nanyang University (1956).

11. The word "Malaya" referred to the geographical region of the Malay Peninsula.

12. Under pressure from the Indian government, the colonial state in British Malaya enacted the Labour Code of 1923, which stipulated that rubber plantations provide schools for children of Tamil workers. Many plantation owners dismissed this legislation as a shifting

of public responsibility that should rightly belong to the state, and responded halfheartedly by installing a rudimentary form of schools. See Loh (1975, pp. 44–47 and 102) and Ponniah (1968, p. 97).

13. *First Education Triennial Survey, 1955–1957* (1959), p. 37. About the background of the UCLES, its role in consolidating imperial power, its connection with the colonial office, and its adjustment to the postwar era of decolonization, see Stockwell (1990).

14. The table of contents of the history series of the World Bookstore was available in *Special Issue for the Twentieth Anniversary of Nan Chiau Girls' High School* (1967, pp. 108–110).

15. The sixth form is part of the British system. It is a two-year course to prepare students who have completed secondary education for the entrance examination of universities.

16. In 1961, the government replaced the old Senior Middle III exam with these two exams.

17. One indicator for the development of this kind of partnership relation was the installation of the Singapore Advisory Committee of the UCLES in May 1960. This advisory committee consisted of representatives from both the Ministry of Education in Singapore and the UCLES, and its function was to cooperate in the administration of local Cambridge exams (MEAR, 1960, p. 7).

Chapter 5

1. See Prop. 1978/79:180 (1978–1979), SOU 1985:30 (1985), Kirke- og undervisningsdepartementet (1974), Kirke- og undervisningsdepartementet (1987), and Utbildningsdepartementet (1980).

2. Apple revises and deepens his analysis in *Educating the "Right" Way* (2001), where he refers to "conservative modernization" as having an additional element—the managerial focus of a particular fraction of the professional and managerial new middle class.

3. Some central official documents introducing educational reforms in Sweden and Norway in the 1990s not directly cited in the text include: Kirke-, utdannings- og forskningsdepartementet (1994; 1996), NOU 1995:9 (1995), NOU 1997:25 (1997), Prop.1988/89:4 (1988–1989), Prop.1990/91:18 (1990–1991), Prop.1991/92:75 (1991–1992), Prop.1992/ 93:220 (1992–1993a), Prop. 1992/93:230 (1992–1993b), Prop.1993/94:183 (1993–1994), Royal Ministry of Education, Research and Church Affairs (1994), Utbildningsdepartementet (1980), SOU 1985:30 (1985), SOU 1990:22 (1990), SOU 1992:94 (1992), SOU 1993:2 (1993), SOU 1993:47 (1993), St.meld. 43 (1988–1989), St.meld. 37 (1990–1991), St.meld. 33 (1991–1992), St.meld. 4 (1992–1993), St.meld. 40 (1992–1993), St.meld. 29 (1994–1995), and St.meld. 47 (1995–1996). For important discussions of educational reforms and reform strategy in Sweden in the 1990s not directly cited in the text, see Ball and Larsson (1989); Berg, Englund, and Lindblad (1995); Carlgren and Kallòs (1997); Dahllöf (1996); Englund (1994; 1995; 1996); Kallòs and Lindblad (1994); and Petterson and Wallin (1995).

Chapter 6

1. The work of the Subaltern Studies Group in India is important in this regard (Parlo Singh, personal communication).

2. Of course, even the use of such phrases as "different contexts" risks naturalizing and exoticizing the distinction.

3. A word on our use of the term "hegemonic project" is necessary here. Like most nations, the state in South Korea is structured both horizontally and vertically. Because of this, we should not assume total unanimity on policies within the state. Horizontally, the Department of Employment may have differences with the Department of Education over the

specific relationship between education and the economy and over the specific policies which regulate it. Thus, even before the current crisis, there were indications of uncertainty about the future directions of education and training policies, although there did seem to be agreement that the pressure to engage in a massive expansion of higher education had to be stemmed. Vertically, there is no guarantee that policies emanating from the central departments will be followed in the manner their proponents advocate. Instead, such policies will be highly mediated, transformed, or resisted to varying extents as they proceed downward through regional and local state institutions and actors. Thus our use of the term "hegemonic project" is grounded in a recognition that the state education policies ultimately generated and acted upon are themselves often based on complex compromises and alliances within the state itself.

4. Further discussions of the methodology of data collection can be found in M. Cho (1997). Of the two authors of this chapter, Cho is Korean. She has spent considerable time investigating how the realities of gender and class work their ways out in the daily lives of Korean students and on how this should be thought about. Apple has lectured widely in Korea and has repeatedly worked with critical scholars and educators there on issues related to critical educational theory, policy, and practice. The data for this chapter were collected by Cho. The theory and interpretations were the result of joint discussions and deliberations over two years.

5. The 3D phenomenon refers to manual labor jobs that are difficult, dangerous, and dirty and that are to be avoided.

6. Some scholars who have been influenced by Foucault may actually be employing Foucauldian terms to make what are basically Parsonian claims about teachers' uses of normative judgments. It is important to use Foucault appropriately and to avoid smuggling in older theories of social control and functionalism under a new language (Frances Schrag, personal communication).

7. On average, a blue-collar worker's total monthly wage was about 75 percent of that of a white-collar worker. Female workers were paid 55.2 percent of male workers' wages (Kli, 1994; Lee, 1995). However, there was also a significant wage differential between large and small factories. When students said that they would go to factories to make money, they meant big factories.

8. Since experience is not social reality itself but is discursively constructed, there is serious debate about whether people's experience is a solid foundation for the construction of their subjectivities. For more on this issue, see Clough (1993) and Scott (1986).

9. The great majority of female students wanted to continue their work after marriage. Many of them considered home and marriage as gender-oppressive sites. See D.M. Cho (1996) for further analysis of the issue of self-employment and educational and gender differences.

10. The problem of how to regulate the ambitions of working-class and lower-middle-class students is of course a very real problem in many societies. Indeed, the power of the idea of self-employment as an escape route from bosses and from many forms of discrimination is well recognized in industrial sociology and in sociological studies of the paid labor process. There are significant similarities between the responses of students studied here and those found in previous research in "Western" contexts. However, although similar in many ways, the gender specificities seem to be more pronounced, as was the salience of "mental labor" and the dream of owning one's own business. This relates to the speckled histories of class relations and paid employment, of agricultural labor and the relationship between big capital and other forms of business, state policies, patriarchal structures, and colonization. The very meaning of these similarities and differences requires further study. However they are studied, it should be clear that, in the context of South Korea, concepts such as resistance once again not only take on all of the rich and contradictory tendencies and meanings they have had in the history of their use in "Western" contexts,

but also require even more nuanced and historically grounded analyses to be understood in "different contexts."

Chapter 7

1. "True education" is the umbrella under which democratic and socially critical educators in Korea have united. It has been a major rallying cry for democratic social movements and for the independent teachers union. Its elements include a critically participatory emphasis, knowledge related to the pressing social and political problems and the national history of the people of Korea, and a clear commitment to extending democracy into all spheres of public life.
2. This document can be accessed at http://sociedu.njoyschool.net but needs Korean language characters to gain access.
3. For further discussion of the uses of and debates over discussion methods in social studies teaching, see Evans (1997), Hemmings (2000), Hess (1998), Larson (1997), and Lockwood (1985). See also Ladson-Billings (1994) on connecting important issues in classrooms to the lived cultures and histories of students.
4. We do not want to naturalize and uncritically accept the tenets of what has been called "critical pedagogy." There is, of course, serious debate about the power relations involved in this kind "emancipatory" education. See, for example, Luke and Gore (1992). For other arguments about the possible weaknesses of some of the literature on critical pedagogy, see Apple (2001).
5. For a more varied range of students and their resistance to other forms of curriculum and teaching in Korea, see the chapter by Cho and Apple in this book.
6. This says something about the dangers of the "genetic fallacy" in critical perspectives. The fact that a procedure such as, say, performance assessment comes both from dominant groups and from perspectives in government does not mean that its use is always guaranteed to uphold dominance. While there is a danger of romanticizing this situation, dominant procedures may embody contradictory tendencies and may create spaces for oppositional work that they cannot control. See, for example, Apple (2000, 2001).

Chapter 8

1. This and all other translations of Brazilian sources are ours.
2. Apart from the public system of education, there are innumerous private schools at all levels (preschool, elementary, middle, high, and college); they enroll almost 10 percent of all Brazilian students in elementary schools.
3. Elementary education is understood here as grades 1 to 8 and high school education as grades 9 to 11. Brazil has 11 grades of school education (plus early childhood education for children from zero to six years old).
4. There are two municipal high schools, but there is no intention of building more of them. They are a legacy of previous administrations.

Chapter 9

1. I do not want to give the impression that this makes Mannheim's work irrelevant for critical educational research. This would be decidedly incorrect. See Whitty (2002) for a clear discussion of Mannheim's continuing importance.

References

Aasen, P. (1994). "Bærekraftig Pedagogikk. Pedagogiske Og Utdanningspolitiske Utfordringer I Velferdsstaten." In P. Aasen and O.K. Haugaløkken (eds.), *Bærekraftig Pedagogikk. Identitet Og Kompetanse I Dr Moderne Samfunnet* (pp. 268–302). Oslo, Norway: Ad Notam Gyldendal.

———. (1997). "Refleksiv Pedagogikk." In J.C. Jacobsen (ed.), *Refleksive Læreprocesser* (pp. 37–59). Copenhagen, Denmark: Politisk Revy.

———. (1999). "Det Sosialdemokratiske Prosjektet. Utdanningsreformer I Sverige Og Norge I Etterkrigstiden." In A.O. Telhaug and P. Aasen (eds.), *Både—Og. 90-Tallets Utdanningsreformer I Historisk Perspektiv* (pp. 13–64). Oslo, Norway: Cappelen Akademisk Forlag.

Abers, R. (1998). "From Clientelism to Cooperation: Local Government, Participatory Policy and Civic Organizing in Porto Alegre, Brazil." *Politics & Society,* 26 (4), pp. 511–537.

Ahmed, S. (1998). "Tanning the Body: Skin, Color, and Gender." *New Formations* 34, pp. 28–42.

Allen, J.V. (1967). *The Malayan Union.* New Haven, CT: Yale University, Southeast Asia Studies Monograph.

———. (1970). "Malayan Civil Service, 1874–1941: Colonial Bureaucracy/Malayan Elite." *Comparative Studies in Society and History,* 12 (1), pp. 149–187.

Amelsvoort, H.V., and J. Schereens. (1996). "Decentralization in Education in Seven European Countries and States." Paper presented at ECER meeting in Seville, Spain.

Ansvaret för Skolan, Government Bill no. 18 199/91, Sveriges Riksdag (1990–1991).

Apple, M.W. (1986). *Teachers and Texts: A Political Economy of Class and Gender Relations in Education.* New York: Routledge & Kegan Paul.

———. (1990). *Ideology and Curriculum.* (2nd ed.) New York: Routledge (original work published 1979).

———. (1993). "The Politics of Official Knowledge: Does a National Curriculum Make Sense?" *Teachers College Record,* 95, pp. 222–241.

———. (1993). "Series Editor's Introduction." In C. McCarthy and W. Crichlow (eds.), *Race, Identity, and Representation in Education* (pp. vii–ix). New York: Routledge.

———. (1994). "Texts and Contexts: The State and Gender in Educational Policy." *Curriculum Inquiry,* 24, pp. 349–359.

———. (1995). *Education and Power.* (2nd ed.) New York: Routledge.

———. (1996). *Cultural Politics and Education.* New York: Teachers College Press.

———. (1996a). *Cultural Politics and Education.* New York: Teachers College Press.

———. (1996b). "Power, Meaning and Identity: Critical Sociology of Education in the United States." *British Journal of Sociology of Education,* 17 (2), pp. 125–144.

———. (1997). "Justifying the Conservative Restoration: Morals, Genes, and Education Policy." *Educational Policy,* 11 (2), pp. 167–182.

———. (1999). *Power, Meaning, and Identity.* New York: Peter Lang.

———. (2000). *Official Knowledge: Democratic Education in a Conservative Age.* (2nd ed.) New York: Routledge.

———. (2001). *Educating the "Right" Way: Markets, Standards, God, and Inequality.* New York: RoutledgeFalmer.

———. (2001a). *Educating the "Right" Way: Markets, Standards, God, and Inequality.* New York: RoutledgeFalmer.

———. (2001b). "Standards, Subject Matter, and a Romantic Past." *Educational Policy,* 15 (2), pp. 323–333.

Apple, M.W., and J.A. Beane (eds.). (1995). *Democratic Schools.* Alexandria, VA: Association for Supervision and Curriculum Development.

Apple, M.W., and J.A. Beane (eds.). (1998). *Democratic Schools: Lessons from the Chalk Face.* Buckingham, England: Open University Press.

Apple, M.W., and L.K. Christian-Smith. (1991). *The Politics of the Textbook.* New York: Routledge.

Apple, M.W., and L. Weis (eds.). (1983). *Ideology and Practice in Schooling.* Philadelphia, PA: Temple University Press.

Archer, M. (1995). "The Neglect of the Educational Systems by Bernstein." In A. Sadovnik (ed.), *Knowledge and Pedagogy: The Sociology of Basil Bernstein* (pp. 211–235). Norwood, NJ: Ablex Publishing.

Arnot, M. (2002). *Reproducing Gender?* New York: Routledge.

Arnot, M., M. David, and G. Weiner. (1999). *Closing the Gender Gap: Postwar Education and Social Change.* Cambridge, England: Polity Press.

Arnot, M., and J. Dillabough (eds.). (2000). *Challenging Democracy.* New York: Routledge.

Aronowitz, S., and H. Giroux. (1992). *Postmodern Education: Politics, Culture and Social Criticism.* Minneapolis, MN: University of Minnesota Press.

Ashley, B. (1996, December 19). "Barbie Goes Ba-a-Ad." *USA Today,* p. 7A.

Avritzer, L. (1999). *Public Deliberation at the Local Level: Participatory Budgeting in Brazil.* Mimeo.

Azevedo, J.C. (1998). "Escola Cidadã: Construção Coletiva E Participação Popular." In L.H. Silva (ed.), *A Escola Cidadã No Contexto Da Globalização* (pp. 308–319). Petrópolis, Brazil: Vozes.

———. (1999). "A Democratização Da Escola No Contexto Da Democratização Do Estado: A Experiência De Porto Alegre." In L.H. Silva (ed.), *Escola Cidadã: Teoria E Prática* (pp. 12–30). Petrópolis, Brazil: Vozes.

———. (2000). *Escola Cidadã: Desafios, Diálogos E Travessias.* Petrópolis, Brazil: Vozes.

Baiocchi, G. (1999). *Participation, Activism, and Politics: The Porto Alegre Experiment and Deliberative Democratic Theory.* Mimeo.

Baldwin, J. (1899). *Our New Possessions: Cuba, Puerto Rico, Hawaii, Philippines.* New York: American Book Company.

Ball, S., R. Bowe, and S. Gerwitz. (1994). "Market Forces and Parental Choice." In S. Thomlinson (ed.), *Educational Reform and Its Consequences.* London: IPPR/Rivers Oram Press.

Ball, S.J. (1990). *Politics and Policymaking in Education: Explorations in Policy Sociology.* London: Routledge.

———. (1994). *Education Reform: A Critical and Post-Structural Approach.* Buckingham, England: Open University Press.

Ball, S.J., and S. Larsson (eds.). (1989). *The Struggle for Democratic Education: Equality and Participation in Sweden.* New York: Falmer Press.

Barbie Nation: An Unauthorized Tour [television series episode]. (1998). Stern, S. (Producer). American Documentary, Inc. (Producer), *P.O.V.* New York: Public Broacasting Service.

Barthes, R. (1967). *Elements of Semiology* (trans. by A. Lavers and C. Smith). London: Cape Editions (original work published 1964).

————. (1972). *Mythologies* (trans. by A. Lavers). London: Paladin (original work published 1957).

————. (1974). *S/Z* (trans. by R. Miller). New York: Hill & Wang.

————. (1977a). "The Death of the Author." (trans. by S. Heath). In *Image-Music-Text* (pp. 142–48). New York: Hill & Wang (original work published 1968).

————. (1977b). "The Rhetoric of the Image." (trans. by S. Heath). In *Image-Music-Text* (pp. 32–51). New York: Hill & Wang (original work published 1968).

Baudet, E.H.P. (1965). *Paradise on Earth: Some Thoughts on European Images of Non-European Man* (trans. by E. Wentholt). Westport, CT: Greenwood Press.

Beck, U. (1992). *Risk Society: Towards a New Modernity.* London: Sage Publications.

Bedlington, S.S. (1978). *Malaysia and Singapore: The Building of New States.* Ithaca, NY: Cornell University Press.

Berg, G. (1992). "Changes in Steering of Swedish Schools: A Step Towards 'Ossification of the State.'" *Journal of Curriculum Studies,* 24 (4), pp. 327–344.

Berg, G., L. Brettell, E. Lindskog, U. Nytell, M. Söderström, and M. Yttergren. (1987). *Skolans Arbetsorganisation—Vad Er Det?* Lund, Sweden: Studentlitteratur.

Berg, G., T. Englund, and S. Lindblad (eds.). (1995). *Kunskap—Organisation—Demokrati. Vänbok Till Erik Wallin.* Lund, Sweden: Studentlitteratur.

Berkwitz, D. (1990, August 13). "Finally, Barbie Doll Ads Go Ethnic." *Newsweek,* p. 48.

Bernstein, B. (1977). *Class, Codes and Control (Volume 3: Towards a Theory of Educational Transmissions).* (rev. ed.) London: Routledge & Kegan Paul.

————. (1986). "On Pedagogic Discourse." In J. Richardson (ed.), *Handbook of Theory and Research for Sociology of Education* (pp. 205–240). New York: Greenwood Press.

————. (1990). *The Structuring of Pedagogic Discourse.* New York: Routledge.

————. (1996). *Pedagogy, Symbolic Control, and Identity: Theory, Research, Critique.* London: Taylor & Francis.

Bernstein, B., and J. Solomon. (1999). "Pedagogy, Identity, and the Construction of a Theory of Symbolic Control." *British Journal of Sociology of Education,* 20 (2), pp. 265–279.

Bhabha, H.K. (1994). *The Location of Culture.* London: Routledge.

Bird of Paradise [motion picture]. (1932). Selznick, D.O., and K. Vidor (Producers), and K. Vidor (Director). United States: RKO Radio Pictures.

Boli, J. (1989). *New Citizens for a New Society.* Elmford, NY: Pergamon Press.

Bougainville, L. (1967). *A Voyage Round the World* (trans. by J.R. Forster). Amsterdam, Holland: N. Israel (reprint of 1772 ed.).

Bourdieu, P. (1984). *Distinction: A Social Critique of the Judgment of Taste.* Cambridge, MA: Harvard University Press.

————. (1996). *The State Nobility: Elite Schools in the Field of Power* (trans. by L. C. Clough). Stanford, CA: Stanford University Press.

————. (1998). *Acts of Resistance: Against the Tyranny of the Market.* New York: New Press.

Bowles, S., and H. Gintis. (1986). *Democracy and Capitalism.* New York: Basic Books.

Brock, D. (2002). *Blinded by the Right.* New York: Crown Publishers.

Bromley, H. (1989). "Identity Politics and Critical Pedagogy." *Educational Theory,* 39, pp. 207–223.

Bromley, H., and M.W. Apple (eds.). (1998). *Education/Technology/Power.* Albany, NY: State University of New York Press.

Broude, N., and M. Garrard (eds.). (1992). *The Expanding Discourse: Feminism and Art History.* New York: Harper Collins Publishers.

Brown, D. (1982). *Hawaii Recalls: Selling Romance to America.* Honolulu, HI: Editions Limited.

Burris, J. (2001, February 11). "Hawai'i Could Set Example for World." *Honolulu Advertiser,* p. B1.

Butler, J.P. (1993). *Bodies That Matter: On the Discursive Limits of "Sex."* New York: Routledge.

Carlgren, I. (1995). "National Curriculum as Social Compromise or Discursive Politics? Some Reflections on a Curriculum Making Process." *Journal of Curriculum Studies*, 27 (4), pp. 411–430.

Carlgren, I., and D. Kallós. (1997). "Lessons from a Comprehensive School System for Curriculum Theory and Research: Sweden Revisited after Twenty Years." *Journal of Curriculum Studies*, 29 (4), pp. 407–430.

Carlson, D., and M.W. Apple (eds.). (1998). *Power/Knowledge/Pedagogy*. Boulder, CO: Westview Press.

Carnoy, M., and J. McDonell. (1990). "School District Restructuring in Santa Fe, New Mexico." *Educational Policy*, 4 (1), pp. 49–64.

Carter, P. (1987). *The Road to Botany Bay: An Exploration of Landscape and History*. Chicago: University of Chicago Press.

Cheah, B.K. (1978). "Malayan Chinese and the Citizenship Issue, 1945–1948." *Review of Indonesia and Malayan Affairs*, 12 (2), pp. 95–122.

———. (1981). "Sino-Malay Conflicts in Malaya, 1945–1946: Communist Vendetta and Islamic Resistance." *Journal of Southeast Asian Studies*, 12 (1), pp. 108–117.

———. (1983). *Red Star over Malaya: Resistance and Social Conflict during and after the Japanese Occupation of Malaya, 1941–1946*. (2nd ed.) Singapore: Singapore University Press.

———. (1997). "Writing Indigenous History in Malaysia: A Survey on Approaches and Problems." *Crossroads: An Interdisciplinary Journal of Southeast Asian Studies*, 10 (2), pp. 33–81.

Cho, D.M. (1994a). "Han-Kook-Kae-Keup-Koo-Jo-Euy Byun-Wha: Kae-Keup-Koo-Jo-Euy Yang-Keuk-Wah-Euy Go-Chal [The Change of Korean Class Structure: The Examination of Class Polarization]." *Korean Journal of Sociology*, 28, pp. 17–50.

———. (1994b). "Petite-Bourgeoisie-Euy Kae-Keup-Juk Sung-Gyuk-Kwha Jae-Sang-San-Kwha-Jeong [The Class Nature and Reproduction Process of the Petite Bourgeoisie]." *Kyung-jae-wha Sahooy [Economy and Society]*, 23, pp. 20–44.

———. (1996). "[Petite-Bourgeoisie and Class Mobility]." Working paper [in Korean].

Cho, M. (1997). *School, Work and Subjectivity: An Ethnographic Study of Two South Korean Commercial High Schools*. Unpublished Ph.D. dissertation, University of Wisconsin-Madison.

Chui, K. (1989). *Changing National Identity of Malayan Chinese*. Xiamen, Fujian: Xiamen University Press.

Chung Nam Provincial School Board. (1991). *The Basic Data for Career Education: High School*. Chung Nam: Chung Nam Provincial School Board.

Clarke, J., and J. Newman. (1997). *The Managerial State*. London: Sage Publications.

Clough, P.T. (1993). "On the Brink of Deconstructing Sociology: Critical Reading of Dorothy Smith's Standpoint Epistemology." *The Sociological Quarterly*, 34, pp. 169–182.

Connell, R.W. (1995). *Masculinities*. Berkeley, CA: University of California Press.

Corrigan, P.R.D., and D. Sayer. (1985). *The Great Arch: English State Formation as Cultural Revolution*. Oxford, England: Blackwell.

Cuban, L. (1990). "Reforming Again, Again and Again." *Educational Researcher*, 19 (1), p. 3.

Culler, J. (1981). "Issues in Contemporary American Critical Debate." In I. Konigsberg (ed.), *American Criticism in the Poststructuralist Age*. Ann Arbor, MI: University of Michigan Press.

Curtis, B. (1988). *Building the Educational State: Canada West, 1836–1871*. Philadelphia, PA: Falmer Press/Althouse Press.

Curtis, B. (1992). *True Government by Choice Men? Inspection, Education, and State Formation in Canada West*. Toronto, Canada: University of Toronto Press.

Dahllöf, U. (1996). "Reformpolitik Och Pedagogisk Forskning I Norge Och Sverige. Notiser Om Svenska Erfarenheter Och Norska Möjligheter." In P. Haug (ed.), *Pedagogikk I Ei Reformtid* (pp. 99–123). Volda, Norway: Høgskulen i Volda/Norges Forskningsråd.

Dale, R. (1989). *The State and Education Policy.* Milton Keynes, England: Open University Press.

DeHart, J.S. (1991). "Gender on the Right: Behind the Existential Scream." *Gender and History,* 3, p. 261.

DelFattore, J. (1992). *What Johnny Shouldn't Read: Textbook Censorship in America.* New Haven, CT: Yale University Press.

Derrida, J. (1982). *Margins of Philosophy* (trans. by A. Bass). Chicago: University of Chicago Press.

Desmond, J. (1999). *Staging Tourism: Bodies on Display from Waikiki to Sea World.* Chicago: University of Chicago Press.

Dewey, J. (1916). *Democracy and Education.* New York: Macmillan.

Dillon, J.T. (1994). *Using Discussion in the Classroom.* Philadelphia, PA: Open University Press.

Dimitriadis, G., and C. McCarthy. (2001). *Reading and Teaching the Postcolonial: From Baldwin to Basquiat and Beyond.* New York: Teachers College Press.

Donald, J. (1992). *Sentimental Education: Schooling, Popular Culture, and the Regulation of Liberty.* London: Verso.

Dore, R.P. (1976). *The Diploma Disease: Education, Qualification, and Development.* Berkeley, CA: University of California Press.

Ducille, A. (1994). "Dyes and Dolls: Multicultural Barbie and the Merchandising of Difference." *differences,* 6 (1), pp. 46–68.

Dyer, R. (1997). *White.* New York: Routledge.

Edmond, R. (1997). *Representing the South Pacific: Colonial Discourse from Cook to Gauguin.* New York: Cambridge University Press.

Ee, J. (1961). "Chinese Migration to Singapore, 1896–1941." *Journal of Southeast Asian History,* 2 (1), pp. 33–51.

Eide, K. (1995a). "Educational Research Policy in the Nordic Countries: Historical Perspectives and a Look Ahead." In A. Tuijnman and E. Wallin (eds.), *School Research at the Crossroads: Swedish and Nordic Perspectives* (pp. 49–62). Stockholm: Stockholm Institute of Education Press.

———. (1995b). *Økonomi Og Utdanningspolitikk.* Oslo, Norway: Utredningsinstituttet for Forskning og Høyere Utdanning.

Eisenman, S. (1996). "Triangulating Racism." *Art Bulletin,* 78 (4), pp. 603–609.

Eliason, L.C. (1989). "School Reform between Rationality and Politics: Expertise and Experimentation as Strategies of Conflict Management in Sweden and the Federal Republic of Germany." Paper presented at the annual meeting of the American Educational Research Association in San Francisco.

En Ny Läroplan för Grundskolan Och Ett Nytt Betygsystem för Grundkolan, Sameskolan, Specialskolan Och Den Obligatoriska Särskolan, Government Bill no. 220 1992/93, Sveriges Riksdag (1992–1993).

Englund, T. (1994). "Education as Citizenship Right—A Concept in Transition: Sweden Related to Other Western Democracies and Political Philosophy." *Journal of Curriculum Studies,* 26 (4), pp. 383–399.

——— (ed.). (1995). *Utdanningspolitiskt Systemskifte?* Stockholm: HLS Förlag.

———. (1996). "The Public and the Text." *Journal of Curriculum Studies,* 28 (1), pp. 1–35.

Epstein, D., and R. Johnson. (1998). *Schooling Sexualities.* Buckingham, England: Open University Press.

Evans, E.J. (1997). *Thatcher and Thatcherism.* New York: Routledge.

Evans, P.B., D. Rueschemeyer, and T. Skocpol. (1985). *Bringing the State Back In.* Cambridge, England: Cambridge University Press.

Evans, R.W. (1997). "Teaching Social Issues: Implementing an Issues-Centered Curriculum." In E.W. Ross (ed.), *The Social Studies Curriculum: Purposes, Problems, and Possibilities* (pp. 197–212). Albany, NY: State University of New York Press.

Ezzy, D. (1997). "Subjectivity and the Labour Process." *Sociology,* 31, pp. 422–444.

Fabian, J.R. (1983). *Time and the Other: How Anthropology Makes Its Object.* New York: Columbia University Press.

Fine, M., L. Weis, L. Powell, and L.M. Wong (eds.). (1997). *Off White.* New York: Routledge.

Fitzgerald, S. (1972). *China and the Overseas Chinese: A Study of Peking's Changing Policy, 1949–1970.* Cambridge, England: Cambridge University Press.

———. (1996). "Hooker Barbie a Hot Seller," *The Capital Times,* December 18.

Fodor, E. (ed.). (1961). *Hawaii 1961.* New York: David McKay Company.

Foley, K. (1997, July 25). "Barbie Sendup Is Riotous, Naughty Bit." *Los Angeles Times,* p. F25.

Foucault, M. (1972). *The Archaeology of Knowledge.* New York: Pantheon Books.

———. (1977). *Discipline and Punish: The Birth of the Prison* (trans. by A. Sheridan). New York: Pantheon Books.

———. (1977a). *Discipline and Punish: The Birth of the Prison* (trans. by A. Sheridan). New York: Pantheon Books.

———. (1977b). *Language, Counter-Memory, Practice.* Ithaca, NY: Cornell University Press.

———. (1980). *Power/Knowledge.* New York: Pantheon Books.

Fraser, N. (1989). *Unruly Practices: Power, Discourse, and Gender in Contemporary Social Theory.* Minneapolis: University of Minnesota Press.

———. (1997). *Justice Interruptus.* New York: Routledge.

Freire, P. (1970). *Pedagogy of the Oppressed.* New York: Herder & Herder.

Freire, P. (1988). "O Partido Como Educador-Educando." In A. Damasceno, et al. (ed.), *A Educação Como Ato Político Partidário* (pp. 16–18). São Paulo, Brazil: Cortez.

Freitas, A.L.S. (1999). "Projeto Constituinte Escolar: A Vivência Da 'Reinvenção Da Escola' Na Rede Municipal De Porto Alegre." In L.H. Silva (ed.), *Escola Cidadã: Teoria E Prática* (pp. 31–45). Petrópolis, Brazil: Vozes.

Furre, B. (1991). *Vårt Århundre. Norsk Historie 1905–1990.* Oslo, Norway: Det Norske Samlaget.

Gandin, L.A. (1994). "Qualidade Total Em Educação: A Fala Mansa Do Neoliberalismo." *Revista de Educação—AEC,* 23 (92), pp. 75–80.

———. (1998). "Para Onde a Escola Está Sendo Levada? (Ou a Escola Pode Ser Levada Para Algum Lugar Diferente Daquele Que O Projeto Hegemônico Quer?)." *Revista de Educação—AEC,* 27 (107), pp. 9–16.

———. (1999). "A Educação Escolar Como Produto De Marketing: Processo Natural?" *Revista de Educação—AEC,* 28 (112), pp. 33–39.

Gans, H.J. (1988). *Middle American Individualism: The Future of Liberal Democracy.* New York: Free Press.

Genro, T. (1999). "Cidadania, Emancipação E Cidade." In L.H. Silva (ed.), *Escola Cidadã: Teoria E Prática* (pp. 7–11). Petrópolis, Brazil: Vozes.

Gilbert, D. (1999). "London in All Its Glory—or How to Enjoy London: Guidebook Representations of Imperial London." *Journal of Historical Geography,* 25 (3), pp. 279–297.

Giroux, H. (1995). "Insurgent Multiculturalism and the Promise of Pedagogy." In D.T. Goldberg (ed.), *Multiculturalism: A Critical Reader* (pp. 325–343). Cambridge, MA: Blackwell.

Giroux, H., and R.I. Simon. (1989). *Popular Culture, Schooling and Everyday Life.* New York: Bergin & Garvey.

Gopinathan, S. (1974). *Towards a National System of Education in Singapore, 1945–1973.* Singapore: Oxford University Press.

Gramsci, A. (1971). *Selections from the Prison Notebooks.* London: Lawrence & Wishart.

Granger, J. (1934, December). "Hawaiian Medley." *Vanity Fair,* 43 (4), pp. 42–45, 62.

Green, A. (1990). *Education and State Formation: The Rise of Education Systems in England, France, and the USA.* New York: St. Martin's Press.

———. (1994). "Education and State Formation Revisited." *History of Education Review,* 23 (3), pp. 1–17.

———. (1997). *Education, Globalization, and the Nation State.* London: Macmillan.

Griffin, C. (1985). *Typical Girls? Young Women from School to the Job Market.* London: Routledge & Kegan Paul.

Hall, S. (1985). "Signification, Representation, Ideology: Althusser and the Post-Structuralist Debates." *Critical Studies in Mass Communication,* 2, pp. 91–114.

———. (1988). "The Toad in the Garden: Thatcherism among the Theorists." In G. Nelson and L. Grossberg (eds.), *Marxism and the Interpretation of Culture* (pp. 35–57). Urbana, IL: University of Illinois Press.

———. (1992). "Cultural Studies and Its Theoretical Legacies." In L. Grossberg, C. Nelson, and P. A. Treichler (eds.), *Cultural Studies* (pp. 277–294). New York: Routledge.

———. (1996). "On Postmodernism and Articulation: An Interview with Stuart Hall—Edited by Lawrence Grossberg." In D. Morley and K. Chen (eds.), *Stuart Hall—Critical Dialogues in Cultural Studies* (pp. 131–150). London: Routledge.

Hannah, M. (2000). *Governmentality and the Mastery of Territory in Nineteenth-Century America.* New York: Cambridge University Press.

Hargreaves, A. (1994). *Changing Teachers, Changing Times: Teachers' Work and Culture in the Postmodern Age.* London: Cassell.

Harp, S.L. (1998). *Learning to Be Loyal: Primary Schooling as Nation Building in Alsace and Lorraine, 1850–1940.* DeKalb, IL: Northern Illinois University Press.

Healy, M. (2000, February 14). "Barbie Gets a New Smile and a New Bellybutton." *Honolulu Advertiser,* p. C5.

Hemmings, A. (2000). "High School Democratic Dialogues: Possibilities for Praxis." *American Educational Research Journal,* 37 (1), pp. 67–91.

Herrnstein, R.J., and C.A. Murray. (1994). *The Bell Curve: Intelligence and Class Structure in American Life.* New York: Free Press.

Hess, D. (1998). *Discussing Controversial Public Issues in Secondary Social Studies Classrooms: Learning from Skilled Teachers.* Unpublished Ph.D. Dissertation, University of Washington, Seattle.

Hobsbawm, E. (1994). *The Age of Extremes.* New York: Pantheon Books.

Hogan, D. (1982). "Education and Class Formation." In M.W. Apple (ed.), *Cultural and Economic Reproduction in Education* (pp. 32–78). Boston: Routledge & Kegan Paul.

Hong, D.S. (1983). "Jik-up-Boon-Suk-Eul Tong-Han Kae-Cheung-Yon-Koo: Han-Kook-Pyo-Joon-Jik-up-Boon-Reu-Reul Joong-Sim-Eu-Ro [A Study on Socio-Economic Status: On the Basis of the Korean Standard Occupational Classification]." *Sa-hooy-kwa-hak-kwa Jeong-check-yon-koo [The Study of Social Science and Policies],* 5, pp. 69–87.

"Hooker Barbie a Hot Seller." (1996, December 18). *Capital Times,* p. C1.

Hula [motion picture]. (1927). Schulberg, B.P. (Producer), and V. Fleming (Director). United States: Paramount Pictures.

Hunter, A. (1988). *Children in the Service of Conservatism: Parent-Child Relations in the New Right's Pro-Family Rhetoric.* Madison, WI: Institute for Legal Studies, University of Wisconsin-Madison Law School.

Hunter, J.D. (1983). *American Evangelicism.* New Brunswick, NJ: Rutgers University Press.

———. (1987). *Evangelicism.* Chicago: University of Chicago Press.

Husén, T. (1988). *Skolreformerna Och Forskningen.* Stockholm: Verbum Gothia.

Husén, T., and M. Kogan (eds.). (1984). *Educational Research and Policy: How Do They Relate?* Oxford, England: Pergamon Press.

Jessop, B. (1990). *State Theory: Putting the Capitalist State in Its Place.* University Park, PA: Pennsylvania State University Press.

Johnson, R. (1983). *What Is Cultural Studies Anyway?* Occasional paper. Centre for Contemporary Cultural Studies, University of Birmingham, England.

Johnston, P. (1997). *Real Fantasies: Edward Steichen's Advertising Photography.* Berkeley, CA: University of California Press.

Kallós, D., and S. Lindblad (eds.). (1994). *New Policy Contexts for Education: Sweden and the United Kingdom.* Umeå, Sweden: Umeå University Educational Reports 42.

Kallós, D., and I. Nilsson. (1995). "Defining and Re-Defining the Teacher in the Swedish Comprehensive School." *Educational Review,* 47 (2), pp. 133–189.

Karlsen, G. (2000). "Decentralized Centralism: Framework for a Better Understanding of Governance in the Field of Education." *Journal of Education Policy,* 15 (5), pp. 525–538.

Katz, M.B. (1989). *The Undeserving Poor: From the War on Poverty to the War on Welfare.* New York: Pantheon Books.

———. (2001). *The Price of Citizenship.* New York: Metropolitan Books.

Kayal, M. (2001, May 6). "ADB Meeting Puts Spotlight on Honolulu." *Honolulu Advertiser,* p. C1.

Khoo, K.K. (1981). "Sino-Malaya Relations in Peninsular Malaysia Before 1942." *Journal of Southeast Asian Studies,* 12 (1), pp. 93–107.

Kim, B.J. (1986). "Hyun-Dae Han-Kook Koo-Joong-Kan-Kae-Keup-Euy Hyung-Sung Mit Jae-Sang-San [The Formation and Reproduction of the Petite Bourgeoisie in Korea]." *Han-kook-sa-hooy-sa-yon-koo-hooy-non-moon-jip [The Studies of Korean Social History],* 3, pp. 259–306.

Kim, E.M. (1993). "Contradictions and Limits of a Developmental State: With Illustrations from the South Korean Case." *Social Problems,* 40, pp. 228–249.

Kim, Y.W. (1993). *A Study on the Educational Enthusiasm of Korean People.* Seoul: Korean Educational Development Institute.

Kimmelman, M. (1996, May 19). "Does It Really Matter Who Sponsors a Show?" *New York Times,* p. C1.

Kincheloe, J.L. (1993). *Toward a Critical Politics of Teacher Thinking: Mapping the Postmodern.* Westport, CT: Bergin & Garvey.

Kirch, P.V., and M. Sahlins. (1992). *Anahulu: The Anthropology of History in the Kingdom of Hawaii* (Vol. 1). Chicago: University of Chicago Press.

Kirke- og undervisningsdepartementet. (1974). *Mønsterplan for Grunnskolen 1974.* Oslo, Norway: Kirke- og Undervisningsdepartementet.

———. (1987). *Mønsterplanen for Grunnskolen 1987.* Oslo, Norway: Kirke- og undervisningsdepartementet.

Kirke- undervisnings- og forskningsdepartementet. (1994). *Reform '94. Videregående Opplæring. Nye Læreplaner.* Oslo, Norway: Kirke-, Undervisnings- og Forskningsdepartementet.

Kirke- utdannings- og forskningsdepartementet. (1996). *Læreplanverket for Den 10-Årige Grunnskolen.* Oslo, Norway: Kirke-, Utdannings- og Forskningsdepartementet.

Klatch, R.E. (1987). *Women of the New Right.* Philadelphia, PA: Temple University Press.

KLI. (1994). *Labor Statistics.* Seoul: Korean Labor Institute.

Knapp, J. (1989). "Primitivism and Empire: John Synge and Paul Gauguin." *Comparative Literature* (41), pp. 53–68.

Kozol, J. (1991). *Savage Inequalities: Children in America's Schools.* New York: Crown Publishers.

Ladson-Billings, G. (1994). *The Dreamkeepers: Successful Teachers of African American Children.* San Francisco: Jossey-Bass.

Lafferty, W. (1989). "The Notion of the Public Sector Class," paper prepared for the IPSA Roundtable on Modernization in the Public Sector, Oslo, August 24–26, 1989.

Larson, B. (1997). "Teachers' Conceptions of Discussion as Method and Outcomes." Paper presented at the annual meeting of the American Educational Research Association.

Lather, P. (1991). *Getting Smart: Feminist Research and Pedagogy within the Postmodern.* New York: Routledge.

Lau, A. (1989). "Mayalan Union Citizenship: Constitutional Change and Controversy in Malaya, 1942–1948." *Journal of Southeast Asian Studies,* 20 (2), pp. 216–243.

———. (1991). *The Malayan Union Controversy, 1942–1948.* Singapore: Singapore University Press.

———. (1992). "The National Past and the Writing of the History of Singapore." In B.K. Choon, A. Pakir, and T.C. Kiong (eds.), *Imagining Singapore* (pp. 48–68). Singapore: Times Academic Press.

———. (1994). "The Colonial Office and the Singapore Merdeka Mission, 23 April to 15 May 1956." *Journal of South Seas Society,* 49, pp. 104–122.

Lauglo, J. (1995). "Forms of Decentralization and Their Implication for Education." *Comparative Education,* 31 (1), pp. 5–29.

Lee, E. (1991). *The British as Rulers: Governing Multiracial Singapore, 1867–1914.* Singapore: Singapore University Press.

Lee, I. (1994). "Teaching to Beat in a Korean Academic High School." *The SNU Journal of Educational Research,* 4 (1), pp. 15–37.

Lee, T.H. (1987). "Chinese Education in Malaya, 1894–1911." In L.T. Lee (ed.), *The 1911 Revolution: The Chinese in British and Dutch Southeast Asia* (pp. 48–65). Singapore: Heinemann Asia.

Lee, Y.H. (1995). *Social Institutions and Skill Formation in Korean Manufacturing Industry: A Comparison with Japan.* Unpublished Ph.D. dissertation, University of Wisconsin-Madison.

Leon, W.M.C. (1994). "Foundations of the American Image of the Pacific." *Boundary,* 2 (21), pp. 7–29.

Lin, J. (1992). *Zhanqian Wunian Xiama Wenxue Lilun Yanjiu [Chinese Literary Theories in Prewar Singapore and Malaya, 1937–1941].* Singapore: Tongan Huiguan.

Lindblad, S., and E. Wallin. (1993). "On Transitions of Power, Democracy and Education in Sweden." *Journal of Curriculum Studies,* 25 (1), pp. 77–88.

Liston, D.P. (1988). *Capitalist Schools: Explanation and Ethics in Radical Studies of Schooling.* New York: Routledge.

Lockwood, A. (1985). "A Place for Ethical Reasoning in Social Studies Curriculum." *The Social Studies,* 76 (6), pp. 264–268.

Loh, P. (1974a). "British Policies and Education of Malays." *Pedagogica Historica,* 14 (2), pp. 355–384.

———. (1974b). "A Review of Educational Development in the Federated Malay States to 1939." *Journal of Southeast Asian Studies,* 5 (2), pp. 225–238.

———. (1975). *Seeds of Separation: Educational Policy in Malaya, 1874–1940.* Kuala Lumpur, Malaysia: Oxford University Press.

Lord, M.G. (1994). *Forever Barbie: The Unauthorized Biography of a Real Doll.* New York: Morrow & Company.

Louis, W.R. (1985). "American Anti-Colonialism and the Dissolution of the British Empire." *International Affairs,* 61 (3), pp. 395–420.

Lovejoy, A., and G. Boas. (1935). *Primitivism and Related Ideas in Antiquity.* Baltimore, MD: Johns Hopkins University Press.

Lovett, R. (1899). *The History of the London Missionary Society* (Vol. 1). London: Henry Frowde.

Luhmann, N. (1981). *Politische Theorie Im Wohlfartsstaat.* Munich, Germany: Olzog.

Luke, C., and J. Gore (eds.). (1992). *Feminisms and Critical Pedagogy.* New York: Routledge.

Lundahl, L. (2000). "A New Kind of Order: Swedish Policy Texts related to Governance, Social Inclusion and Exclusion in the 1990s." In S. Lindblad and T.S. Popkewitz (eds.), *Public*

Discourses on Education Governance and Social Integration and Exclusion: Analysis of Policy Texts in European Context (pp. 166–204). Uppsala Reports on Education, No. 36. Uppsala, Sweden: Department of Education, Uppsala University.

Mac an Ghaill, M. (1994). *The Making of Men: Masculinities, Sexualities, and Schooling.* Buckingham, England: Open University Press.

Maclennan, C. (1995). "Foundations of Sugar's Power: Early Maui Plantations, 1840–1860." *Hawaiian Journal of History,* 29, pp. 33–57.

Man, G. (1991). "Hollywood Images of the Pacific." *East-West Film Journal,* 5 (2), pp. 16–29.

McCarthy, C., and M.W. Apple. (1988). "Class, Race, and Gender in Educational Research." In L. Weis (ed.), *Race, Class, and Gender in American Education* (pp. 9–39). Albany, NY: State University of New York Press.

McCarthy, C., and W. Crichlow. (1993). *Race, Identity, and Representation in Education.* New York: Routledge.

McGouch, R. (1989). "The Lake." In J. Booth (ed.), *Thread the Needle* (pp. 150–151). Toronto, Canada: Holt, Rinehart & Winston.

McGrath, D.J., and P.J. Kuriloff. (1999). "They're Going to Tear the Doors Off This Place: Upper-Middle-Class Parent School Involvement and the Educational Opportunities of Other People's Children." *Educational Policy,* 13 (5), pp. 603–629.

McGregor-Alegado, D. (1980). "Hawaiians: Organizing in the 1970s." *Amerasia,* 7 (2), pp. 29–55.

McLaren, P. (1995). "White Terror and Oppositional Agency: Towards a Critical Multiculturalism." In D.T. Goldberg (ed.), *Multiculturalism: A Critical Reader* (pp. 45–74). Cambridge, MA: Blackwell.

McNeil, L.M. (1986). *Contradictions of Control.* New York: Routledge.

———. (2000). *Contradictions of School Reform: Educational Costs of Standardized Testing.* New York: Routledge.

Mediås, O.A. (1999). "Fra Veiledning Til Resultatoppfølging. Den Statlige Regionale Styring Av Skoleverket før Og Etter 1992." In A.O. Telhaug and P. Aasen (eds.), *Både—Og. 90-Tallets Utdanningsreformer I Historisk Perspektiv* (pp. 114–136). Oslo, Norway: Cappelen Akademisk Forlag.

Mediås, O.A., and A.O. Telhaug. (2000). *Fra Sentral Til Desentralisert Styring. Statlig, Regional Styring Av Utdanning Fram Mot År 2000* (Report No. 2). Steinkjer/Trondheim, Norway: Utdanning som Nasjonsbygging.

Mellor, P.A., and C. Shilling. (1997). *Re-Forming the Body: Religion, Community and Modernity.* London: Sage Publications.

Melton, J.V.H. (1988). *Absolutism and the Eighteenth-Century Origins of Compulsory Schooling in Prussia and Austria.* Cambridge, England: Cambridge University Press.

Melucci, A., J. Keane, and P. Mier. (1989). *Nomads of the Present: Social Movements and Individual Needs in Contemporary Society.* Philadelphia, PA: Temple University Press.

Meyer, J.W., D.H. Kamens, and A. Benavot (eds.). (1992). *School Knowledge for the Masses: World Models and National Primary Curricular Categories in the Twentieth Century.* Washington, DC: Falmer Press.

Mills, C.W. (1997). *The Racial Contract.* Ithaca, NY: Cornell University Press.

Mitchell, C., and J. Reid-Walsh. (1995). "And I Want to Thank You Barbie: Barbie as a Site for Cultural Interrogation." *Review of Education/Pedagogy/Cultural Studies,* 17 (2), pp. 143–155.

Modleski, T. (ed.). (1986). *Studies in Entertainment: Critical Approaches to Mass Culture.* Bloomington, IN: Indiana University Press.

Morris, K. (1998, May 25). "The Rise of Jill Barad." *Business Week* (3579), pp. 112–119.

Mouffe, C. (1992). "Preface: Democratic Politics Today." In C. Mouffe (ed.), *Dimensions of Radical Democracy: Pluralism, Citizenship, Community.* London: Verso.

Murphy, J. (1991). *Restructuring Schools: Capturing and Assessing the Phenomena.* New York: Teachers College Press.

Murray, M. (1995). "Från Fullbordan Till Upplösning Och . . . ? Svensk Skolpolitik 1980–1995." *Didaktika Minima,* 9 (4), pp. 6–27.

Nam, H. (1994). *Analysis of School Knowledge in South Korea Textbooks (1965–1991).* Unpublished Ph. D. Dissertation, University of Alberta, Canada.

Nan Chiau Girls' High School. (1967). "Special Issue for the Twentieth Anniversary of Nan Chiau Girls' High School."

Nanyang University. (1956). *Nan-Yang Ta Hsueh Ch'uang Hsiao Shih [The History of Nanyang University Inauguration].* Singapore: Nanyang Cultural Publishing.

Neave, G. (1998). "The Evaluative State Reconsidered." *European Journal of Education,* 33 (3), pp. 265–284.

Negt, O. (1982). *Den Indre Naturs Industrialisering: Kapitalisme Og Borgligt Samhälle* (Tekla no. 12–13). Lund, Sweden: Røda Bokforlaget.

Ng-Lun, N.H., and C.Y. Chang. (1989). "China and the Development of Chinese Education in Hong Kong." In N.H. Ng-Lun and C.Y. Chang (eds.), *Overseas Chinese in Asia Between the Two World Wars* (pp. 169–185). Hong Kong: Chinese University of Hong Kong, Overseas China Archives.

NOU 1988:28. (1988). *Med Viten Og Vilje* (commissioned report/Green Paper No. 28). Oslo, Norway: Statens Forvaltningstjeneste.

NOU 1995:9. (1995). *Identitet Og Dialog. Kristendomskunnskap, Livssynskunnskap Og Religionsundervisning* (commissioned report/Green Paper No. 9). Oslo, Norway: Statens Forvaltningstjeneste.

NOU 1997:25. (1997). *Ny Kompetanse. Grunnlaget for En Helhetlig Etter- Og Videreutdanning* (commissioned report/Green Paper No. 25). Oslo, Norway: Statens Forvaltningstjeneste.

OECD. (1988). *Review of Educational Policy in Norway.* Paris: OECD.

Offe, C. (1995). "Some Skeptical Considerations on the Malleability of Representative Institutions." In J. Cohen and J. Rogers (eds.), *Associations and Democracy* (pp. 114–132). London: Verso.

Offe, C., and J. Keane. (1984). *Contradictions of the Welfare State.* London: Hutchinson.

Oliver, A.O. (1993). *The Politics of Textbook Controversy: Parents' Challenge of the Implementation of a Reading Series.* Unpublished Ph.D. dissertation, University of Wisconsin-Madison.

Om Lärarutbildning m.m., Government Bill no. 75 1991/92, Sveriges Riksdag (1991–1992).

Om Läroplan för Grundskolan m.m., Government Bill no. 180 1978/79, Sveriges Riksdag, (1978–1979).

Om Skolans Utveckling Och Styrning, Government Bill no. 4 1988/89, Sveriges Riksdag, (1988–1989).

Omi, M., and H. Winant. (1994). *Racial Formation in the United States.* New York: Routledge.

Osborne, P. (1996). "Introduction: Philosophy and the Role of Intellectuals." In P. Osborne (ed.), *A Critical Sense* (pp. vii–xxviii). New York: Routledge.

Pagenhart, P. (1994). "Queerly Defined Multiculturalism." In L. Garber (ed.), *Tilting the Tower* (pp. 177–185). New York: Routledge.

Perlez, J. (1996, August 26). "A Museum for the 90's That Laughs at the 90's." *New York Times,* p. A4.

Petterson, S., and E. Wallin. (1995). "The Research Programme of the Swedish National Agency of Education." In A. Tuijnman and E. Wallin (eds.), *School Research at the Crossroads: Swedish and Nordic Perspectives* (pp. 26–35). Stockholm: OECD/National Agency for Education/Stockholm Institute of Education Press.

Pettersson, O. (1991). "Democracy and Power in Sweden." *Scandinavian Political Studies,* 14 (2), pp. 173–191.

Pollack, A. (1996, December 22). "Barbie's Journey in Japan." *New York Times,* p. E3.

Ponniah, S.M. (1968). "The Poverty of Tamil Education in Singapore, 1946–66." *Intisari*, 3 (4), pp. 95–106.

Popkewitz, T., and M. Brennan (eds.). (1998). *Foucault's Challenge.* New York: Teachers College Press.

Poulantzas, N.A. (1978). *State, Power, Socialism.* London: Verso.

Press, E. (1996). "Barbie's Betrayal." *Nation*, 263 (22), pp. 11–16.

Purcell, V. (1966). *The Chinese in Southeast Asia.* (2nd ed.) London: Oxford University Press.

Rand, E. (1995). *Barbie's Queer Accessories.* Durham, NC: Duke University Press.

Ravitch, D. (2000). *Left Back.* New York: Simon and Schuster.

RCKCT. (1994). *Jae-6cha-Kyo-Yook—Kwa-Jung-Aeeuy-Hanhak—Kyo-Kyo-Yook-Kwa-Jung Pyun-Sung Woon-Young-Euy Sil-Jae [The Sixth Revision of National Curriculum and Its Organization and Practices].* Seoul: Dong-A.

Reinarman, C. (1987). *American States of Mind: Political Beliefs and Behavior among Private and Public Workers.* New Haven, CT: Yale University Press.

Resch, R.P. (1992). *Althusser and the Renewal of Marxist Theory.* Berkeley, CA: University of California Press.

Robertson, S., and H. Lauder. (In press). "A Class Choice." In R. Phillips and H. Lauder (eds.), *Education, Reform and the State.* London: Routledge.

Rose, N.S. (1990). *Governing the Soul: The Shaping of the Private Self.* London: Routledge.

Royal Ministry of Education, Research and Church Affairs. (1994). *Core Curriculum for Primary, Secondary and Adult Education in Norway.* Oslo, Norway: Royal Ministry of Education, Research and Church Affairs.

Rydell, R. (1984). *All the World's Fair: Visions of Empire at American International Expositions 1876–1916.* Chicago: University of Chicago Press.

Salzinger, L. (2000). "Manufacturing Sexual Subjects." *Ethnography*, 1 (1), pp. 67–92.

Santos, B.S. (1998). "Participatory Budgeting in Porto Alegre: Toward a Distributive Democracy." *Politics and Society*, 26 (4), pp. 461–510.

Saussure, F. de. (1959). *Course in General Linguistics* (trans. by W. Baskin). New York: McGraw-Hill Book Company.

Scase, R., and R. Goffee. (1981). "Traditional Petite-Bourgeoisie Attitudes: The Case of Self-Employed Craftsmen." *Sociological Review*, 29, pp. 729–747.

Schaeffer, F.A. (1990). *The Francis A. Schaeffer Trilogy.* Westchester, IL: Crossway Books.

Schmitt, R. (1977). *Historical Statistics of Hawai'i.* Honolulu, HI: University of Hawai'i Press.

Schwoch, J., M. White, and S. Reilly. (1992). *Media Knowledge: Readings in Popular Culture, Pedagogy and Critical Citizenship.* Albany, NY: State University of New York Press.

Scott, J.W. (1986). "Gender: A Useful Category of Historical Analysis." *American Historical Review*, 91, pp. 1053–1075.

Selden, S. (1999). *Inheriting Shame.* New York: Teacher's College Press.

Shilling, C. (1993). *The Body and Social Theory.* London: Sage Publications.

Shor, I. (1986). *Critical Teaching and Everyday Life.* Boston: South Shore Press.

———. (1992). *Empowering Education: Critical Teaching for Social Change.* Chicago: University of Chicago Press.

Silva, N. (1998). "Kanaka Maoli Resistance to Annexation." *'Oiwi*, 1 (1), pp. 40–75.

Silverman, K. (1983). *The Subject of Semiotics.* New York: Oxford University Press.

Slagstad, R. (1994). "Arbeiderpartistaten Som Skolestat." *Nytt Norsk Tidsskrift*, 11 (3–4), pp. 221–233.

———. (1996a). "Norig, Ein Folkedanningsheim." *Nytt Norsk Tidsskrift*, 13 (3–4), pp. 308–326.

———. (1996b). "Skolens Oppgaver—Hva Slags Lærere Trenger Vi." Paper presented at the Norwegian Teachers' Union's Conference on Teacher Education in Oslo.

Slater, D., and F. Tonkiss. (2001). *Market Society.* Malden, MA: Polity Press.

SMED [Secretaria Municipal de Educação]. (1993). *Projeto Gestão Democrática* (Lei Complementar No. 292).

———. (1999a). *Boletim Informativo—Informações Educacionais*, 2 (5).

———. (1999b). "Ciclos De Formação—Proposta Político-Pedagógica Discourse Analysis Escola Cidadã." *Cadernos Pedagogicos*, 9 (1), pp. 1–111.

———. (1999c). "Official Homepage of the S.M.E.D." Accessed December 15, 1999 at http://www.portoalegre.rs.gov.br/smed/.

Smith, B. (1985). *European Vision and the South Pacific, 1768–1850.* New Haven, CT: Yale University Press.

Solomon-Godeau, A. (1991). "The Primitivism Problem." *Art in America,* 79 (2), pp. 41–45.

———. (1992). "Going Native: Paul Gauguin and the Invention of Primitivist Modernism." In N. Broude and M. Garrard (eds.), *The Expanding Discourse: Feminism and Art History* (pp. 312–329). New York: HarperCollins Publishers.

Sopiee, M.N. (1974). *From Malayan Union to Singapore Separation: Political Unification in the Malaysia Region, 1945–65.* Kuala Lumpur, Malaysia: Penerbit Universiti Malaya.

SOU 1973:48. (1973). *Skolans Regionala Ledning: Betänkande Avgivet Av Länsskolnämndsutredningen* (commissioned report/Green Paper No. 48). Stockholm: Utbildningsdepartementet.

SOU 1985:30. (1985). *Skola för Delaktighet* (commissioned report/Green Paper No. 30). Stockholm: Allmänna Förlaget.

SOU 1988:20. (1988). *En Förändrad Ansvarsfördelning Och Styrning På Skolområdet: Betänkande Från Beredningen Om Ansvarsfördelning Och Styrning På Skolområdet* (commissioned report/Green Paper No. 20). Stockholm: Utbildningsdepartementet.

SOU 1990:22. (1990). *Utbildning för 2000-Tallet* (commissioned report/Green Paper No. 22). Stockholm: Allmänna Förlaget.

SOU 1990:44. (1990). *Demokrati Och Makt I Sverige* (commissioned report/Green Paper No. 44). Stockholm: Allmänna Förlaget.

SOU 1992:94. (1992). *Skola för Bildning* (commissioned report / Green Paper No. 94). Stockholm: Allmänna Förlaget.

SOU 1993:16. (1993). *Nya Villkor för Ekonomi Och Politik. Ekonomikommissionens Förslag* (commissioned report/Green Paper No. 16). Stockholm: Fritzes.

SOU 1993:2. (1993). *Kursplaner för Grundskolan. Läroplankommitténs Slutbetäkning* (commissioned report/Green Paper No. 2). Stockholm: Allmänna Förlaget.

SOU 1993:47. (1993). *Konsekvenser Av Valfrihet Inom Skola, Barnomsorg, Äldreomsorg Och Primärvård* (commissioned report / Green Paper No. 47). Stockholm: Allmänna Förlaget.

Souza, D.H., E.A. Mogetti, M. Villani, M.T.C. Panichi, R.P. Rossetto, and S.M.R. Huerga. (1999). "Turma De Progressão E Seu Significado Na Escola." In S. Rocha and B.D. Nery (eds.), *Turma De Progressão: A Inversão Da Lógica Da Exclusão* (pp. 22–29). Porto Alegre, Brazil: Secretaria Municipal de Educação.

Spurr, D. (1993). *Rhetoric of Empire.* Durham, NC: Duke University Press.

St.meld. no. 29. (1994–1995). *Om Prinsipper Og Retningslinjer for 10-Årig Grunnskole—Ny Læreplan* (report to Parliament/White Paper No. 29). Oslo, Norway: Kirke-, Utdannings og Forskningsdepartementet.

St.meld. no. 33. (1991–1992). *Kunnskap Og Kyndighet. Om Visse Sider Ved Videregående Opplæring* (report to Parliament/White Paper No. 33). Oslo, Norway: Kirke-, Utdannings og Forskningsdepartementet.

St.meld. no. 37. (1990–1991). *Om Omorganisering Og Styring I Utdanningssektoren* (report to Parliament/White Paper No. 37). Oslo, Norway: Kirke-, Utdannings og Forskningsdepartementet.

St.meld. no. 4. (1992–1993). *Langtidsprogrammet* (report to Parliament/White Paper No. 4). Oslo, Norway: Kirke-, Utdannings og Forskningsdepartementet.

St.meld. no. 40. (1992–1993). —*Vi Smaa En Alen Lange; Om 6-Åringer I Skolen—Konsekvenser for Skoleløpet Og Retningslinjer for Dets Innhold* (report to Parliament/White Paper No. 40). Oslo, Norway: Kirke-, Utdannings og Forskningsdepartementet.

St.meld. no. 43. (1988–1989). *Mer Kunnskap Til Flere* (report to Parliament/White Paper No. 43). Oslo, Norway: Kirke-, Utdannings og Forskningsdepartementet.

St.meld. no. 47. (1995–1996). *Om Elevvurdering, Skolebasert Vurdering Og Nasjonalt Vurderingssystem* (report to Parliament/White Paper No. 47). Oslo, Norway: Kirke-, Utdannings og Forskningsdepartementet.

Stallybrass, P., and A. White. (1986). *The Poetics and Politics of Transgression*. Ithaca, NY: Cornell University Press.

Stam, R. (1995). "Eurocentrism, Polycentrism, Multicultural Pedagogy: Film and the Quincentennial." In R. Campra, E.A. Kaplan, and M. Sprinker (eds.), *Late Imperial Culture* (pp. 97–121). London: Verso.

Steinmetz, G., and E.O. Wright. (1989). "The Fall and Rise of the Petite Bourgeoisie: Changing Patterns of Self-Employment in the Post-War United States." *American Journal of Sociology*, 94, pp. 973–1018.

Stevenson, R. (1975). *Cultivators and Administrators: British Educational Policy towards the Malays, 1875–1906*. Kuala Lumpur, Malaysia: Oxford University Press.

Stockwell, A.J. (1990). "Examination and Empire: The Cambridge Certificate in the Colonies, 1857–1957." In J.A. Mangan (ed.), *Making Imperial Mentalities: Socialization and British Imperialism* (pp. 203–220). Manchester, England: Manchester University Press.

Suh, K.M. (1984). *Kae-Keup Hyung-Sungkwa Kae-Keup-Bun-Wha [Class Formation and Class Division]*. Seoul: Hanul.

Tan, L.E. (1997). *The Politics of Chinese Education in Malaya, 1945–1961*. Kuala Lumpur, Malaysia: Oxford University Press.

Tarling, N. (1993). *The Fall of Imperial British in South-East Asia*. Singapore: Oxford University Press.

Tarrow, S.G. (1994). *Power in Movement: Social Movements, Collective Action and Politics*. Cambridge, England: Cambridge University Press.

Tavares, H. (1996). "Classroom Management and Subjectivity." *Educational Theory*, 46, pp. 189–201.

———. (2002). *Schooling, Work, and the Body*. Unpublished Ph. D. dissertation, University of Wisconsin-Madison.

Telhaug, A.O. (1990). *Den Nye Utdanningspolitiske Retorikken. Bilder Av Den Internasjonale Skoleutviklingen*. Oslo, Norway: Universitetsforlaget.

———. (1992). *Norsk Og Internasjonal Skoleutvikling*. Oslo, Norway: Ad Notam Gyldendal.

———. (1994). *Norsk Skoleutvikling Etter 1945*. Oslo, Norway: Didaktika Norsk Forlag.

———. (1997a). "Restructuring in Education—Scandinavia in the Eighties and Nineties." Paper presented at Keynote Address of the 6th National Conference in Education in Oslo.

———. (1997b). *Utdanningsreformene: Oversikt Og Analyse*. Oslo, Norway: Didaktika Norsk Forlag.

Terry, J., and J. Urla. (1995). *Deviant Bodies*. Bloomington, IN: Indiana University Press.

The Secret Lives of Barbie [television broadcast]. (1998, June 11). R. Stearns and B. Vardell (Producers). *ABC News Thursday Night*. New York: American Broadcasting Company.

Tiffin, C. (ed.). (1978). *South Pacific Images*. Brisbane, Australia: South Pacific Association for Commonwealth Literature and Language Studies.

Tilly, C. (1995). *Popular Contestation in Britain*. Cambridge, MA: Harvard University Press.

Touraine, A. (2001). *Beyond Neoliberalism*. Malden, MA: Blackwell.

Trask, H.K. (1987). "The Birth of the Modern Hawaiian Movement: Ḳalama Valley, O'ahu." *Hawaiian Journal of History*, 21, pp. 126–153.

———. (2000). "The Struggle for Hawaiian Sovereignty." *Cultural Survival Quarterly*, 21, pp. 8–11.

Tregonning, K.G. (1990). "Tertiary Education in Malaya: Policy and Practice." *Journal of the Malayan Branch of the Royal Asiatic Society,* 63 (Part 1), pp. 1–14.

Tyack, D., and L. Cuban. (1995). *Tinkering toward Utopia: A Century of Public School Reform.* Cambridge, MA: Harvard University Press.

Urla, J., and A.C. Swedlund. (1995). "The Anthropometry of Barbie: Unsettling Ideals of the Feminine Body in Popular Culture." In J. Terry and J. Urla (eds.), *Deviant Bodies* (pp. 277–313). Bloomington, IN: Indiana University Press.

Utbildningsdepartementet. (1980). *Läroplan för Grundskolan 1980.* Stockholm: Skolöverstyrelsen.

Utvecklingsplan för Skolväsendet, Government Bill no. 183 1993/94, Sveriges Riksdag (1993–1994).

Valfrihet I Skolan, Government Bill no. 230 1992/93, Sveriges Riksdag (1992–1993).

Valli, L. (1985). *Becoming Clerical Workers.* London: Routledge & Kegan Paul.

Vlieland, C.A. (1932). *British Malaya: A Report on the 1931 Census and on Certain Problems of Vital Statistics.* London: Waterlow.

Walkerdine, V. (1990). *Schoolgirl Fictions.* London: Verso.

Watson, K. (1993). "Rulers and Ruled: Racial Perceptions, Curriculum, and Schooling in Colonial Malaya and Singapore." In J.A. Mangan (ed.), *The Imperial Curriculum: Racial Images and Education in the British Colonial Experience* (pp. 147–174). London: Routledge.

Weiler, H.N. (1990). "Decentralization in Educational Governance: An Exercise in Contradiction?" In M. Granheim, M. Kogan, and P. Lundgren (eds.), *Evaluation as Policymaking* (pp. 42–72). London: Jessica Kingsley.

Wexler, P. (1992). *Becoming Somebody: Toward a Social Psychology of School.* London: Falmer Press.

White, T. (1898). *Our New Possessions.* Chicago: J.S. Ziegler & Company.

Whitney, H.M. (1970). *The Hawaiian Guide Book.* Honolulu, HI: Henry M. Whitney (original work published 1875).

Whitty, G. (1985). *Sociology and School Knowledge.* New York: Methuen.

———. (1997). "Creating Quasi-Markets in Education." In M.W. Apple (ed.), *Review of Research in Education* (Vol. 22). Washington, DC: American Educational Research Association.

———. (2002). *Making Sense of Education Policy.* London: Paul Chapman.

Whitty, G., A.D. Edwards, and S. Gerwitz. (1993). *Specialisation and Choice in Urban Education: The City Technology College Experiment.* London: Routledge.

Whitty, G., S. Power, and D. Halpin. (1998). *Devolution and Choice in Education: The School, the State and the Market.* Buckingham, England: Open University Press.

Williams, R. (1961). *The Long Revolution.* London: Chatto and Windus.

———. (1977). *Marxism and Literature.* Oxford, England: Oxford University Press.

———. (1983). *The Year 2000.* New York: Pantheon Books.

———. (1989). *Resources of Hope: Culture, Democracy, Socialism.* London: Verso.

Willis, P. (1977). *Learning to Labor* (repr. ed.). New York: Columbia University Press.

Willis, P., S. Jones, J. Canaan, and G. Hurd. (1990). *Common Culture: Symbolic Work at Play in the Everyday Cultures of the Young.* Boulder, CO: Westview Press.

Willis, P., and M. Trondman. (2000). "Manifesto for Ethnography." *Ethnography,* 1 (1), pp. 5–16.

Wilson, H.E. (1978). *Social Engineering in Singapore: Educational Policies and Social Change, 1819–1972.* Singapore: Singapore University Press.

Wong, L.K. (1971, December). "The New Primary History Syllabus: Purpose and Scope." *Journal of the Historical Society of the University of Singapore,* pp. 16–21.

Wong, T.-H. (2000). "State Formation, Hegemony, and Nanyang University in Singapore, 1953–1965." *Formosan Education and Society,* 1 (1), pp. 59–85.

———. (2002). *Hegemonies Compared: State Formation and Chinese School Politics in Postwar Singapore and Hong Kong.* New York: RoutledgeFalmer.

Wright, E.O. (1985). *Classes.* New York: Verso.

Yen, C.H. (1982). "Overseas Chinese Nationalism in Singapore and Malaya, 1877–1912." *Modern Asian Studies,* 16 (3), pp. 397–425.

———. (1984). "Chang Yu-Nan and the Chaochow Railway, 1904–1908: A Case Study of Overseas Chinese Involvement in China's Modern Enterprise." *Modern Asian Studies,* 18 (1), pp. 119–135.

Yeo, K.W. (1973a). "The Anti-Federation Movement in Malaya, 1946–1948." *Journal of Southeast Asian Studies,* 4, pp. 31–51.

———. (1973b). *Political Development in Singapore, 1945–55.* Singapore: Singapore University Press.

Yeo, K.W., and A. Lau. (1991). "From Colonialism to Independence, 1945–1965." In E.C.T. Chew and E. Lee (eds.), *A History of Singapore* (pp. 117–153). Singapore: Oxford University Press.

Young, M.F.D. (ed.). (1971). *Knowledge and Control.* London: Collier-Macmillan.

Published Official Documents

[Fenn-Wu Report]. *Chinese Schools and the Education of Chinese Malayans: The Report of a Mission Invited by the Federation Government to Study the Problems of Education of Chinese in Malaya.* Kuala Lumpur, Government Printer, 1951.

[FETS] *First Education Triennial Survey, Colony of Singapore.* 1955–1957.

[MEAR] *Ministry of Education, Annual Report.* 1959, 1960, 1962, 1963, 1964, 1965, and 1967.

[All-Party Report]. *Report of the All-Party Committee of the Singapore Legislative Assembly on Chinese Education.* Singapore Government Printer, 1956.

[Wong Gung-Wu Report]. *Report of the Nanyang University Curriculum Review Committee.* Singapore: Nanyang University, 1965.

Singapore Legislative Assembly Debate, Official Report. 1956–1958.

Syllabus for Geography in Primary and Secondary Schools, 1957 [in Chinese]. Reprinted by the Singapore Ministry of Education, 1959.

Syllabus for Geography in Primary and Secondary Schools [in Chinese]. Singapore, Ministry of Education, 1961.

Syllabus for History in Primary and Secondary Schools, 1957 [in Chinese]. Reprinted by the Singapore Ministry of Education, 1959.

Syllabus for History in Primary and Secondary Schools [in Chinese]. Singapore, Ministry of Education, 1961.

Declassified Official Files

CO (Colonial Office) 825/90/7 and 1022/285.

SCA (Secretary for Chinese Affairs, Singapore) 15/54.

Newspaper Sources

Sin Chew Jit Poh (SCJP), 1945–1965.

Standard, 1959.

Straits Budget (SB), 1946–1965.

Straits Times (ST), 1960.

Contributors

Petter Aasen is head of the Norwegian Institute for Studies in Research and Education (NIFU) in Oslo. He is also adjunct professor in education and former Dean of Faculty of Social Sciences and Technology Management at the Norwegian University of Science and Technology in Trondheim. He has written extensively on the relationship between government policy and educational reform in Scandinavia.

Michael W. Apple is John Bascom Professor of Curriculum and Instruction and Educational Policy Studies at the University of Wisconsin, Madison. He is the author of many books, including the recently published *Educating the "Right" Way* (Routledge, 2001).

Misook Kim Cho is a researcher on the staff of the Korean Educational Development Institute and has written on gender, power, and education in journals such as *Gender and Society.*

Luís Armando Gandin teaches at the Federal University of Rio Grande do Sul in Porto Alegre, Brazil. He has published a number of books on the politics of education.

Anita Oliver teaches at La Sierra University in Riverside, California. Her research has focused on the power of social movements in determining the content and form of textbooks.

Youl-Kwan Sung is a researcher on the staff of the Korean Educational Development Institute. He has written on the processes and possibilities of democratization in education in nations that have strongly authoritarian traditions.

Hannah Tavares has taught at the University of Hawaii and has published a number of articles on the relationship between education and the disciplined body.

Ting-Hong Wong teaches at Nan Hwa University in Taiwan. He is the author of *Hegemonies Compared* (Routledge, 2002).

Index